PLOTS AND CHARACTERS
IN MAJOR RUSSIAN FICTION

THE PLOTS AND CHARACTERS SERIES

Robert L. Gale
General Editor

PLOTS AND CHARACTERS
IN MAJOR RUSSIAN FICTION

Volume I
Pushkin, Lermontov, Turgenev, Tolstoi

Thomas E. Berry

Archon Books
Dawson

First published in 1977

Archon Books, The Shoe String Press Inc.
995 Sherman Avenue, Hamden, Connecticut 06514 USA

Wm Dawson & Sons Ltd, Cannon House
Folkestone, Kent, England

Library of Congress Cataloging in Publication Data

Berry, Thomas Edwin.
     Plots and characters in major Russian fiction.

     (The Plots and characters series)
     CONTENTS: v. 1. Pushkin, Lermontov, Turgenev, Tol-
stoi.
     1. Russian fiction—Stories, plots, etc. 2. Characters
and characteristics in literature. I. Title.
PG3095.B4   891.7'3'03   76-58458

Archon ISBN 0-208-01584-1 (v. 1)
Dawson ISBN 0 7129 0759 9 (v.1)

Printed in the United States of America

To Kira and Valia

CONTENTS

PREFACE

Students and scholars of literature are often confused by the names and numerous characters in Russian fiction. *War and Peace* alone presents so many generals and statesman that a reader can quickly lose track of the historical and fictional figures. This book is designed to help and encourage the reading of Russian literature.

As a reference book or reader's guide, this book has various functions:

1. Part I, the plots, can serve to recall plots and themes in famous Russian novels. Character lists are given after each plot: last names only for historical personages; full names for fictional characters.

2. Part II, the characters, is an index to fictional and historical characters in Russian literature. Biographical information (dates, etc.) is given for historical personages to assist the reader in seeking additional information in other sources. If a reader is looking for a particular historical personage or cannot remember where the figure appeared in a particular novel, he can find the information in the character section: for instance, Julius Caesar is listed in *War and Peace* (1, 1, 5) which means Book I, Part I, Chapter 5. Another example would be the German philosopher Schelling, who is listed in *Anna Karenina* (8, 9), meaning Part 8, Chapter 9.

3. Part II can help a reader identify the multitudinous generals, statesmen, and mythological references that abound in Russian literature. If a reader is not acquainted with Russian names, he is advised to read the following explanation of names in this book.

Russian Names

Russians have three names: first name, patronymic, and surname: for instance, Ivan Ivanovich Ivanov. The patronymic has the ending "ich" (son of) if it is a male name and "ovna" (daughter of) if it is a female. In alphabetizing, if a Russian has no surname, his name will be alphabetized by the first name. The patronymic will be given with the first name, but it does not affect the alphabetizing. Consequently, Ol'ga Ivanovna will appear in the "O" section, not the "I" section.

The Library of Congress transcription system is used for the names in this volume. It should be pointed out that the system is different for French, German, Italian, English, and Russian names.

For instance, Peter in English is spelled Petr in the Russian system. Alexander is Aleksandr. The spelling will depend on the country the name is from. A reader should have no trouble, but some common names are given under both spellings with cross references to avoid any confusion.

A further understanding of Russian titles can be found in Part II, the character section, under the name "Riurik."

Acknowledgements

I am grateful to the Graduate School of the University of Maryland for its financial assistance during my work on this volume.

I used the following editions of Soviet publications during the preparation of this work:

> Pushkin, A. S., *Polnoe sobranie sochinenii v desiati tomakh*. Izdanie tret'e. (Moskva: Izdatel'stvo Akademia Nauk SSSR, 1962).
>
> Tolstoi, L. N., *Polnoe sobranie sochinenii v devianosta odnom tome*. (Moskva: Izdatel'stvo Akademia Nauk SSSR, 1964).
>
> Turgenev, I. S., *Polnoe sobranie sochinenii i pisem v dvadtsati vos'mi tomakh*. (Moskva: Izdatel'stvo Akademia Nauk SSSR, 1961).

I also wish to thank the librarians of the McKeldin Library of the University of Maryland for their assistance during my work on this volume.

Thomas E. Berry

Slavic Department
University of Maryland

CHRONOLOGY

Aleksandr Sergeevich Pushkin, 1799-1837
Mikhail Iur'evich Lermontov, 1814-1841
Ivan Sergeevich Turgenev, 1818-1883
Lev Nikolaevich Tolstoi, 1828-1910

1799 Pushkin born to Nadezhda Osipovna (née Gannibal) and Sergei L'vovich Pushkin. Grandson of Ethiopian Abram Petrovich Gannibal.
1811 Pushkin entered newly founded lyceum at Tsarskoe Selo.
1814 Lermontov born to Maria (née Arsen'eva) and Iurii Petrovich Lermontov. A descendant of Scottish mercenary, George Learmont.
1815 Pushkin praised by poet G. R. Derzhavin at poetry reading.
1816 Pushkin joined literary group "Arzamas" as supporter of N. M. Karamzin's literary and linguistic reforms.
1817 Pushkin attached to ministry of foreign affairs. Attended meetings of semi-literary and semi-political group "The Green Lamp." Lermontov placed in custody of grandmother, a member of wealthy Stolypin family.
1818 Turgenev born to Varvara Petrovna (Lutovinova) and Sergei Nikolaevich Turgenev. Reared at mother's estate, Spasskoe. Lermontov taken to Caucasus to improve health.
1820 Pushkin finished "Ruslan and Liudmila." Exiled to Caucasus for daring poem "Ode to Liberty." Had sentimental attachment for Maria Raevskaia. Settled in Kishinev and began *Evgenii Onegin*. Lermontov taken on second trip to Caucasus to improve health.
1821 Pushkin wrote blasphemous poem "Gavriliada."
1823 Pushkin transferred to Odessa. Had affairs with Countess Elizabeth Vorontsova and Amalia Riznich.
1824 Pushkin accused of atheism. Exiled to estate, Mikhailovskoe.
1825 Pushkin saddened by loss of friends in Decembrist Revolution.
1826 Pushkin promised Tsar Nicholas I not to write rebellious literature.
1827 Lermontov moved to Moscow. Privately tutored. Pushkin wrote poem "André Chenier," in honor of the Decembrists.

1828   Tolstoi born to Countess Maria Nikolaevna (née Bolkon-
        skaia) and Count Nikolai Il'ich Tolstoi.
        Lermontov entered Gentry Pension.   Called "Frog" by
        classmates.
1829   Pushkin visited younger brother in Caucasus.
1830   Pushkin spent summer at estate, Boldino, Finished *Evgenii
        Onegin*, "The Little Tragedies" and other works.
        Lermontov entered Moscow University.   Wrote poems in
        Byronic style and loved Natal'ia Ivanova.
1831   Pushkin married Natal'ia Goncharova.   Entered government
        service.
1832   Lermontov had sentimental attachment for Varvara Lopuk-
        hina. Went to St. Petersburg and entered School of Ensigns
        of the Guards.
1833   Pushkin wrote "The Bronze Horseman" and published
        "The Queen of Spades."   Turgenev entered Moscow Uni-
        versity.
1834   Lermontov received commission in Life Guard Hussars.
        Turgenev transferred to University of St. Petersburg.
1835   Pushkin appointed "gentleman of the bedchamber" by Tsar
        Nicholas I to keep the poet closer to court.
1836   Pushkin started the journal the *Contemporary* and pub-
        lished *The Captain's Daughter*.
        Tolstoi moved to Moscow and lived with father.
1837   Pushkin killed in duel with Baron Georges D'Anthes.
        Aleksandra Osten-Saken appointed Tolstoi's guardian at
        father's death.   Lermontov wrote elegy on death of Pushkin
        which attacked despotism in government.   Exiled to fighting
        in the Caucasus.
1838   Through grandmother's efforts, Lermontov reassigned to
        hussars. Turgenev's first verses published in the *Contemporary*.
        Went to Berlin to study philosophy.
1839   Lermontov joined the "Sixteen," a secret society for the dis-
        cussion of philosophy and politics.
1840   Lermontov finished *A Hero of Our Time*. Sent to Caucasus after
        a duel with French Ambassador, Erneste de Barante.
1841   Tolstoi moved to relative in Kazan after death of guardian.
        Lermontov ordered to front lines in Caucasus by Tsar
        Nicholas I. Lermontov provoked N. S. Martynov into a duel
        and was killed.   Turgenev wrote poem "Parasha" and was
        considered a poet of promise.
        "Dubrovskii," by Pushkin published.
1844   Tolstoi entered Kazan University. Studied law.
1845   Turgenev began affair with singer Pauline Garcia (Mme.
        Viardot).

1847 Tolstoi left university and returned to estate, Iasnaia Po-
     liana. Turgenev followed Mme. Viardot to Europe. Pub-
     lished stories in the *Contemporary*.
1849 Tolstoi withdrew from examinations at University of St.
     Petersburg and returned to estate, Iasnaia Poliana.
1850 Turgenev returned to Russia. Received inheritance at
     mother's death.
1851 Tolstoi went to Caucasus with brother Nikolai.
1852 Tolstoi passed examination for noncommissioned officer.
     Wrote "The Raid" and *Childhood*.
     Turgenev banished to estate for his obituary on Gogol' and
     the official reception of *A Hunter's Sketches*.
1855 Tolstoi wrote Sevastopol stories. Promoted to lieutenant.
1856 Turgenev published *Rudin*.
1857 Mme. Viardot gave birth to child, allegedly Turgenev's.
1859 Tolstoi traveled in Europe. Wrote *Family Happiness*. Founded
     school for peasant children on his estate, Iasnaia Poliana.
     Turgenev published *A Gentry Nest*.
1860 Turgenev published *On the Eve* and "First Love."
1862 Tolstoi married Sofia Behrs. Gave her his personal diary.
     Turgenev published *Fathers and Sons*.
1863 Turgenev exonerated from charge of aiding London group
     of expatriates.
     Tolstoi began *War and Peace*.
1867 Turgenev published *Smoke*.
1869 Financial difficulties forced Turgenev to sell villa at Baden.
     Tolstoi had famous nightmare about death in Arzamas. His
     War and Peace published.
1870 Tolstoi began novel on Petr I. Unfinished.
1872 Turgenev published *Spring Freshets*.
1873 Tolstoi began *Anna Karenina*.
1877 Turgenev published *Virgin Soil*. *Anna Karenina* published.
1878 Tolstoi began novel on Nicholas I. Unfinished.
1879 Tolstoi wrtoe *Confession* and *A Critique of Dogmatic Theology*.
     Turgenev received honorary degree from Oxford.
1880 Turgenev took active part in Pushkin festival in Moscow.
1881 Tolstoi wrote "What Men Live By" and moved family to
     Moscow.
1882 Tolstoi wrote "What I Believe." Bought house in Moscow.
     Turgenev became seriously ill with cancer of spine.
1883 Turgenev died with Mme. Viardot and her children near him.
1885 Tolstoi wrote stories for the *Intermediary*, founded by his
     disciple, V. G. Chertkov.
1886 Tolstoi wrote "The Death of Ivan Il'ich" and "The Power of
     Darkness."

1890   Tolstoi began to write *Fruits of Enlightenment* and "The Kreutzer Sonata."
1892   Tolstoi divided his property between his wife and children.
1899   Tolstoi wrote *Resurrection* and donated profits to Dukhobors for their departure from Russia.
1901   Tolstoi excommunicated by Russian Orthodox Church.
1902   Tolstoi resumed work on *The Light in the Darkness* but did not finish it.
1902-1910   Tolstoi suffered many quarrels and intrigues because of disagreements with his wife and fellow Tolstoians. Left Iasnaia Poliana on October 28, 1910, and died at Astopova, November 9, 1910.

PLOTS

Anna Karenina, L. N. Tolstoi, 1877.

"All happy families are alike, but an unhappy family is unhappy in its own way." Learning that Dolly, a sister-in-law, had discovered a trist between her maid and her husband Stephan, Anna Karenina left her spouse and son in imperial St. Petersburg and traveled to metropolitan Moscow for a short visit with the Oblonskiis. At the station, Anna witnessed the death of a man who fell under the train. In spite of the grim incident, the beautiful visitor reunited the quarreling mates, fascinated Dolly's sister Kitty, and created a pleasant impression wherever she went. Kitty Shcherbatskaia had two suitors: Prince Levin, a member of an old aristocratic family who loved her desperately and wanted to marry her; and Count Vronski, a dashing page of the imperial corps, who flirted with her but had not declared his intentions. When Levin made his fated proposal, Kitty refused, feeling that Vronskii would also propose. However, at a grand ball, Kitty watched in horror the beginning of a romantic situation between the Count and the beautiful visitor, Anna. Fearing that she could not trust her heart, Anna left for home the next day, satisfied that she had fulfilled her mission. On the train, she was pleased and horrified to find Vronskii, who had followed her and who now professed his love. St. Petersburg society contained the smart, liberal set of the Princess Betsy Tverskoi, at whose home Anna began to see Vronskii; and a conservative set headed by the Countess Lidia Ivanovna, a hostess greatly admired by Anna's husband Karenin. Rumors about Anna and Vronskii began to circulate, and Karenin worried about their social position. When Vronskii was injured in a horse race and Anna cried, Karenin accused her of infidelity. He considered a duel, divorce and separation; but fearful of his own position, he merely forbade Anna to see Vronskii again. The lovers, however, continued to meet in private. Kitty became ill after losing Vronskii and went abroad for a cure. In a German spa, she became a close friend of Varenka, who promised to visit her in Russia after Kitty was married. Levin returned to his estate after Kitty's refusal and busied himself in improving his property. He worked in the fields with the serfs and devised economic improvements. When he found that Kitty had not married and was visiting a farm nearby, he wanted to visit her; but his pride restrained him. Later he went to Moscow in hopes of seeing her. When Anna realized that she was pregnant, she expected Vronskii to be elated. He was secretly disappointed but asked her to petition for a divorce so that they could marry. Karenin refused her request and decided to accept the child as his own to avoid scandal. Anna had to agree because Karenin threatened to take away their son if she pressed for separation. One evening Karenin accidentally met Vronskii in his own home. Incensed, he announced that he would divorce Anna; but second thoughts about his position changed his mind. After the birth of her daughter, Anna became gravely ill. Vronskii, distraught, attempted suicide, but inflicted only a slight wound with a single shot. Karenin, believing that Anna was dying, agreed to allow Vronskii to visit. In her delirium, Anna asked the two men to forgive her and be on good terms. They agreed. After her recovery, she and Vronskii took their daughter to Italy. They tried to build new interests and met the artist Mihailov. Levin and Kitty married, thus joining two of the most prominent Moscow families. They moved to Levin's country estate, where Kitty matured into a capable gentlewoman. She helped Levin nurse his brother Nikolai before his death, and she bore him three children. Anna and Vronskii returned to Russia, but were not accepted by society and could not obtain a divorce. After a snubbing by former acquaintances at the opera and a sad reunion with her son, Anna moved to a country estate with Vronskii. Fearful of losing her beloved, Anna wanted him with her at all times. When he was away, she fretted and imagined that she was losing his love. When Vronskii was invited to his mother's estate and Anna found out that the Princess Sorokin was there, she decided to go and bring him home. At the train station she concluded that she had lost his love and was living a life of deceit. When a train came, she threw herself under a wagon, extinguishing her life as she would a candle. Levin's other brother, the writer Koznyshev, saw Vronskii on a train when he was heading for the Turkish frontier. It was evident that the officer had lost his will to live, and he was also suffering from a toothache. Levin's family welcomed his brother at their estate. He showed Koznyshev his economic developments. Levin was content with his life. He had accepted

Christianity. He knew that the religion would not answer life's questions for everybody, but it had finally given him inner peace.

Adam, Agafia, Aleksandr, Tsar Aleksandr II, Alesha, Aleshka, Anishkin, Annushka, Apraksina, Evgenii Ivanovich Apukhtin, Automedon, Avenev, Aveneva, Bach, Balakirev, Bartnianskii, Beethoven, Beist, Bentham, Bertenev, Bertha, Bezzubova, Biriuzovskii, Petr Petrovich, Bohl, Bobrishchev, Borozdina, Bovina, Brenteln, Brianskii, Briantsev, Buslaev, Buzulukov, Canut, Card, Chagin, Charskii, Chechenskii, Masha Chibisova, Chirikov, Corday, Cordelia, Darialov, Daudet, Demin, Dickens, Dogovushin, Dolly, Dram, Duniasha, Edwards, Egor, Egorov, Empress Ekaterina II, Eletskii, Enoch, Ermil, Prohor Ermilin, Eve, Fedor, Fedot, Fentinkov, Filipp, Finogen, Flerov, Fokanych, Fomich, Fomin, Franklin, Emperor Frederich II, Gagin, Galtsin, Gautier, Goethe, Gogol', Golenishchev, Grabovskii, Gretchen, Grimm, Grinevich, Grisha, Gritskii, Hegel, Hannah, La Belle Hélène, Heine, Hull, Iashvin, Ignat, Isaac, Ivan, Ivan Ivanovich, Ivan Petrovich, Ivanov, John, St. John, Joseph, Mishka Kaluzhskii, Kamerovskii, Kant, Kapitonich, Karr, Kartasov, Aleksei Aleksandrovich Karenin, Serezha Karenin, Anna Karenina, Anna Arkad'evna Karenina, Karibanov, Katavasov, Katerina Petrovna, Kaulbach, Kedrov, Kirilov, Khomiakov, Khliustov, Komisarov, Konsunskaia, Kornei, Lidia Korsunskaia, Egor Korsunskii, Korzinskaia, Sergei Ivanovich Koznyshev, Kostia, Kritskii, Krivin, Krivtsov, Krupov, Krylov, Kuz'ma, Kuzovlev, Kvytskii, Landau, Lankovskii, Lassalle, Laura, Lavrentii, Konstantin Ivanovich Levin, Nikolai Levin, Lili, Lille, Linon, Lizaveta Petrovna, King Louis XV, Lucca, Arsenii L'vov, Lidia Ivanovna, Makhotin, Malteshcheva, Malvinskii, Mamonov, Mamonova, Marfa Efimova, Maria Borisovna, Maria, Maria Nikolaevna, Marie, Mariette, Masha, Maslova, Matrena Filimonovna, Matvei, Mazankov, Menelaus, Liza Markalov, Merzhkov, Metrov, Miakhaia, Bibish Miakhii, Miakhov, Miaskin, Mikhailov, Mileev, Mill, Mishka, Mitia, Mitiukha, Mordvinskii, Moses, Nadenka, Nastia, Iulis Neledinskaia, Lisa Neptunova, Nevedovskii, Filipp Nikitin, Nikolaeva, Nikolenka, Nillson, Noah, Mary Nordston, Dar'ia Aleksandrovna Oblonskaia, Petr Oblonskii, Stepan Arkadievich Oblonskii, Offenbach, Parfan, Ivan Parmenov, Paskudin, Patti, Tsar Petr I, Petritskii, Petrov, Petrova, Petrovskii, Pierre, Pilate, Plato, Platon, Poltavskii, Pravdin, Priachnikov,

Pugachev, Putiatov, Ivan Ivanich Ragozov, Rambouillet, Raphael, Rebecca, Renan, Fedor Rezunov, Riabinin, Ristich-Kudzhitskii, Rolandaki, Maria Evgenievna Rtishchev, Rubens, Samovar, Samson, Sarmatskii, Schelling, Schopenhauer, Schulze-Delitsch, Schuzburgs, Semen, Semenov, Serpukhovskoi, Sestrin, Shakespeare, Shakhovskaia, Shcherbatskaia, Kitty Shcherbatskaia, Natal'ia Shcherbatskaia, Aleksandr Shcherbatskii, Nikolai Shcherbatskii, Shilton, Shirkov, Shuraev, Sigonin, Siniavin, Skorodumov, Mikhail Slyndin, Snetkov, Socrates, Sorokina, Spencer, Spinoza, Stahl, Stiva, Sappho Stolz, Strauss, Stremov, Nikolai Ivanovich Sviazhskii, Svintich, Taine, Talleyrand-Périgord, Tania, Tartar Tereshchenko, Thérèse, Tintoretto, Titian, Titus, Topor, Turovtsyn, Tushkevich, Betsy Tverskaia, Tyndall, Vania, Varenka, Varia, Varvara, Vasil'chikov, Vasil'chikova, Vasil'ev, Vasilii, Vasilii Lukich, Vaska, Vatkovskaia, Venevskii, Grisha Veselovskii, Vasenka Veslovskii, Petr Vinovskii, Vlaseva, Voitov, Vorkuev, Vronskaia, Aleksandr Kirillovich Vronskii, Aleksei Kirillovich Vronskii, Kiril Ivanovich Vronskii, Wagner, Werther, Wilson, Wrede, Zhivakhov, Zipporah, Zola.

The Captain's Daughter, A. S. Pushkin, 1836.

While Petr Andreich Grinev was enlisted as a sergeant in the Semenovskii regiment when he was a boy, he remained at the family estate and completed his studies. At seventeen he started out for Fort Orenburg accompanied by his faithful servant, Savel'ich. The naive young gentleman learned much from incidents during the trip: he played billiards with a traveling soldier, Zurin, and lost one hundred roubles; he decided to travel against the advice of his servant, and they were soon snowbound in their carriage; he allowed a stranger to lead them to an inn and rewarded him the next day with his hareskin jacket, much to the chagrin of Savel'ich. When Grinev reported to the commander at Orenburg, the wise old man feared the young man would fall into dissipation at the large fortress and sent him to the Belogorsk fortress under Captain Mironov. Petr soon learned that the small, wooden fort at Belogorsk was under the command of the captain's wife, Vasilisa Egorovna, who managed with a firm hand. The captain's daughter, Mar'ia, made a fine impression on Petr, and he spent much time in their home. A fellow officer, Shvabrin, was a good friend until Petr called Shvabrin a liar and was challenged to a duel. They met the next morning in a field, but Vasilisa Egorovna sent troops and stopped them. The enemies agreed to carry out the duel at their earliest convenience. Petr learned from Mar'ia that Shvabrin was her rejected suitor. Although he understood his adversary's ridicule of Mar'ia, the next day he went ahead with the duel and was wounded in the chest. For five days he lay unconscious. Mar'ia took care of him; and when he revived, he asked her to marry him. Petr wrote his father about Mar'ia, but his father sent back word that he did not approve of the match and asked that Petr be transferred to another fortress. Savel'ich assured Petr that he had not written anything derogatory to his father. The logical culprit was Shvabrin, who had been jailed after the duel but had written Petr's father about the affair. Petr was in great despair and did not know what to do. Events decided for him. A peasant rebellion broke out led by the Yaikian cossack Emel'ian Pugachev. Many of the cossacks in the area joined the rebel, and the Belogorsk fortress was in great danger. When Captain Mironov received a manifesto from the cossack leader ordering him to surrender the fort, he decided to send Mar'ia to safety at Orenburg. Before she could leave, the rebels attacked. Traitors in the fortress helped give a quick victory to the insurgents. Pugachev, claiming to be the dead Tsar Petr III, demanded that all officers bow to him. Captain Mironov refused and was hanged. When his wife interfered, she was struck down with a sword and killed. Petr recognized the rebel leader as the man to whom he had given the hareskin coat. Through Savel'ich's intercession, Petr's life was spared. Shvabrin proclaimed that the rebel leader was the tsar and joined his forces. Although the traitor knew that Mar'ia was hiding at the home of the village priest, he did not tell anyone. Summoned before Pugachev, Petr refused to join the Cossacks. The rebel leader respected Petr for his steadfastness and gave him a sheepskin coat and a horse for safe conduct to Orenburg. Arriving at the large fortress, Petr alerted the forces to an oncoming attack by the rebels. When it occurred, he found out that Shvabrin was forcing Mar'ia to marry him. Petr wanted to lay siege to Belogorsk, but the Orenburg Commander felt that the mission was too dangerous and refused permission. Fearing for Mar'ia's safety, Petr and Savel'ich again started out for the remote fortress. They were quickly taken prisoner by Pugachev's rebels. Petr again impressed the rebel leader by his fearlessness and persuaded him to give him and Mar'ia safe conduct to Orenburg. During the return trip, they encountered a detachment led by Captain Zurin. The officer persuaded Petr to send Mar'ia with Savel'ich to his family while he joined the forces at Orenburg. The rebel army surrounded the large fortress, and the siege lasted a long time. During a search for rebel units, Petr found himself near his family's estate and went for a visit. He was confronted by a rebellion. The peasants had risen against their masters and were holding them captive. Shvabrin arrived with his rebel forces and planned to hang everyone except Mar'ia. Suddenly Captain Zurin's troops appeared and drove off the renegades. Shvabrin was wounded and taken prisoner to stand trial. Petr joined Captain Zurin's forces, planning to marry Mar'ia with his parents' consent after the rebellion was over. When Shvabrin accused Petr of spying for Pugachev, the young officer was arrested. Mar'ia could have helped clear his name, but he would not draw her into the matter. The rebel leader's kindness to Petr was not understood, and the young officer was sentenced to exile in Siberia. Mar'ia went to St. Petersburg, where she hoped to appeal to the Empress Ekaterina II. Walking in a park one day, she met an older lady who was soon impressed by her story about her loved one. The next day Mar'ia was summoned to court and presented to the lady she had met in the park, the Empress Ekaterina II. Petr was pardoned and married the captain's daughter.

Akulina Pamfilovna, Akul'ka, Andriushka, Anna Vlasevna, Arinushka, B____, Beaupré, Beloborodov, Fomka Bikbaev, Bulanin, Chumakov, Empress Ekaterina II, Father Gerasim, Nastas'ia Gerasimova, Golitsyn, Andrei Petrovich Grinev, Petr Andreevich Grinev, Avdotia Vasil'evna Grineva, Ivan Ignatich, Karolinka, Krushchov, Taras Kurichkim, Semen Kuzov, Lizaveta Kharlovna, Maksimich, Ivan Ivanovich Mikhelson, Minikh, Ivan Kuzmich Mironov, Maria Ivanovna Mironova, Vasilisa Egorovna Mirovova, Ustinia Negulina, Grishka Otrep'ev, Palashka, Stepan Paramanov, Ivan Polezhaev, Prokhorov, Pugachev, Andrei Karlovich R____, Petr Aleksandrovich Rumiantsov, Arkhip Savel'ich, Aleksei Ivanovich Shvabrin, Afanasii Sokolov, Aleksandr Petrovich Sumarokov, Timofeich, Trediakovskii, Vania, Volynskii, Ivan Ivanovich Zurin.

"The Death of Ivan Il'ich," L. N. Tolstoi, 1886.

Three colleagues of Ivan Il'ich were discussing law cases when one of them, Petr Ivanovich, read in the paper about their co-worker's death. They speculated about the recipient of Ivan's position. Petr called on the widow and met an acquaintance, Schwartz, with whom he arranged to play cards. Before he could leave, the widow trapped him in a conversation about her husband and her pension. Petr finally slipped away and made the card game for a second hand. Ivan Il'ich had passed away, not missed by anyone. His childhood had been ordinary, and he had held responsible positions with the government. When he had attained the position of examining magistrate, he met Praskov'ia Golovina and married her without any burning passion. She became jealous and demanding; so he devoted his life to his official work and avoided her. He received promotions; but after quarreling with his superiors, he was passed over for a raise in rank. Feeling unappreciated, he became depressed. To save money, he moved to his wife's family for the summer. Becoming more restless, he went to St. Petersburg in search of employment. Luckily, he received an appointment two levels higher than his former colleagues. He moved to the city ahead of his family in order to decorate their new lodgings. While standing on a ladder hanging drapes, he fell and bruised his left side. The incident was soon forgotten. His family joined him and was very pleased with their new furnishings even though they reflected middle-class taste. Ivan Il'ich became a petit-bourgeois and led a very orderly life. Cards became his favorite pastime. Young men began to give his daughter attention, and his son did well in school. Life was running smoothly when Ivan Il'ich suddenly began noticing pains in the left side of his stomach and a queer taste in his mouth. As the pain increased, he became more irritable and argued frequently with his wife. Finally he visited a doctor who gave him some medicine and a diet. Ivan Il'ich became obsessed with ailments and went from doctor to doctor, always receiving a different diagnosis. Shortly before the New Year, his brother-in-law visited and was shocked at the change in Ivan. The latter visited another doctor and was told he had a problem in the caecum. Ivan Il'ich finally admitted to himself that he was dying and found the idea difficult to accept. During the third month of his illness, the thought of his death was on everyone's mind in the household. He was given opium and morphine, but his greatest consolation came when the peasant Gerasim held his legs up, alleviating the pain. Ivan Il'ich's last days were poisoned by the falsity around him. Everyone acted as if his illness would soon pass. He began hating his wife for her fine health. One morning when the family

was away he was frantic from being left alone. He sent Gerasim
away and cried like a child, berating God. He thought of his life
and realized that his only pleasant memories were from his childhood. He concluded that he had misspent his life and accepted
holy sacraments. Two weeks passed. Petrishchev proposed to his
daughter. Ivan Il'ich's condition became worse and he screamed
for three days. When he quieted down, he felt his hand being
kissed by his son. His wife was crying by his bed. He felt sorry for
them and wanted to ease their pain. He realized that his death
would give them relief, and then he accepted the inevitable.
Suddenly he was no longer fearful. In place of death, there was
light; and he felt joy. Two hours later he died.

   Alekseev, Bernhardt, Caius, Dmitrii, Fedor Petrovich, Fedor
Vasil'evich, Gerasim, Il'ia Efimovich Golovin, Ivan Il'ich
Golovin, Liza Golovina, Praskov'ia Fedorovna Golovina,
Grev, Happe, Helena, Il'in, Ivan Semenovich, Jean, Katen'ka,
Kiezewetter, Krasovskii, Lecouvreur, Leshchetitskii, Melin-
skii, Mikhail Danilovich, Mikhail Mikhailovich, Miller,
Mitia, Nikolaevich, Petr, Petr Ivanovich, Petr Petrovich,
Petrishchev, Dmitrii Ivanovich Petrishchev, Scharmer,
Schwartz, Ivan Egorovich Shebek, Shtabel, Sokolov, Trufon-
ova, Vinnikov, Volodia, Zakhar Ivanovich, Zola.

"Dubrovskii," A. S. Pushkin, 1833.
Kiril Petrovich Troekurov, an old, spoiled and uneducated
landowner, was harsh with his serfs and proud of his wealth. He
respected no one except for his poor neighbor Andrei Gavrilovich
Dubrovskii. They had been in the service together and had met a
similar fate. They both married for love but soon became wid-
owers, each left with one child. One day Troekurov started a hunt
by taking his guests on a tour of his splendid kennels. Dubrovskii
was the only one who did not express rapture over the dogs because
he was envious. During the tour, one of Troekurov's whips made
an insulting joke at Dubrovskii's expense and the guest went home
offended. Troekurov twice sent a servant to fetch Dubrovskii,
but he refused to return, saying that he deserved an apology.
Troekurov became angered and pondered revenge. Several days
later another incident occurred which thwarted any hope of
reconciliation. When Dubrovskii caught Troekurov's peasants
stealing his lumber, he took their horses and punished them.
Furious, Troekurov sought revenge. When the rural assessor told

him he could take over his enemy's estate because the ownership
papers had been burned, Troekurov started proceedings. Dubrovskii went to court unworried. He was sure that justice would
prevail. Such was not the case; and when he discovered that he
would lose his property, he hurled an inkstand at the assessor.
Once he had returned home, his health began deteriorating rapidly.
Egorovna, an old nurse, informed his son Vladimir, a military
officer, of all that had happened. Vladimir, a man of extravagant
habits, received the news with horror and set out for home with
his servant, Grisha, two days later. Upon arrival, the young officer
found the peasants afraid of becoming Troekurov's property. He
wanted to help them, but his father's condition had worsened and
he had to spend time with him. When the term for appealing cases
expired, the estate belonged to Troekurov. One day the rich
neighbor was conscience stricken and drove to Dubrovskii's estate
to make peace. The ailing man saw his enemy's approach and had
a heart attack. Vladimir ordered Troekurov to leave, which he did,
enraged. The elder Dubrovskii soon died. After the funeral,
Vladimir walked through a woods in search of peace. Arriving
home, he found that magistrates had come to take the servants.
The peasants began a revolt, but the young Dubrovskii stopped
them by promising to take a petition to the tsar. In the night, when
the officials were sleeping, Dubrovskii sent his people out of the
house and set it on fire. All the magistrates perished. Dubrovskii
fled. Soon there was gossip of a gang of brigands. At this time,
Troekurov decided to employ a tutor for his son, Sasha. The boy
had been born to a Mademoiselle Mimi, once a tutoress for Troekurov's beautiful daughter Mar'ia. When the tutor, Monsieur
Deforges, arrived, he was locked in a room with a chained bear.
Troekurov found bear baiting and human fear quite amusing.
The new tutor simply shot the animal and thus gained the master's
respect. Mar'ia also began to respect the fine qualities of the tutor.
When a rural official discovered that the tutor was Dubrovskii,
the hero began making plans for departure. He revealed his true
identity to Mar'ia and confessed his love. He departed just as the
sheriff came for his arrest. The next year, the old Prince Vereiskii
visited Troekurov and proposed marriage with Mar'ia. The girl
found the idea repulsive and kept a secret rendezvous with Dubrovskii. He gave her a ring to place in the hollow of a tree if she
should decide to go away with him. Mar'ia wrote the prince that
she did not wish to marry, and the old man showed the letter to her

father. Troekurov locked her in a room and announced the marriage for the next day. Mar'ia gave her ring to Sasha; but when he
put it in the tree, Mitia, a peasant boy, took it out. They fought
and Sasha accidentally told his father that Mar'ia had given him the
ring. Troekurov decided that Mitia was one of Dubrovskii's band
and locked him up. The marriage took place as scheduled though
Mar'ia expected Vladimir to save her. Driving home, Mar'ia and
her new husband were stopped by Dubrovskii's band. She could
be free, but Mar'ia was married in the church and replied that she
could not leave her husband. Dubrovskii's band was attacked by
soldiers but won the battle. With their position very dangerous,
Dubrovskii said goodbye to his comrades and suggested that they
should give up their life of robbing the rich and giving to the poor.
    Agafia, Anton, Arkhip, Anton Pafnutich, Orina Egorovna
Buzyreva, Deforge, Andrei Gavrilovich Dubrovskii, Vladimir
Andreevich Dubrovskii, Egorovna, Fedotovna, Ivan An-
dreevich Dubrovskii, Egorovna, Fedotovna, Ivan Andreevich
Globov, Vanusha Globov, Anna Savishna Globova, Grisha,
Khariton, Ivan Danilovich Kul'nev, Laventer, Lukeria, Masha,
Mikita, Mimi, Mitia, Pakhomovna, Paromoshka, Rinaldini,
Rodia, Sasha, Savel'ich, Shabashkin, Sidorich, Spitin, Stepka,
Timoshka, Kiril Petrovich Troekurov, Mar'ia Kirilovna Troe-
kurova, Taras Alekseevich, Vereiskii, Vasilisa.

Evgenii Onegin, A. S. Pushkin, 1832.
    In a prefatory stanza, Pushkin gave a collection of cold and
light-hearted observations on his time before beginning the story
of his hero, Evgenii Onegin.
    Receiving word that his uncle was ill, Onegin left post haste for
the country estate of his old relative. The young man regretted
leaving St. Petersburg's balls, theaters and amusements. Society
bored him, but he loved being bored in society. He was a dandy,
dressed in fashions from London and Paris; he was a snob, educated
enough to drop Latin anecdotes and speak French impeccably; and
he was a lover, racing from one coquette to another, hoping to
embarrass a husband on the way. So that no reader would identify
the author with the hero, Pushkin wrote that he, too, knew Onegin
and had planned to travel with him until the hero's creditors interfered. The possibility of an inheritance took Onegin to his uncle,
and as luck would have it, there was no wait: the relative's demise
preceded Onegin's arrival. At first the young squire enjoyed his

new estate, but boredom soon set in and his conduct drove off his friendly neighbors. They complained that the newcomer was a boor and a Freemason, and did not observe proper etiquette. In contrast to the general dislike of Onegin in the region, the arrival of a new landowner, Vladimir Lenskii, brought praise from the rural gentry: he was handsome and educated; he had compassion and fine manners; and he was wealthy and unmarried. When Onegin and Lenskii met, they found each other dull, but from nothing else to do, they developed a mutual admiration. Onegin listened to his friend's outpourings of the heart and considered him naive. Lenskii enjoyed the domestic circle more than the fashionable world. He was a poet and was desperately in love with Ol'ga Larina, the daughter of a neighboring family. Lenskii had known the deceased head of the family and wanted Onegin to meet the widow and her daughters. The proud young St. Petersburg dandy refused at first but finally consented. The estate of the Larins was nearby. The widow who managed the property had been a society debutante in her youth, but she had grown old in the ways of a country matron. Her daughter Ol'ga, the beloved of Lenskii, was beautiful, carefree and gay. Tat'iana, the eldest daughter, was not a beauty. She loved reading foreign writers and was inspired by nature. Neither daughter made a great impression on Onegin, and when he left the estate he asked, "Which one was Tat'iana?" Yet Onegin had made a great impression on the melancholy Tat'iana. Her imagination overwhelmed her reasoning, and she saw the new acquaintance as a knight in shining armor. Unable to eat or sleep, she wrote a secret letter and poured out her heart to the proud young neighbor. She apologized sincerely for her boldness, but her sincerity excused the rashness of the act. Onegin had awakened hidden joys; she would never be the same again. Could he possibly come and save her heart's desires? Onegin was moved by Tat'iana's letter, but he did not wish to deceive an innocent soul's trustfulness. He went to the Larins and found Tat'iana in a garden. He treated her embarrassment kindly, with genuine nobility of the soul, but he also explained that the domestic life was not in his interests. Such delights were for Lenskii and Ol'ga. Onegin did not deceive Tat'iana, but the tender maiden was crushed by his refusal. She wasted away in silence, and neighbors whispered that it was time for her to marry. Lenskii and Ol'ga blissfully lived through the carefree summer and colorful fall. When the first snow swirled, Lenskii saw Onegin and passed on the

Larins' invitation to Tat'iana's names-day party. Onegin scoffed at the local gentry that would be there but agreed to attend. The Larin household was filled with guests. A Monsieur Triquet embarrassed Tat'iana with a stanza in her honor. Onegin, bored, began flirting with Ol'ga during the dancing. Lenskii, incensed, left the party when Ol'ga told him the dance he wanted was taken by his friend. Lenskii solicited the former brawler Zaretskii for his second. When the latter delivered Lenskii's challenge to Onegin, the young dandy's first reaction was that he was always ready. The duel was set for the next day. Lenskii went to Ol'ga and was surprised when she asked why he had left the party so early. He was still loved, but he felt that he had to defend his honor. Early the next morning, he and his second waited on a country dam. Onegin had overslept. When he arrived with his valet for a second, Zaretskii argued that a menial was not suitable for the position. Onegin asked if he should leave, and the matter was dropped. The duelists marked their paces. Onegin fired first and Lenskii fell, mortally wounded. Onegin hastened to him, but the youthful poet had met an untimely end. Ol'ga did not grieve long. She was soon married to another and left the family. Onegin abandoned the country and traveled as an escape in the fashion of a Byronic hero. Tat'iana visited Onegin's estate and read his books. She realized that he was a parody of Childe Harold and slowly outgrew his tortured soul. In Moscow, she was introduced to society. When a general from a princely family made an offer, Tat'iana accepted. In time she became a grand matron of society. At a ball, Onegin met the transformed country girl and fell madly in love with her. He sent her a missive but was spurned. A second and third note received no reply. In desperation, he went to her stately home and entered her private quarters. Tat'iana, in tears, admitted that she still cared for him but that she would never be his. The remorseful hero left to face a life of disillusionment.

Pushkin bade his reader farewell with remorse, which he also felt in saying goodbye to his hero, Onegin.

Abbé, Agafon, Akul'ka, Albano, Alina, Andriushka, Anisia, Apollo, Apuleius, Armida, Aurora, Automedon, Baratinskii, Bayle, Bentham, Bichat, Bogdanovich, Buianov, Byron, Chaadaev, Chadskii, Chamfort, Chateaubriand, Childe Harold, Cicero, Circes, Clarissa, Cleopatra, Corsair, Cypris, Delphine, Del'vig, Demon, Derzhavin, Diana, Didelot, Don Juan, Elena, Elvina, Eol, Eve, Faublas, Filip'evna, Finmush, Flianov, Flora,

Fontenelle, Fonvizin, Fortuna, Freischutz, Giaour, Gibbon, Goethe, Grandison, Grimm, Guillot, Gulnare, Gvozdin, Herder, Homer, Horace, Hymen, Iazykov, Istomina, Ivan Petrovich, Julie, Juvenal, Kant, Katenin, Kaverin, Panfil Khalikov, Kniazhnin, La Fontaine, Dmitrii Larin, Ol'ga Larina, Pashette Larina, Tat'iana Larina, Lel', Lenore, Vladimir Lenskii, Levshin, Liubov' Petrovna, Liudmila, Lovelace, Lukeria L'vovna, Malek-Adel', Malvina, Manzoni, Marmontel, Melmoth, Melpomene, Moëna, Morpheus, N___, Napoleon I, Nereid, Nina Omir, Evgenii Onegin, Ovid, Ozerov, Paris, Parny, Pelagea Nikolaevna, Petrarch, Petushkov, Phaedra, Phillis, Phoebus, Pradt, Praskovia, Priam, Prolasov, Pustiakov, Pykhtin, Racine, Regulus, Richardson, Romulus, Rousseau, Ruslan, Saadi, Say, Sbogar, Schiller, Scott, Semen Petrovich, Semenova, Seneca, Sen-Pri, Shakhovskoi, Shishkov, Smith, Sotinin, Stael, Svetlana, Tasso, Terpsichore, Thalia, Theocritus, Tissot, Tolstoi, Triquet, Vandyke, Vania, Venus, Viazemskii, Virgil, Voronskaia, Wandering Jew, Werther, Wolmar, Yorick, Zadeck, Zaretskii, Zeus, Zizi.

Fathers and Sons, I. S. Turgenev, 1862.

Having graduated from St. Petersburg University, Arkadii Kirsanov returned to his family's estate accompanied by a friend, Eugene Bazarov, a taciturn liberal and nihilist. The lack of respect for authority expressed by the two young men greatly distressed the conservative members of the household: Arcadii's father, Nikolai, and his uncle, Pavel. Nikolai admitted to his son that he had taken a mistress, Fenichka, who lived in the manor house. Arkadii congratulated his father and was pleased to learn later that he had an infant half-brother. Pavel was an aristocrat bound by tradition who lived in retirement after a disappointing career as an army officer. He had forsaken his military career to be the lover of a famous beauty, Princess R___. Bazarov considered him a superfluous man. Pavel was irritated by the guest's abuse of the state, church, and pan-Russianism, and regretted his influence on his nephew. Fortunately Bazarov kept busy collecting frogs and infusoria which he was always dissecting and observing under a microscope. Nikolai showed his son their estate and explained his problems. He had divided his farm into smaller plots which the peasants rented on a sharecropping basis. Yet they cheated him and were slow in paying their rent. Growing bored with life on the estate, Bazarov suggested a trip to the provincial capital. With introductions to the governor, Arkadii and his friend went to town, where they met a fellow liberal, Sitnikov. The self-esteemed acquaintance introduced the newcomers to provincial society. At a ball they were overwhelmed by a young widow, Madame Odintsov. Arcadii found that his mother had been an intimate friend of the beautiful widow's mother. A friendship developed between them, and Madame Odintsov invited him and his friend for a visit to her estate. In a few days they became favored guests in her wealthy household. The hostess's younger sister, Katia, was especially attracted to Arkadii. Bazarov became the companion of Madame Odintsov. Long discussions led the nihilist to the conclusion that he was in love. When he professed his feelings and proposed marriage, Madame Odintsov politely refused. Perturbed by his rejection, Bazarov persuaded Arkadii to leave. They traveled on to the Bazarov's modest estate, where they were received with great enthusiasm by the nihilist's doting mother and admiring father, a retired army doctor. With nothing to do, the young men soon became bored and quarreled. Abruptly they left for the Kirsanov estate. On a whim they decided to stop at Madame Odintsov's. She received them coolly. Feeling unwanted, they soon went on their way. Bazarov continued his research at the Kirsanov estate and developed a friendship with Fenichka. Once, as they sat in the garden, Bazarov kissed her unexpectedly, causing her confusion and distress. Pavel accidentally witnessed the scene and challenged Bazarov to a duel even though he did not consider him a gentleman. In the encounter, Pavel was wounded in the leg. He told his brother that they had fought over political disagreements, but he was greatly embarrassed that he had been wounded by a nihilist. After urging Nikolai to marry Fenichka, Pavel returned to his old life as a dandy in Dresden. Bazarov moved back to his family's estate and helped his father treat peasants. Convinced that Arkadii was in love with Madame Odintsov, Bazarov stopped at her estate to help his friend with his suit. The hostess ridiculed him. Arkadii proposed marriage with Katia. When one of Bazarov's patients became ill with typhus, Bazarov accidentally scratched himself with a scalpel he had used. Although his father cauterized the wound, Bazarov became ill with a fever. Dying, he asked that Madame Odintsov be summoned. She came for a visit shortly before his death. Arkadii married Katia, and Madame Odintsov eventually became the bride of a successful lawyer. Nikolai made his union with Fenichka legal and became a magistrate during the liberation of the serfs. The Bazarovs often visited the grave of their son, who once had shown great promise.

Aesop, Tsar Aleksandr I, Alexisa, Anfisushka, Evgenii Vasil'ich Bazarov, Vasilii Ivanich Bazarov, Arina Vlas'evna Bazarova, Bourdaloue, Brown, Brühl, Büchner, Bunsen, Byron, Castor, Cincinnatus, Condillac, Cooper, Croesus, Debrett, Don Juan, Duniasha, Durdoleosova, Egorovna, Empress Ekaterina II, Elisevich, Emerson, Eniusha, Ermolov, Erofei, Fedka, Fedos'ia Nikolaevna, Fedot, Fenichka, Filipp, Foma, Frémy, Galignani, Ganot, Goethe, Gogol', Guizot, Hegel, Heine, Hoffman, Horace, Hufeland, Ivan, John the Baptist, Avdotia Stepanovna K____, Katia, Lidia Khostatova, Arcadii Nikolaevich Kirsanov, Nikolai Petrovich Kirsanov, Pavel Petrovich Kirsanov, Petr Kirsanov, Agafakleia Kuzminishna Kirsanova, Masha Prepolovenskaia Kirsanova, Kisliakov, Kolia, Il'ia Koliazin, Matvei Il'ich Koliazin, Agafeia Koliazina, Avdotia Nikitishna Kukshina, Lazarus, Liebig, Sergei Nikolaevich Loktev, Katerina Sergeevna Lokteva, Lothario, Louis, Louis Philippe, Macaulay, Massalskii, Matthew, Michelet, Mitia, Mitiukha, Mozart, Napoleon I, Napoleon III, Nelly, Saint Nikolai, Anna Sergeevna Odintsova, Peel, Pelouse, Petr, Porfirii Platonich, Pollux, Prepalovenskii, Prokovich, Proudhon, Pushkin, R____, Radcliffe, Raphael, Robert le Diable, Rodemacher, Rousseau, Sand, Sapozhnikov, Anna Savishna, Schiff, Schiller, Schubert, Shonlein, Sidor, Victor Sitnikov, Speranskii, Suvorov, Svechin, Taniushka, Timofeich, Toggenburg, Vaska, Saint Vladimir, Wellington, Wittgenstein, Zhukovskii.

"First Love," I. S. Turgenev, 1860.

After a party, three men decided that each should tell the story of his first love. The first man fell in love with his nanny; the second fell in love with his present wife; the third said his story would be put into writing and read to them at their next encounter. Vladimir, the third man, was a sixteen-year-old boy when his family moved from Moscow to their estate in the country for the summer. His parents paid him little attention. His father was a handsome man who had married for money. His mother was a nervous and jealous type. Vladimir had full freedom to do as he chose. Their nearest neighbors were the impoverished Zasekin family. The Princess Zasekina had a daughter, Zinaida, who was beautiful and charming.

Vladimir became one of her admirers, and was duly teased and flirted with. Vladimir went from ecstasy to despair, depending on the caprices of Zinaida. When she told him that he should be her page, he took the matter seriously, spying on her day and night. To his surprise, his father turned out to be a nocturnal visitor at Zinaida's. Soon thereafter, an anonymous letter revealed the affair between Zinaida and Vladimir's father to Vladimir's mother. The family returned to Moscow. Once Vladimir went riding with his father. When told to stay with the horses, Vladimir disobeyed and watched his father make a rendezvous with Zinaida. He saw his father stroke her arm with his whip, and she raised her arm and kissed it. Vladimir was in awe of the scene before him. Later, Vladimir entered the university and his father died. When Vladimir learned that Zinaida was in St. Petersburg with her husband, he waited a week before going to see her. When he went, he learned that she had died in childbirth.

Anna Ivanova, Antony, Maria Nikolaevna B____, Petr Vasilich B____, Vladimir Petrovich B____, Barbier, Victor Egorych Belovzorov, Byron, Caesar, Cleopatra, Dolskaia, Duniashka, Ermak, Fedor, Filipp, Freitag, Hugo, Kaidunov, Khomiakov, Lushin, Maidanov, Malek-Adel', Malevskii, Masha, Matilda, Saint Nikolai, Nirmatskii, Othello, Polonius, Pushkin, Rarey, Schiller, Sergei Nikolaevich, Sonia, Tonkosheev, Vladimir Petrovich, Vladimir Sergeich, Vonifatii, Zasekin, Vladimir Zasekin, Zasekina, Zinaida Aleksandrovna Zasekina, Zinaida.

A Gentry Nest, I. S. Turgenev, 1859.

After her husband's death, Mar'ia D. Kalitina filled her life with small-town gossip and the care of her son and her two daughters, Liza, a teen-age beauty, and Elena, a small child. An old aunt, Marfa T. Pestova, lived with them but did not approve of their frivolous acquaintances, the busybody Gedeonovskii and the dashing young suitor Panshin. Liza had considerable musical talent and studied piano with an old German, Mr. Lemm. When a distant relative, the landowner Fedor Lavretskii, returned from abroad, the family welcomed him. They felt sorry for the man whose wife, Varvara, had become a notorious Parisian courtesan. They had separated when he discovered her infidelity even though she was pregnant at the time. Lavretskii, who had been reared a Spartan, took over his estates after the death of his maiden aunt Grafira. He visited the Kalitins often and through his interest in music developed a friendship with Lemm. Mar'ia

wanted Liza to marry Panshin, who proposed for her hand; but
Marfa objected to the match.   Lavretskii also disapproved of
Panshin and fell in love with Liza, a love she returned.   Suddenly,
Lavretskii learned of his wife's death through a Parisian news-
paper.   He did not regret the news; he was now free to marry Liza.
An old school friend, Mikhalevich, visited Lavretskii at his estate
and warned him that happiness is rarely given once to a man, and
more rarely twice.   The two school friends realized that everything they once scorned, they now respected.   Their views had
changed with time.   Lavretskii wanted to marry Liza, but his wife
Varvara made a sudden return and his dream was shattered.
Varvara asked to be forgiven and soon involved herself in the
evening parties at the Kalitins.   She and Panshin became close.
When Lavretskii took his wife to one of his estates, Panshin visited
her from time to time.   The love between Liza and Lavretskii was
doomed, and she entered a convent.   Varvara returned to Paris,
and Lavretskii spent his time traveling and overseeing his estates.

   In the epilogue, the heirs to the Kalitin home, Mar'ia's son, and
daughter, Elena, have filled the house with love and happiness.
After eight years, Lavretskii went to Liza at the monastery, but he
caught only a glimpse of her.   He was comforted by their up-
holding their noble duty.

   Agaf'ia Vlas'evna, Alcides, Tsar Aleksandr I, Ambodik, Anton,
Apraksia, Bach, Balzac, Barbe, Baudran, Beethoven, Belenit-
syna, Bellini, Betsy, Bolius, Boutet, Chopin, Delaunay,
Demosthenes, Depré, Diderot, Doche, Donizetti, Dorval,
Dumas, Empress Ekaterina II, Ernest, Fedia, Fedor Avksent'-
evich, Féval, Fridolin, Sergei Petrovich Gedenovskii, Handel,
Helvétius, Herz, Ivan the Terrible, Jouvin, Jules, Justine,
Kalitin, Elena Mikhailovna Kalitina, Elizaveta Mikhailovna
Kalitina, Maria Dmitrievna Kalitina, Katrin, Khomiakov,
Kock, Mikhail Petrovich Kolyshev, Petr Vasil'evich Kolyshev,
Pavel Petrovich Korob'in, Kalliope Karlovna Korob'ina,
Varvara Pavlovna Korob'ina, Kubenskaia, Lais, Ada Lavret-
skaia, Anna Pavlovna Lavretskaia, Glafira Petrovna Lavret-
skaia, Malania Sergeevna Lavretskaia, Varvara Pavlovna
Lavretskaia, Andrei Afanas'evich Lavretskii, Fedor Ivanich
Lavretskii, Ivan Petrovich Lavretskii, Petr Andreevich Lavret-
skii, Kristopher Theodor Gottlieb Lemm, Lenochka, Lepic,
Lermontov, Liszt, Mars, Metternich, Mikhailevich, Mochalov,
Moreau, Mozart, N____, Nastia, Oberon, Odry, Ogarkova,
Palashka, Vladimir Nikolaevich Panshin, Parcae, Peel, Dmi-

trii Pestov, Marfa Timofeevna Pestova, Petito, Phryne, Prozorovskii, Pushkin, Rachel, Raynal, Richelieu, Rossini, Rousseau, Praskovia Fedorovna Saltykova, Sand, Schiller, Schlegel, Schubert, Scott, Scribe, Sénancour, Shakespeare, Shurochka, Skurekhin, Sonnenberg, Stratelates, Sue, Theodore, Titus, Van'ka, Vaucelles, Voltaire, Woldemar, Zakurdalo-Skubyrnikov.

A Hero of Our Time, M. Iu. Lermontov, 1840.

"Bela"

While traveling from Georgia to Russia in 1837, a Russian officer met Maksim Maksimich, a junior captain who had worked himself up from the lower ranks. Inclement weather forced them to spend the night in a smoky hut on the Mountain of the Cross in the Caucasus. After much tea with rum, Maksim Maksimich told an adventurous tale from his past. In June of 1832 he was stationed in a fort beyond the Terek River. One day a young ensign named Pechorin arrived with a supply convoy. He was a charming fellow but a little odd. He could hunt in the cold all day and never be exhausted, and became friends with Azamat, the son of a Circassian prince. The boy greatly admired the horse of a bandit named Kazbich, and Pechorin agreed to obtain the steed for him if he would kidnap his sister, Bela, for Pechorin. The dastardly act was carried off. Azamat brought his beautiful sister to the ensign and Pechorin helped the boy steal the horse. In the beginning life was difficult for the captive Circassian girl, but she finally fell in love with Pechorin. After a few weeks of bliss, he began to tire of her and took up hunting. Once while he was away, the saddened Bela went outside the fort to the river. The bandit Kazbich slipped up and abducted her. At that moment Pechorin and Maksim Maksimich returned and gave chase. Kazbich stabbed Bela in the spine and ran off. Pechorin took the wounded girl back to the fort, where she had a painful death. He buried her and became ill in his sadness. Later he was transferred to Georgia. Maksim Maksimich ended his story, and the two parted.

"Maksim Maksimich"

The traveling officer and Maksim Maksimich met again in 1837 at an inn in Vladikavkaz. As they were talking, a coach entered the courtyard and Maksim Maksimich recognized Pechorin in the vehicle. He sent word by his valet that he was at the inn and was eager to see his old friend. Maksim Maksimich waited a long time. He thought that Pechorin would come as soon as he received his note, but he arrived late and acted rather coolly. He was not interested in talk about the old days. When he abruptly left, Maksim Maksimich was offended. He mentioned that he had kept Pechorin's private journal and would now discard it. The traveling officer asked for the notes, and Maksim Maksimich readily gave them to him when they parted.

"Introduction to Pechorin's Journal"

When the traveling officer learned that Pechorin had died while returning from Persia in 1838, he decided to publish the journal of the deceased. His reason for making the private notes public was that he believed in the sincerity of the man who so mercilessly exhibited his own failings and vices. The journal was an instructive testament of a human soul; it could serve mankind as much as a history of a country. The officer's opinion of Pechorin was expressed in the ironic title he gave the book.

"Taman'"

One evening in 1830 while on travel orders, Pechorin and his cossack aid arrived in Taman', the grimmest seacoast town in Russia. The only quarters available were by the edge of the sea in a shanty known as an evil place. When a blind boy opened the door of the hut, Pechorin was filled with disgust at the sight of the misfortunate. The boy's reticence to communicate aroused Pechorin's enmity, but he settled down in a dark, dank corner. Awakened by noises during the night, he secretly followed the blind boy down to the sea. A girl like an undine met the boy, and they waited until a pirate rowed ashore. The three dragged something up on the beach. The next day Pechorin met the old landlady, who pretended deafness. His cossack warned that they were in the midst of bad people. When Pechorin tried to force the blind boy to explain his activities in the previous night, the old woman rebuked him for harming a child. Pechorin went outside and heard the undine singing on the roof. She danced and sang around the hut most of the day. That evening she lured Pechorin down to the sea and into a boat. He was overpowered by her attractions; but once they were at sea, she tried to throw him overboard. Although she fought like a man, Pechorin was able to grab her by the hair and toss her into the water. He could not swim and had to row ashore with a broken oar. On a cliff near the sea, Pechorin heard voices. The pirate Yanko had returned. When the undine warned that there was danger, the brigand gave instructions: the undine would go with him, the old woman could die and the blind boy could forage for himself. The boy began crying, and Yanko tossed him a few coins. Pechorin discovered that his personal belongings had been taken by the smugglers. He berated his cossack for sleeping during the robbery and left Taman' the next day.

"Princess Mary"
On May 10, 1832, Pechorin told in his diary about his arrival in Piatigorsk, a Caucasian spa. He met an acquaintance, Grushnitskii, whom he did not like. Strolling together, they came upon Princess Ligovskaia and her beautiful daughter, Princess Mary. Grushnitskii was in love with Mary. A Russian doctor at the spa, Werner, a friend of Pechorin's, told him that the older princess had inquired about him. Pechorin refused his offer of introduction to the Ligovskiis and delighted in ignoring the young princess when they occasionally met. She began to despise him and felt kindly toward Grushnitskii. About the nineteenth of May, Pechorin accidentally met an old love, Vera. She was married to an old man and was a guest in the Ligovskii household. Pechorin decided to befriend Princess Mary as a means of seeing Vera in her home. On May 22nd, a ball was held in the Club of the Nobility. During the dancing, a Captain of the Dragoons insulted Princess Mary and Pechorin saved her reputation by throwing him out of the hall. The Princess Ligovskaia introduced herself to Pechorin, and he became a frequent visitor at her home. The young ensign expressed a romantic philosophy, claiming that happiness was accentuated ego and that we live only out of the curiosity that things will become better. Mary became captivated by Pechorin and lost interest in Grushnitskii even through he was promoted to an officer's rank. The spurned suiter blamed Pechorin and sought vengeance. When Pechorin moved to Kislovodsk along with several members of the nobility, Grushnitskii began spreading rumors about him and Princess Mary. Pechorin overheard a plot Grushnitskii made with the Captain of the Dragoons against Pechorin. The spurned suiter was to pick a fight with Pechorin so that he would challenge Grushnitskii to a duel. The Captain would not put a shot in Pechorin's gun, and he would

thus be at Grushnitskii's mercy. That evening Pechorin visited
Vera. As he was climbing out of her window, someone grabbed
him. Pechorin knocked Grushnitskii to the ground and ran off
in the dark. When Grushnitskii related that Pechorin had come
out of the Princess Mary's room, the accused proposed a duel.
On June 17th, the adversaries met on a cliff above a ravine. Werner
was Pechorin's second, and the Captain was Grushnitskii's. Werner
knew about the plot, but went along with Pechorin's plan. Grushnitskii was ashamed to fire at an unarmed man, but he fired and
wounded Pechorin in the knee. Before firing, Pechorin asked if
Grushnitskii wanted to apologize and forget the matter. He refused. Pechorin then asked that a bullet be put in his gun as the
Captain had failed to load his pistol. The latter protested, but
Grushnitskii agreed, completely ashamed. Pechorin fired, and his
adversary fell to his death. Vera left Pechorin a note that she
was leaving him forever. He tried to follow her, but his horse
went lame. He confessed to Princess Mary that he did not love
her. She suffered from his rebuke. On June 19th, Pechorin was
transferred to a fort in the upper Caucasus.

"The Fatalist"
In December, 1832, Pechorin went to a cossack settlement north of
the Terek River. During a card game, predestination became the
topic of conversation. Lieutenant Vulich, a Serb who loved cards,
asked if anyone would bet with him that a man cannot dispose of
his life by his own will. In jest, Pechorin offered a wager, saying
that he did not believe in predestination. Vulich went to a bedroom and took a gun from the wall. Pechorin thought the young
man looked as if he would die that night. Vulich put the muzzle to
his forehead, pulled the trigger, but no shot fired. The next cham-
ber of the gun held a bullet. Vulich collected his money and left.
Walking home, Pechorin nearly tripped over a pig that had been
slashed by a sword. Two cossacks came running down the road in
search of a drunken friend who could easily harm himself. At four
in the morning, Pechorin was awakened by some fellow officers.
Vulich had been murdered. A drunken cossack had struck him on
the head and killed him. Pechorin knew that his intuition had not
betrayed him, for he had forseen Vulich's end. The assassin locked
himself in an empty hut. Pechorin broke in through a back window
and bound him. Pechorin contemplated fate and decided that man
can never be sure of anything. He mistakes for conviction an error

of reasoning. Pechorin preferred to have doubts about everything. He returned home and told Maksim Maksimich about his experience.

Apfelbaum, Azamat, Bela, Blind Boy, Captain of Dragoons, Chelakhov, Cicero, Efimich, Eremeich, Eromolov, Aleksei Petrovich Ermolov, Semen Vasil'evich, G____v, Vera G____v, Gamba, Grushnitskii, Ianko, Ivan Ignatevich, Kazbich, Mary Ligovskaia, Maksim Maksimovich, Mitka, N____, Napoleon, Narrator, Nastia, Nero, Old Woman, Grigorii Aleksandrovich Pechorin, Tsar Petr I, Raevich, S____, Tasso, Undine, Vasilii Petrovich, Vulich, Werner.

A Hunter's Sketches, I. S. Turgenev, 1852.

"Khor' and Kalinych"
A hunter visited the landowner Polutykin and met two peasants with completely different personalities. The first, Kalinych, was an idealist and a romantic, who was exalted and enraptured by nature and life itself. The second, Khor', was a prosperous peasant, who was a realist and enjoyed the snug nest he had created. Kalinych lived from hand to mouth, had once married, but had no children. Khor' lived comfortably and had a large family. The romantic had feared his wife; the realist had no fear or respect for women. Kalinych was in awe of their master; Khor' saw through the landowner. In spite of their differences, Khor' loved Kalinych and patronized him; Kalinych loved and respected Khor'. The special friendship between the two peasants impressed the hunter during his stay at Polutykin's.

Alliluev, The Eagle, Fedia, Kalinych, Khor', Miniaich, Nakhimov, Tsar Petr, Pichukov, Pinna, Polutykin, Nikolai Kuzmich Polutykin, Potap, Sidor, Socrates, Vasia.

"Ermolai and the Miller's Wife"
Ermolai, a respected huntsman, accompanied the narrator on a hunt in a deep forest. In the evening, they requested lodging at a miller's, who protested at first, but finally made a small shed available to the strangers. The miller's wife, Arina Timofeevna, brought them some food and Ermolai struck up a conversation with her. She had been the servant of a wealthy squire, Zverkov, but had been sent to the country in rags when she wanted to marry a man whom her owner did not find worthy. Later she was bought

by a burgher for his wife. They had one child, but it died. Ermolai sensed that Arina was not happy and asked her to visit him at his lodgings, promising to drive out his own wife while Arina was there. The miller's wife did not refuse the invitation. By coincidence, the narrator had once met her previous owner, Zverkov, and had a low opinion of the man who had so carelessly denied Arina happiness. Her sad fate was due to the whim of a thoughtless landowner.

Arina Timofeevna, Ermolai, Malania, Petr Vasilevich, Savelii Alekseevich, Sofron, Aleksandr Silych Zverkov.

"Raspberry Spring"

While hunting, the narrator stopped in a ravine to refresh himself at a brook known as Raspberry Spring. Two peasants were sitting in the cove created by the spring water. The author knew one of them, Stepushka, who was from Shumikhino, an estate that had once been prosperous. After the manor house on the estate burned, the masters departed and now cared only for the money they received from the labors of the serfs. Stepushka lived in a cubbyhole of the henhouse on the estate and survived in a meager fashion by doing odd jobs. The narrator joined the peasants and recognized the second as a man called Fog, who was a liberated serf of Count Petr Il'ich ____. The peasants told stories about their former masters which indicated why the aristocrats had lost their wealth. Extravagance and ignorance had ruined the landowners. When the narrator departed, he better understood the sad life of peasants left on ruined estates.

Aksin'ia, Akulina, Aleksei Romanych, St. Damian, Filipp, Gerasim, Kintil'ian Semenych, St. Koz'ma, Mikhailo Savel'ich (Fog), Mitrofan, Petr Il'ich, Stepushka, Trofimich, Valerian Petrovich, Vlas.

"A Country Doctor"

Catching a cold during a hunt, the narrator went to a country doctor, who related a remarkable incident. He was once called to the bedside of a beautiful girl, Alexandra, who was unconscious and had a high temperature. He prescribed a remedy, assured the girl's mother that her daughter would live, and took a rest. When the mother retired, the doctor looked in on his patient. He found the maid asleep and the girl raving. He quieted the beauty, woke up the maid, and retired. The next day the patient showed no im-

provement and the doctor spent much time with her. Alexandra
was educated and clever. Slowly they both realized their mutual
attraction and fell in love. For three days and nights, he battled
her illness. He could not send for help because the weather had
made the roads impassable. When he confessed his love and proposed, the girl accepted even though she was near death. She told
her mother of her betrothal before she passed away. The doctor
was despondent for a long time but finally took a wife. She did not
bring him happiness.

Akulina, Aleksandra Andreevna, Kalliopin, Pavel Lukich
Mylov, Trifon Ivanovich.

"My Neighbor Radilov"

Ermolai, a huntsman, and the narrator once entered a neglected
park and killed a partridge. A landowner, Radilov, appeared.
He was perturbed that they were hunting near his home. The
narrator, having thought the area was long vacant, apologized and
offered his catch to the landowner. Radilov accepted the bird on
the condition that the narrator would agree to dine with him. The
hunter accepted and went to the modest manor house, where he
met the host's aged mother, a ruined old nobleman named Fedor
Mikheich, and a young girl, Ol'ga, the sister of Radilov's deceased
wife. Although Radilov quoted Voltaire that everything was for
the best in this world, the narrator soon discerned that his host
was not a happy man. When Radilov related the details of his
wife's death, Ol'ga's face gave a memorable expression. Some time
later, the narrator learned that Radilov had run away with Ol'ga
abandoning his old mother. Ol'ga's expression had been more of
jealousy than sorrow. When the narrator visited the old woman,
he asked about her son, but received only tears in answer. The
narrator remembered Voltaire's ironic remark. The hunter knew
that it was illegal in Russia at that time for a man to marry his
sister-in-law.

Ermolai, Fedor Mikheich, Ol'ga, Luka Petrovich Ovsianikov,
Michailo Mihailovich Radilov, Radilova, Voltaire.

"Ovsianikov, the Freeholder"

The Russian gentry had declined steadily after the eighteenth
century. It was difficult to distinguish a petty squire from a muzhik. Such was not the case, however, with the landowner Luka

Petrovich Ovsianikov. He resembled one of the old order of Russian nobles: dignified, well groomed, and respected by his serfs and landed neighbors. The narrator visited this fine example of noble qualities and heard several interesting tales about the olden days. The narrator's grandfather had cheated the Ovsianikovs out of some land; a lout named Komov had drunk himself into the grave while ruining his estate; the narrator's grandfather had offered to sell his wife before he would part with his favorite dog; and the nobleman Korol'ev had urged the gentry to consider the peasants when they were establishing their land boundaries, but Korol'ev himself would not give an inch of his own land to help the serfs. Ovsianikov had a nephew, Mitia, who was always causing trouble through his good intentions. But good though Mitia was, Ovsianikov knew he accepted bribes. The landowner felt his kind-hearted nephew represented the decline of the landed gentry.

Baush, Bespandin, Dmitrii Aleksandrovich, Fedos'ia Mikhailovna, Anton Parfenych Funtikov, Garpenchenko, Anton Karasikov, Stefan Niktopolenych Komov, Aleksandr Vladimirovich Korol'ev, Krylov, Franz Ivanych Lejeune, Vasilii Nikolaich Liubozvonov, Marfa Dmitrievna, Maria Vasil'evna, Mitia, Nikifor Il'ich, Aleksei Grigorievich Orlov-Chesmenskii, Porfirii Ovchinikov, Luka Petrovich Ovsianikov, Petr Ovsianikov, Tat'iana Il'inichna Ovsianikova, Bor'ka Perekhodov Radilov.

"Lgov"

Because they were tired of running after partridges in their own vicinity, Ermolai, the huntsman, persuaded the narrator to go hunting ducks in the Lgov region. Lgov was a large settlement in the steppes along a swampy little river. Once the two had arrived there, a local hunter named Vladimir offered his services. He was a young freed serf with some education but lived without any steady occupation. His eloquence amused the narrator but bothered Ermolai. When the hunting party decided to use a boat, Vladimir went for Suchok, a peasant who owned a small, battered vessel. While calking was being applied to the holes in the boat, the narrator questioned Suchok about his life. The peasant had been a gardener, a page, a whipper-in, a cook, and a coachman, and was now listed as his mistress's fisherman even though he did not fish. His mistress had decided that he should be a fisherman, and so he was, even though there were no fish in the swampy water. When the hunting party set out, they floated over quiet water. Soon they were busy shooting ducks and paid little attention to the water rising in the boat. It suddenly sank to the bottom. The hunters held their guns and birds above the water and walked out to the bank. They dried themselves in a hayloft as the sun set and songs came floating in from the settlement.

Afanasii Nefedych, Alena, Blangy, Ermolai, Iegudiil, Sergei Sergeich Pekhterkhov, Andrei Pupyr, Suchok, Tatiana Vasil'-evna, Vasilii Semenovich, Vladimir.

"Bezhin Meadow"
On a warm July evening, the narrator lost his way while hunting in a deep forest. When he came upon some young boys at a campfire in Bezhin Meadow, he realized how far he had gone astray and that he would have to wait until morning to return home. He joined the young lads around their fire. At first the boys were quiet, but soon they were talking among themselves. Fedia, a handsome, well-built boy, was about fourteen. He asked Iliusha, a hump-nosed, sickly looking boy of twelve, if he had seen the hobgoblin at the paper mill. An animated conversation took place about the supernatural creature. Pavel, a dark-haired, pock-marked lad of twelve, could not understand why the creature coughed. The smaller boys, Kostia, ten, and Vania, nine, listened to their elders in awe. Sounds in the distance were interpreted as emanating from nixies, wolves and whatever else their heightened imaginations envisioned. They spoke of death, forest creatures and haunted buildings. Once a dog barked and ran into the dark. Pavel went for water and reported that the soul of a drowning victim had called out to him. The smaller boys were disturbed, but Pavel warned that no one can escape his fate. A crescent moon rose, and the narrator smelled the burning embers and listened to the boys talk into the night. Waking up early, the hunter left the boys asleep, save for Pavel, who looked up as the narrator nodded to him and left. Later that year, Pavel died in a fall from a horse.

Akim, Aniutka, Avdiusha, Dorofeich, Ermil, Fedia, Feklista, Gavrila, Il'iusha, Ivanushka from Red Knolls, Ivanushka Kosoi, Ivashka Fedosiev, Kostia, Fedor Mikheevskii, Nazarov, Pavlushka, Ivanushka Sukhorukii, Trishka, Trofimich, Vania, Vassia, Vavila, Ul'iana.

"Kassian of Fair Strath"

Returning from a hunting trip, the narrator noticed that his driver, Erofei, a superstitious young man, was hurrying to pass an intersection before a funeral procession turned down the lane. Many considered it an ill omen to meet a corpse on the road. Erofei managed to beat the procession, but an axle broke and he had to stop. The funeral slowly went by them. The driver worked on the axle and was finally able to pull the cart into a village. There the narrator went to a small figure sleeping on the ground and asked for help. The awakening small man, Kassian, turned out to be a dwarf of about fifty years. Learning the inquirer was a hunter, the little wrinkled man shamed the narrator for killing God's creatures. Reluctantly, Kassian agreed to guide the hunter to some offices where he might buy a new axle. While the carriage was being prepared, the narrator went hunting and Kassian tagged along. When a bird was killed, the dwarf became morose and finally accused the hunter of killing for sport, not for food. A young girl gathering mushrooms appeared, and Kassian spoke to her as to a daughter. The narrator tried to inquire about Kassian's past, but the dwarf gave little information. When they returned to the village, Erofei was ready for departure. On the road, the driver commented that Kassian had always been a strange little man.

Annushka, Erofei, Kassian, Martin.

"The Steward"

Arcadii Pavlich Penochkin, a fancified and sophisticated neighbor of the narrator, was considered one of the most respected members of the gentry in the area. However, in spite of his excellent taste, exceptional manners and resplendent hospitality, the narrator was reluctant to visit him. Something was lacking; a disquietude permeated his household. Once while visiting Penochkin, the narrator was obliged to share a ride to a nearby estate of the pampered host. When they arrived, the steward, Sophron Iakovlich, put on a great air of servitude and humbleness. Penochkin proclaimed the steward unsurpassable and took the narrator for a tour of the estate. Sophron had an explanation for everything and worded his remarks so that they complimented his master. When the party met two muzhiks who begged for attendance and bowed to the ground before them, Penochkin condescended to listen. However, when the men complained bitterly

against Sophron, the master refused to accept a different concep-
tion of his steward than the one he had. He dismissed the peasants.
The narrator learned later that the steward was famous for abusing
the serfs and had grown rich at his master's expense.

Anpadist, Antip, Carême, Egor Dmitrich, Fedoseich, Fedor,
Mikholai Mikholaich, Arkadii Pavlych Penochkin, Sofron
Iakovlich.

"The Office"

To escape a drizzling rain, the narrator ducked into a small,
delapidated hut to inquire about the whereabouts of the nearest
village. An ancient man who could hardly see or hear was serving
as a watchman over a pea storage bin. Receiving some vague instructions, the hunter went up the road and came upon a small
building. Entering, he was informed that he was in the office of
the estate of Elena Nikolaevna Losniakova. The narrator said he
was prepared to pay for a place to dry out and have tea. The men-
tion of money brought out a man from another room, who offered
a small, adjoining enclosure to the narrator. During his rest in the
office building, the hunter learned various things about the running of the estate: the office was overrun with clerks; the proprietress issued formal orders for trivial affairs; the steward was
cheating the landowner in the sale of her grain; and the peasants
were mistreated. The narrator recorded a long argument between
two of the office staff and then apologized to the reader for possibly offending his sensibilities. The disorder and pathetic lives
at the Losniakov estate were evident from the quarreling overheard in the office.

Agrafena, Aksin'ia Nikitishna, Mme. Engeni, Fediushka,
Gavrila Antonich, Iagushkin, Ivan, Nikolai Eremeich Khvostov, Konstantin Narkizych, Kupria, Karlo Karlich Lindamandol, Elena Nikolaevna Losniakova, Nazar Tarasych,
Pavel Andreich, Petr, Robinson Crusoe, Sidor, Tat'iana,
Timofei, Tiutiurev, Vasilii Nikolaevich, Viktor Aleksandrovich, Mikhailo Vikulov.

"Biriuk, the Morose One"

Driving through a forest, the narrator was suddenly caught in a
downpour. A large muzhik came out of the woods and directed
the carriage to his own hut. The narrator found out that he was
in the squalid home of a well-known woodsman called Biriuk. A
small girl looked after a baby in a crib in the one-room abode.

Biriuk's wife had run off with a city fellow. When the rain slackened, the woodsman offered to lead his guest out of the forest. Their departure was interrupted when Biriuk heard someone illegally chopping down a tree in the distance. The narrator decided to accompany the woodsman when he went to investigate. Biriuk soon had the thief tied and brought back to the cabin. The narrator offered to pay for the tree, but Biriuk would not free the criminal. The poor muzhik, who was evidently in a state of poverty, pleaded with the woodsman, but Biriuk refused him freedom. When the thief's pleas turned to abuse, Biriuk would have physically harmed him had the narrator not intervened. After some time, the woodsman freed the thief and led the narrator out of the woods.

Ermolai, Foma Kuzmich, Ulita.

"Two Landowners"

The retired General Khvalynskii was a dreadful fussbudget and middle-aged skinflint who managed his own estate. While he was a bachelor, he admired the fair sex and was considered an eligible candidate for marriage. The general was quite a contrast to another landowner named Stegunov. The latter was also a bachelor, but he paid little heed to the running of his estate. He was an excellent host who liked fussing around his manor house. During a visit there, the narrator witnessed a great upheaval which occurred when Stegunov noticed some chickens in his garden. The entire household was put into commotion until the owner of the chickens was identified and the birds were removed from the garden. When the guest heard someone being whipped, the host informed him with the kindliest of smiles that Vassia the butler was being punished for improper behavior. Later when the narrator was leaving the estate, he saw Vassia and asked why he had been whipped. The peasant did not explain but assured the enquirer that he had deserved the punishment. "That's old Russia for you," thought the narrator.

Avdotia, Ermil, Iushka, Vlacheslav Illarionovich Khvalynskii, Mikhailo Ivanovich, Mishka, Natal'ka, Parasha, Pavel Vasil'-evich, Pushkin, Saadi, Mardarii Apollonych Stegunov, Vasia.

"Lebedian'"

In a rural fair at Lebedian', the narrator met all manner of men, including a certain Victor Khlopakov. The swarthy little man of thirty smoked, drank and created mots that brought him much attention. However, his remarks were not very clever and the narrator was puzzled by Khlopakov's popularity. It turned out that the jokester had ruined his own estate and lived at the expense of his friends. The narrator watched the popular figure play billiards with the Grand Duke N____, who greatly appreciated the mots of the ingratiating Khlopakov. The next day the narrator went to look over the horses being sold at the fair. He was dickering over a price with the horse trader Sitnikov when the Grand Duke and Khlopakov drove up in a fine troika. Sitnikov immediately dropped the narrator and favored his new guests. The storyteller went to another dealer and bought a horse which he found to be lame after he had led it home. He went back to the dealer, but was not able to return the horse. Laughing at the lesson he had learned, he went to a coffeehouse. The Grand Duke was there, but he had seemingly dropped Khlopakov and taken up another friend. When Khlopakov tried to be funny, the exalted personage frowned and the jester retired to a corner by himself.

Aeneas, Baklaga, Anastasii Ivanych Chernobei, Il'iusha, Tsar Ivan Vasil'evich, Victor Khlopakov, Nazar Kubyshkin, Kuzia, N____, Petia, Sitnikov, Soniakova, Steshka, Vasilii, Verzhembitskaia.

"Tat'iana Borisovna and Her Nephew"
In a remote village there lived a rather remarkable widow named Tat'iana Borisovna Bogdanova. She was uneducated, unaffected, hard working, and immune to the vices of country women: she never gossiped, became excited or caused trouble. Consequently, she was sought after for advice, and she was known as a good listener. The tranquillity of her household was destroyed when her nephew, Andrei Belozorov, returned from St. Petersburg. When the relative was a boy, he had lived with Tat'iana, but she had sent him to art school in St. Petersburg on the advice of her friend Belevolenskii. For the first three years, the boy wrote regularly; then the letters became rarer. In the seventh year, he asked his aunt for money because Belevolenskii had passed away. She sent all she could until she could send no more. When she stopped sending funds, Andrei arrived at her doorstep. He had become a slothful, impudent ignoramus who rarely painted and then poorly. Tat'iana tolerated and loved Andrei, who became fatter and lazier. Many acquaintances quit calling at the estate.

Agaf'ia, Bettina von Arnim, Petr Mikhailovich Belevolenskii,

Andrei Belozorov, Tat'iana Borisovna Bogdanova, Napoleon
Bonaparte, Correggio, Goethe, Aleksei Nikolaevich K——,
Mlle. K——, Kutuzov, Mikhei, Polezhaev, Policarp, Raphael,
Schiller, Terteresheneva, Vasia, Viotti.

"Death"

The narrator and his neighbor, Ardalion Mikhailich, went to
see the felling of some trees in a forest owned by the latter. The
forest had been ruined by the terrible, snowless winter of 1840.
They were suddenly met by a peasant who reported an accident:
Maxim the contractor had been crushed by a tree. The group went
to the scene of the tragedy and witnessed Maxim's death. The narrator commented that the Russian peasant died as if performing
a rite: coolly and simply. The narrator had witnessed several such
scenes. At a secondary-grade medic's, a large miller came and asked
for help. He had ruptured himself. The medic told the large peasant that he had waited too long but that he would try to save him.
Hearing that his problem was grave, the peasant refused to stay
and went home. Four days later he died. A tutor the narrator respected accepted death calmly, wishing to smoke his pipe once
more before going on. And a landed proprietress tried with her
last effort to thrust her hand under a pillow for a rouble she had
kept to pay the priest for her last rites. Russians die in amazing
ways!

Aksenia, Ardalion Mikhailich, Arkhip, Dasha, Efim, Désiré
Fleury, Hegel, Kapiton Timofeich, Kardon-Kitaeva, Kasatkin,
Kasatkina, Kleopatra Aleksandrovna Kasatkina, Gottlieb von
der Koch, Kondachovy, Kol'tsov, Gur Krupianikov, Fofa
Krupianikova, Zeza Krupianikova, Maksim, Malania, Melek-
trissa, Onisim, Pavel, Schopenhauer, Seliverstych, Avenir
Sorokoumov, Vasilii Dmitrich.

"The Singers"

The hamlet of Kolotovka was miserably ugly. It was located on
the slope of a bare knoll which overlooked a ravine full of pits and
washouts. Only a tavern, the Hunter's Rest, offered solace to the
villagers. The host, Nikolai Ivanich, had the ability to attract
and keep his customers. He gave counsel to peasants and burghers
alike. Yet he was a bystander compared to his hard-working wife.
The narrator happened to visit the pothouse when a singing contest was being held. The Shopman from Zhizdra, a robust man, was

the first to sing. When he opened his mouth, the highest of fal-
settos rang out. He was a "tenore de grazia." At first his voice
did not arouse too much response, but soon the tavern was full of
listeners. Even the Wild Squire, a taciturn and clumsily built
Hercules who rarely expressed pleasure, softened the expression
on his face. When the Shopman finished, he was highly praised.
It was the turn of Iakov the Turk. He started weakly, almost afraid.
Slowly his voice became firm. A Russian soul, true and ardent,
expressed itself in heartfelt sounds. The sincerity and beauty of
the voice soon had the tavern-keeper's wife in tears. The host and
others stood with mouths gaping. Art had transcended the ugliness
of the village, taking the listeners into the realm of beauty. A tear
came down the iron face of the Wild Squire. When Iakov finished,
he was a hero. The narrator, moved by what he had heard, left the
tavern and went back into the ugliness of the world. A boy's voice
called in the distance as the narrator walked out of the ravine.

Antropka, Blinker, Dockmaned Filly, Hercules, Iashka the
Turk, Nikolai Ivanich, Evgraf Ivanov (Featherbrain), Perevlessov (Wild Squire), Shchepetenko, Shopman from Zhizdra.

"Petr Petrovich Karataev"

Waiting for fresh horses at a relay station, the narrator met Petr
Petrovich Karataev. Over tea, the new acquaintance revealed that
he had ruined his estate and was heading to Moscow for work in
the civil service. The wait for horses was long, and so Petr told the
reasons for his fate. He had once fallen in love with a marvelous
wench named Matrena, who belonged to an old landowner near his
own estate. When he pleaded with the old crone for the girl, the
yellowed old woman refused the sale, thinking that Petr would be
a good match for a pale-faced relative. He would not give up the
idea and persuaded Matrena to run away with him. For a while
they lived in bliss on his estate. Matrena loved to drive a sleigh
over snow. One day, in a devil-may-care frame of mind, she insisted on driving past the estate of her old mistress. Unfortunately,
she met the old crone on the road and the old lady's sleigh turned
over. A police inspector soon called on Petr. Bribes helped in the
beginning, but soon Petr was deeply in debt. To save him, Matrena
gave herself up. Petr did not know her fate. The narrator's horses
were readied, and the two acquaintances parted. A year later the
storyteller accidentally met Petr in a Moscow tavern. The former
landowner had degenerated into a drunken carouser.

Sergei Bobrov, Pantelei Gornostaev, Katerina Karpovna, Petr Petrovich Karataev, Fedor Kulika, Matrena Fedorovna Kulikova, Stepan Sergeich Kuzovkin, Maria Il'inichna, Mochalov, Polezhaev, Pushkin, Vasia.

"The Meeting"
Resting in a birch grove to escape a drizzling rain, the narrator fell asleep. When he awoke, the sun was shining. As he started to rise, he spied a pleasant-looking peasant girl sitting about twenty paces away. She was evidently waiting for someone. Soon a male figure appeared, but he was a dandified valet who put on airs. To the girl's distress, the young man, Victor, informed her that his master was leaving the next day for perhaps a year. "You'll forget me," she cried, but he warned her against shedding tears. His answers to her questions were brusque, giving her no comfort. She presented him with some cornflowers. He took them but dropped the bouquet when he took a monocle out of his pocket. He allowed her to look through the glass but quickly grabbed it back when she failed to handle it correctly. When he started to leave, she resorted to tears. Her broken heart did not move him, and her tears only caused him irritation. When she could not control herself, he walked away in great strides. The narrator rushed toward the girl, but she saw him coming and bounded away with her last bit of strength. The storyteller took the blue cornflowers and treasured them long after they had withered.
Akulina, Viktor Aleksandrovich.

"Hamlet of the Shchigrovskii District"
Aleksandr Mikhailovich G____ was a wealthy landowner, who loved to give stag parties at his fine estate. The narrator arrived for such an event and found the host greatly excited: a particularly important person was coming. When he did arrive, all the guests fawned over him. A local wit, Lupikhin, was considered a great tease; but he confessed to the narrator that he was really being malicious and yet was not taken seriously. The wearisome evening finally ended, and the narrator retired to his room which he had to share with a stranger. Neither the narrator or the other guest could sleep, and the latter suddenly began discoursing on his life. He felt that he was not very original and believed that the world belonged to those who were. His own life was a shambles. He had been well educated but could not succeed in any of the three

areas open to a landowner: civil service, military service, or estate management. He had disintegrated from a respected member of the gentry to a nobody. Even his attempts at writing had failed. He began to enjoy the humiliations inflicted on him by his neighbors. He even refused to give the narrator his name, saying that he was just the Hamlet of the Shchigrovskii District. His life had no meaning. The next morning when the narrator awoke, the stranger was gone.

Beethoven, Dalai Lama, Filipovich, Aleksandr Mikhailovich G____, Iakov, Kantagriukhin, Kiril Selifanych, First Kliukhan, Koltun-Babura, Kozel'skii, Vasilii Kudriashev, Linchen, Petr Petrovich Lupikhin, Minchen, Orbassanov, Schiller, Sofia, Vasilii Vasil'evich, Vera, Voinitsin.

"Chertopkhanov and Nedopiuskin"

The Chertopkhanov estate had been ruined by various impractical enterprises: the construction of a church so large that it would have qualified for a cathedral had it ever been finished, and the creation of a coach of such dimensions that it fell apart on a hill. Pantelei Chertophanov inherited his family's pride but little else. Robust and self-assured, Chertopkhanov was considered unusual by his neighbors, but he gave no care to their sentiments. At the reading of an uncle's will, a brash, conceited relative began to tease a young, nervous man, Nedopiuskin, who had been left some money by his benefactor. Chertopkhanov soon put his snobbish relative in his place and made him apologize to the meek little man. Nedopiuskin felt indebted to his rescuer for the rest of his life. They even began to live together: Chertopkhanov became the strength and will of Nedopiuskin, and the latter became an audience for the proud aristocrat. When the narrator visited Chertopkhanov, he met a gypsy woman, Masha, who was "sort of a wife" for the host. Chertopkhanov ordered Masha and Nidopiuskin around, but they bowed to his will as if they appreciated his supervision. The narrator witnessed a lively songfest in an evening "at home" on the Chertopkhanov estate.

Birkopf, Eremei Lukich Chertopkhanov, Pantelei Eremeich Chertopkhanov, Rostislav Adamych Chtoppel, Derzhavin, Ermolai, Frederick the Great, Karp, Khriaka-Khrupenskii, Marlinskii, Masha, Mitrodora, Nedopiuskin, Tikhon Ivanych Nedopiuskin, Vasilisa Vasil'evna, Voltaire.

"The End of Chertopkhanov"

To the surprise of the proud Chertopkhanov, Masha, his gypsy, became weary of living with him and decided to move on, as was her nature. Threats, entreaties, and sobs did not dissuade her. Chertopkhanov was saddened by her departure but then faced another woe: his friend, Nedopiuskin, died. Left alone, Chertopkhanov turned to drink until a wonderful steed, Malek-Adel', came into his life. Chertopkhanov rescued a Jew from a vicious mob, and the grateful man presented his rescuer with the fine horse. Chertopkhanov was too proud to accept the animal and made arrangements to pay the owner something in six months. Malek-Adel' revived Chertopkhanov's spirits. Just before the proud new owner had to pay for the horse, he received an inheritance from an aunt which replenished his resources. However, Malek-Adel' was stolen on the eve of the payment. Chertopkhanov disappeared for a year, searching for the black steed. When he returned with a fine animal, he was apprehensive. He was not sure the horse was Malek-Adel'. Events proved that the new animal was a coward, and Chertopkhanov shot him. Again the proud aristocrat withdrew and drank. When he died, two people followed his coffin to its grave: a servant and the man he saved from the mob.

Eremai Lukich Chertopkhanov, Flora, Foma, Iav, Leiba Moshel, Masha, Nedopiuskin, Perfishka, Vasia.

"Living Relics"

Caught in a rain while hunting with Ermolai, the narrator decided to change locations and went to a remote village on his mother's estate. He spent the night in a small lodge and awoke early the next morning. Standing in the dawn light and enjoying the beautiful natural surroundings, he saw some beehives in a small ravine and started walking toward them. A small, wattled shed stood near the hives. When the narrator glanced through the open door of the building, he was startled. Something was moving on a platform in a dark corner. "Master, oh, master," a voice called out. The narrator entered and saw a small, withered brownish figure. He did not recognize it. The invalid explained that she was the Lukeria who used to be a house serf at his mother's manor house. It was impossible! The narrator remembered Lukeria as a young, joyful girl who was always singing and dancing. After he went away to school, he had forgotten about her. Yet it was she before him. Just before she was to marry the man she loved, she

fell and injured herself internally. Soon her body began to dry up
and shrink. Doctors could not help. She saw her lover marry
another and was then moved to the remote village where she lived
in squalor. The narrator promised her help, but she pleaded to be
left alone. Life had been cruel, but she had adjusted to it. She now
had the joys of nature, and her body deserved no more. The description of life she presented humbled the narrator. He left saddened. Soon afterwards, she passed away.

   Agrafena, Aleksei, Ermolai, Jeanne d'Arc, Lukeria, Petr
   Petrovich, Vasilii Poliakov, Semen Stolpnik.

"Rattling Wheels"
Having run out of bird shot, the narrator decided to take a night-
time trip to Tula for supplies. He hired a peasant, Filofei, to drive
him, and they set out over smooth territory. The narrator went to
sleep and awoke with the realization that the cart was in the middle
of a river. Fiolofei was fording the waterway in the dark by relying
on his horses' judgment. The narrator was not pleased with the
idea, but it worked. They were soon going over hills and dales.
Suddenly in the distance they heard rattling wheels. Filofei
warned of bandits, but the passenger belittled his fears. However,
apprehension soon possessed the narrator and he allowed Filofei
to race the horses. It was to no avail. They were soon overtaken by
a gang of drunken peasants who passed them and then stopped
ahead on a small bridge. "Just the way holdup men do," Filofei
warned. When they came to the peasants, one of them said that
they had "put a lad to bed." It was evident they were drunk.
When one asked for money for more drink, the narrator paid
quickly. Filofei then drove off. The next day the storyteller heard
that a merchant had been murdered on the road. Was it not the
person whom the peasants had "put to bed"? Every time the
narrator met Filofei, they both indicated how lucky they had been
on the road that night.

   Ermolai, Filofei, Kamenskii, Zhukovskii.

"The Kreutzer Sonata," L. N. Tolstoi, 1890.
   On a train traveling across the Russian countryside, a small group
of people became involved in a discussion concerning the rightful
place of women in marriage and society. One woman mentioned
that true marriage was sanctified by love. Another traveler, a
haggard gentleman, seemingly oppressed by loneliness, questioned

the validity of love. He scoffed at the notion of spiritual affinity and described life in marriage as a fearful hell. He deplored physical love and was confident that if the present generation did not attain pure, sexless love, the next one would. He maintained that mankind had to overcome its sex drive because it had demeaned and humiliated the human race. If the human species ended, it would not matter, because the church predicted an eventual end for man. He felt man was enslaved by sex. After his outburst ended with "I am Pozdnyshev and I killed my wife," the narrator listened to his story. When Pozdnyshev was young, he drank and enjoyed himself in society. Finally he married, but from the start the marriage was empty. The couple realized that they were caught in a trap and further, that their feigned font of happiness was actually a burden. Admitting that he was presently a trifle insane, Pozdnyshev painted a vivid picture of the changes in his state of mind before the murder: suspicion, hatred, jealousy and rage. His confession was pitiful, yet candid and honest. He and his wife had five children. The hate and hostility which grew between them was only temporarily suppressed by concern for their offspring. When the burden of the children lessened, the husband and wife seemed to turn on each other. Pozdnyshev saw no reason to have physical relations if they were not going to have more children. His wife became healthier and stronger, causing him to be more spiteful and jealous. When a friend of his, Trukhachevskii, became friendly with his wife through their common interest in music, Pozdnyshev began to suspect her of infidelity. He listened with agony when the two played Beethoven's "Kreutzer Sonata" together. Once when he was away on business, she wrote that Trukhachevskii had called on her. Pozdnyshev was enraged and immediately left for his home. When he arrived, he found his wife dining with his former friend while the children were asleep upstairs. Sending their lackey away so that they would be alone, he took a knife and entered the dining room. The expression on his wife's face seemed to imply her guilt, and he tried to stab her; but Trukhachevskii stopped him. Pozdnyshev turned on his rival, but his wife pulled him back, assuring him that nothing had happened between them. Trukhachevskii ran out of the room, and the husband and wife began quarreling. Enraged, Pozhnyshev stabbed at her, but the knife caught on her corset stays. Freeing the weapon, he wounded her fatally. Then he went to his room and rested. After a few hours, his wife's sister came and asked if he would see his wife before she died. When he entered her room, the enormity of what he had donè came over him and he begged her forgiveness. She refused to forgive him and said that their children would go to her sister. She died, hating him. Pozdnyshev broke into sobs as he finished his tale. At the station, he bid the narrator good-bye.

Andriusha, Beethoven, Buddha, Charcot, Don Juan, Egor, Ernst, Hartmann, Ivan Zakharych, Katerina Semenovna, Liza, Maria Ivanovna, Masha, Phryne, Vasilii Pozdnyshev, Pozdnysheva, Rigulboche, Schopenhauer, Sisyphus, Trukhacherskii, Uriah, Van'ka, Vasia, Venus of Milo, Virsavia.

"On the Eve," I. S. Turgenev, 1860.

One pleasant day two friends, Berseniev and Shubin, lay on the grass discussing life. Berseniev was a student who wanted to become a professor of history or philosophy. Shubin was a sculptor, an artist, as everyone called him. They dined at the house of Anna Stakhova, Shubin's patroness. She was married to Nikolai Stakhov, who spent most of his time in Moscow with his German mistress. Both Berseniev and Shubin were in love with the Stakhovs' daughter, Elena; but she loved Insarov, a Bulgarian studying in Russia. The foreigner's aim was to liberate his country. He met Elena through Berseniev; but when he realized that he loved her, he left. He could be devoted only to his cause. Since he did not say good-bye, Elena went to him. They met in an old chapel and revealed their love for each other. Insarov returned to Moscow, but the Stakhovs waited till the end of summer. News from Bulgaria about an oncoming war caused Insarov to prepare his departure. Elena decided to join him. Since she did not have a passport, he went to an acquaintance during a storm to make arrangements. He did not find his contact and became deathly ill. Berseniev stayed with Insarov during his recovery and reported his progress to Elena. When Insarov recovered, he and Elena secretly married. Her father discovered their union and threatened to complain and annul the marriage. Anna persuaded him to abandon his threats. Elena and Insarov left Russia. In Venice they were awaiting a ship for the final part of their journey when Insarov became ill and died. Elena, a strong-willed Russian woman, went on to Bulgaria as a nurse. She was never heard of again. Berseniev continued his studies, Shubin, his sculpture. Nikolai finally separated from his German mistress.

Agatha, Alfredo, Andriusha, Annushka, Avgustina Khris-
tianovna, B____, Andrei Petrovich Bersenev, Boboshin, Bolgin,
Maria Bredikhina, Brutus, Bustrapa, Byron, Caesar, Canaletto,
Chirkurasova, Arkadii Chikurasov, Conegliano, Dantan, Daria,
E____, Falieri, Fediushka, Granovskii, Grote, Guardi, Homer,
Horatio, Hugo, Dmitrii Nikanorovich Insarov, Katia, Kon-
stantin Pavlovich, Krum, Egor Andreevich Kurnatovskii,
Lupoiarov, Khalampy Lushchikin, Maecenas, Maria Petrovna,
Max, Mignonette, Zoia Nikitishna Muller, Niedermeyer,
Oberon, Palmerston, Perepreevskii, Pifagor, Pinselchen,
Podsalaskinskii, Proudhon, Raumer, Rendich, Schelling,
Schiller, Pavel Iakovlich Shubin, Nikolai Artemevich Stakhov,
Uvar Ivanovich Stakhov, Anna Vasil'evna Stakhova, Elena
Nikolaevna Stakhova, Stavasser, Swedenborg, Tat'iana, The-
mistocles, Timofei Nikolaevich, Tintoretto, Titian, Vanka,
Vasilii, Venelin, Verdi, Viazemskii, Violetta, Karolina Vogel-
mayer, Volgin, Washington, Weber, Werther.

"The Queen of Spades," A. S. Pushkin, 1834.

At a card party in the rooms of Narumov, events followed their
usual order: Surin was losing and Hermann refused to play because it was not his habit "to sacrifice the necessary in the hope
of winning the superfluous." Suddenly Tomskii began talking
about his wealthy grandmother, the Countess Anna Fedotovna.
Once a famous beauty and gambler, she now lived in her memories,
an old and cantankerous woman. Sixty years ago in Paris she
gambled away a large sum of money and her husband refused to
pay the debt. Horrified at the possible loss of honor, she appealed
to the charlatan St. Germain. Because of his admiration for her,
he gave her a card secret which won all her money back. Later she
shared the secret with Tomskii's uncle when he was in debt. Hermann scoffed at Tomskii's story but slowly became obsessed with
the amazing win. He decided to escape his poverty by securing the
trick from the old lady. Standing in front of the countess's mansion,
he was finally able to catch the attention of the old aristocrat's
ward, Lizaveta. He began standing outside the house daily and
Lizaveta continually looked for him. She was curious about the
young man who gave some novelty to her sad life. Though of the
upper class, she was impoverished and forced to live with her old
benefactress. Her days were spent reading and carrying out the
whims of the old lady. Once while entering a carriage with the

countess, Lizaveta saw Hermann run up and put a note in her hand. She was distracted and frightened, but could hardly wait to read the epistle. She did not know the tender message was copied from a German novel. She answered in a noncommittal way by throwing a note out the window. Undaunted, Hermann sent another letter by a servant requesting a meeting. Lizaveta was distraught and told the servant not to bring any more notes. Hermann continued writing. Finally the infatuated girl sent instructions on how to enter her room while she was with the countess at a ball. Hermann slipped into a room next to the old lady's and awaited her return. He watched her enter and undress. When she was alone, he went to her and asked for the secret. The startled old lady said it was a joke, but when Hermann pulled out a gun and threatened her, she died from fright. Hermann went to Lizaveta and confessed. Horrified that she was an accomplice to murder and realizing that she had been used, Lizaveta showed Hermann a secret staircase for his escape. At the countess's funeral, Hermann walked up to the casket and fainted. He thought the old lady had winked at him. That night a white figure entered his room. It was the countess. She would forgive him her death if he married her ward. In return, she gave him the winning series of cards: the three, seven and ace. The cards preyed on Hermann's mind. When a wealthy gambler, Chekalinskii, came to St. Petersburg, Hermann went to Narumov's to play cards. The game was faro; and to the amazement of all, Herman bet 47,000 roubles and won with a three. The next evening he wagered his winnings and won with a seven. The third evening was tense with excitement. Many gathered to watch. The dealer turned up a queen in his slot and an ace in the player's slot. Hermann thought he had won, but when he looked at his card, it was the Queen of Spades with the face of the old countess. He stared and the royal figure winked. The dealer said, "Your Queen has lost. The old lady's been killed." Hermann went mad. Lizaveta married well and became the benefactress of an impoverished young lady. Tomskii married the Princess Polina.

Anna Fedorovna, Casanova, Chaplitskii, Cheralinskii, Dante, Daria Petrovna, Eletskaia, Hermann, Ivan Il'ich, Lebrun, Lerois, Lizaveta Ivanovna, Mephistopheles, Mesmer, Montgolfier, Napoleon I, Narumov, Duc d'Orleans, Paulina, Richelieu, St. Germain, Surin, Pavel Aleksandrovich Tomskii.

Resurrection, L. N. Tolstoi, 1899.

Katiusha Maslova, a buxom twenty-seven-year-old prostitute, was led from her jail cell to stand trial for the murder of a client, the merchant Smekov. Sure of her innocence, she went to the ordeal with confidence. Her problems had begun at the age of sixteen when she was seduced by Prince Dmitrii Ivanich Nekhliudov, the nephew of her employer and benefactress. He gave the girl a hundred roubles and left her pregnant. Leaving her position, Katiusha gave her newborn child to an orphanage, where it died; she then entered a life of prostitution. As she walked to her trial, her seducer, Prince Nekhliudov, was resting at home. He was an idle young dandy of thirty who was breaking off an affair with the wife of the Marshal of the Nobility of his district in order to marry the wealthy Princess Korchagina. A note from the princess reminded him of his jury duty, and off he went to the court. When Katiusha was led into the courtroom, Nekhliudov was shocked and found it difficult to breathe. His concern for the role he had played in Katiusha's downfall was not so great as his anxiety over whether the coincidence that had brought them together might compromise his position and name. But a change developed in his feelings as the trial wore on. He became convinced of his own baseness and developed a desire to help the girl he had wronged. The trial went well and an acquittal seemed assured; however, the jurors found Katiusha innocent of theft, but failed to specify that she was not guilty of premeditated murder. She was sentenced to four years of penal servitude in Siberia. Nekhliudov learned that a clever lawyer could create some basis for an appeal; so he engaged Anatole Fanarin to prepare petitions on Maslova's behalf. During a dinner at Princess Korchagina's, Nekhliudov sensed his growing dissatisfaction with the society in which he lived. He went to visit Katiusha in prison but had difficulty establishing his identity over the din of the other visitors. In a more private interview, the inmate seemed interested only in the immediate gains to be derived from Nekhliudov. He became convinced of his moral obligation to bring about the spiritual regeneration of the prisoner. To cleanse his own soul, he decided to marry her; but she rejected him with derision. She did ask that he intercede for a woman and her son who were imprisoned for arson. Nekhliudov agreed and managed to have Katiusha transferred to the hospital as a nurse. She was expelled after being unjustly accused of enticing a medical assistant.

Nekhliudov went to St. Petersburg when Katiusha's petition came
before the senate, but the appeal was denied. Deciding to join her
in exile to Siberia, Nekhliudov attempted to dispose of his property
in accordance with the maxims of Henry George. At his Kuz-
minskoie estate, Nekhliudov tried to transfer the land to the
peasants under terms which reduced their rent and established a
community fund. The skeptical peasants showed little gratitude
but finally accepted the plan. At his other estate, Panovo, Nekhliudov again relinquished his land at terms disadvantageous to
himself. His sacrifices caused him to feel like a new man, and he
began to help other prisoners. When Katiusha departed with a
gang of convicts for Siberia, Nekhliudov arranged to start on the
same day. He witnessed the death of prisoners from sunstroke and
the harsh treatment of others. He obtained permission for Katiusha
to travel with political prisoners so that her lot would be easier.
The prince became acquainted with the political exiles and began
to respect them. One of the exiles, Vladimir Simonson, fell in
love with Katiusha and desired to marry her. Nekhliudov continued to help the prisoners and arranged medical treatment for
a consumptive. Katiusha's petition was accepted favorably, and
soon her sentence was changed to exile in a district of Siberia.
She decided to marry Simonson and relieve Nekhliudov of his
great sense of obligation toward her. The prince turned to his
religion for consolation and found the answers for all the problems
that had given him great concern.

Agrafena Petrovna, Tsar Aleksandr III, Aline, Anatolii Petro-
vich, Anisia, Anna Vasil'evna, Viktor Apraksin, Petr Bakla-
shov, Beethoven, Beh, Beliavskaia, Bernov, Bertha, Taras
Birukov, Feodosia Birukova, Efimia Ivanovna Bochkova,
Bogatyrev, Vera Efremovna Bogodukhova, Breve, Nadine
Bukshevden, Buzovkin, Aksutka Buzovkina, Charcot, Eka-
terina Ivanovna Charskaia, Ivan Mikhailich Charskii, Mikhail
Ivanovich Chernov, Mariette Chervianskaia, Chervianskii,
Clementi, Comte, Crooks, Iurii Dmitrich Danchenko, Dar-
win, Makar Devkin, Dostoevskii, Dufar, Vera Efremova, Emma,
Anatolii Petrovich Fanarin, Fedka, Fedorov, Fedotov, Ferry,
Filipp, Finashka, Garshin, George, Girofalo, Gladstone,
Governor of Siberia, Grabets, Grisha, Grishin, Gurkevich,
Hegel, Hertzen, Howard, Nikolenka Irtenev, Ivan Ivanovich,
Ivanenko, Ivan Semenich Ivanov, Ivashenko, Jeanne d'Arc,
St. John, Kamenskaia, Karchagin, Karmanov, Katerian Alekse-

evna, Katia, Semen Petrov Kartinkin, Khaltiupkina, Khomia-
kov, Khoroshavka, Kiesewetter, Kirimova, Karolina Albertovna
Kitaeva, Klara Vasil'evna, Kolia, Ivan Ivanich Kolosov, Markel
Kondratiev, Korableva, Petia Korchagin, Mary Korchagina,
Sofia Vasil'evna Korchagina, Kornei, Kornilova, Kriegsmuth,
Anatolii Kriltsov, Gregorii Efimovich Kuleshov, Laska, Levush-
ka, Liszt, Lizanka, Lombroso, Lozinskii, St. Luke, Semen
Makarov, Malania, Marfa, Maria Karlovna, Maria Vasil'evna,
Marks, Marusia, Mary Magdalene, Mikii Maslennikov, Anna
Ignatevna Maslennikova, Katerina Mikhailovna Maslova
(Katiusha), Maria Ivanovna Maslova, Sofia Ivanovna Maslova,
St. Matthew, Matrena Kharina, Matrena Pavlovna, Matvei
Ivanovich, Matvei Nikitich, Maudsley, Mavra, Medintsev,
Dmitrii Menshov, Menshova, Michelangelo, Mikhail, Mikhail
Petrovich, Mikishin, Missy, Mitin, Mitinka, Fedka Moloden-
kov, Moses, Nabatov, Dmitrii Ivanich Nekhliudov, Elena
Nekhliudova, Natasha Nekhliudova, Nepomniashchii, Neverov,
Nikiforov, Nikiteno, Nikitin, Tsar Nikolai I, Novodvorov,
Okhotin, Osten, Tsar Pavel I, Pelin, St. Petr, Petr Gerasimo-
vich, Petrov, Pozen, Pugachev, Rabelais, Emily Rantseva,
Rayner, Razin, Repin, Natal'ia Ivanovna Rogozhinskaia, Ig-
natii Nikiforovich Rogozhinskii, Rozovskii, Salamatov,
Samanov, Schopenhauer, Selenin, Semen, Semen Ivanovich,
Semenenko, Semenov, Shchegklov, Maria Pavlovna Shchen-
tinnina, Shenbok, Lidia Shustova, Sidorov, Valdimir Simon-
son, Skovorodnikov, Ferapont Smelkov, Sokolov, Spencer,
Starikov, Stepan, Taporov, Tarde, Mikhail Sergeevich Telegin,
Thoreau, Timokhin, Turgenev, Ustinov, Vakulov, Vania,
Vaseek, Vasil'ev, Vasilii Karlich, Vaska, Vinet, Voltaire,
Vorobev, Voronzova, Wolf, Zakharov.

Rudin, I. S. Turgenev, 1856.
   In a provincial Russian manor house some distance from Moscow,
a circle of acquaintances often met at Dar'ia Lasunskaia's, a wealthy
landowner who had a piquant interest in the unusual. Her household contained tutors for her sons, Vania and Petr, and a French
governess for her seventeen-year-old daughter, Natal'ia. The local
gentry that made up her group of acquaintances consisted of
Aleksandra Lipina, a young widow; Sergei Volyntsev, a retired
cavalry captain; Lezhnev, a wealthy landowner who dressed as a
commoner; Pigasov, a caustic misanthropic man who had failed at

nearly everything; and Pandalevskii, a bright young man who served as Dar'ia's secretary. One day Dmitrii Rudin came to read for the group an educational article by a mutual friend. Rudin was scoffed at by Pigasov, but the newcomer's brilliant intellect soon gained him the upper hand. For the next few months he became Dar'ia's favorite and practically ran the household. While Rudin was secure in Dar'ia's affection, Lezhnev maintained that Rudin was not all he seemed. He based his remarks on experiences which he and Rudin had shared as students. Rudin had destroyed Lezhnev's first love affair by his meddling. Rudin's eloquence and intellect greatly influenced Natal'ia, and she became infatuated with him. Volyntsev, who had courted Natal'ia for some time, watched with dismay her interest in Rudin. Natal'ia interpreted a chance remark by Rudin as a sign of his love for her. When she confronted him about his comment, he gave no encouragement, much to Natal'ia's distress. Seeing Natal'ia's disappointment, Volyntsev accused all intellectuals of being despots. Rudin avoided the challenge. Later, Natal'ia told Rudin, "I will be yours." Rudin made a clumsy attempt to establish better relations with Volyntsev, but the latter rejected his explanations as meddling. Rudin ceased his efforts, ashamed of his impetuosity. When Dar'ia learned from Pandalevskii about Natal'ia's affections for Rudin, she was shocked that her daughter could consider such a nobody and ordered her not to see him anymore. In a last meeting, Rudin counseled Natal'ia to obey her mother's wishes. She accused him of cowardice, and they parted forever. In later years, Aleksandra Lipina married Lezhnev, and Natal'ia married Volyntsev. Rudin wandered from place to place and patron to patron searching for new intellectual ideas and causes. He died in a lost cause, the Paris uprising of 1848.

Aibulat, Archimedes, Aristophanes, Bettina von Arnim, Basistov, Beethoven, Boncourt, Cambyses, Canning, Elena Antonovna Chepuzova, Copernicus, Demosthenes, Diogenes, Don Quixote, Dumas, Filipp Stepanich, Gagarin, Goethe, Griboedov, Fredrich von Hardenberg, Hegel, Hoffman, Jeanne d'Arc, Kant, Karchagin, Koltsov, Roksolan Mediarovich Ksandryk, Kurbeev, La Rochefoucauld, Dar'ia Mihailovna Lasunskaia, Natal'ia Alekseevna Lasunskaia, Petia Lasunskii, Vania Lasunskii, Mikhail Mikhailovich Lezhnev, Misha Lezhnev, Aleksandra Pavlovna Lipina, King Louis XIV, Maecenas, Manfred, Masha, Matrena, Mephistopheles, Muffel, N____ N____, Napoleon, Newton, Novalis, Orpheus,

Konstantin Diomidych Pandelevskii, Pavel, Pechorin, Afrikan
Semenich Pigasov, Pokorskii, Priazhentsov, Pushkin, Ras-
trelli, Recomier, Rosen, Dmitrii Nikolaevich Rudin, Sancho,
Schubert, Shchitov, Stepan, Subbotin, Tartuffe, Terlakhov,
Thalberg, Tocqueville, Virginia, Sergei Pavlich Volyntsev,
Zhukovskii.

Smoke, I.S. Turgenev, 1867.

In Baden on August 10, 1862, several well-dressed women and
men were promenading in front of a fashionable hall. Turgenev
commented: "May the Lord send them relief from the ennui which
torments them." Gregorii Litvinov, whose mother was of noble
birth and whose father was a merchant, was on vacation in Baden
where he awaited his fiancée, Tat'iana Shestova. He had studied
progressive farming methods and hoped to improve his family's
estate as a gentleman farmer after his marriage. An ebullient
acquaintance, Bambaev, once introduced Litvinov to Gubarev, the
idol of the intellectual set in Baden, who asserted that Russia pro-
duced nothing good, that everything of value was in Europe and
that the emancipation of serfs was not wise. The young men were
joined by an older lady, Matrena Sukhanchikova, who brought
gossip and pseudo-intellectual themes into their conversation.
One boorish guest, Bindasov, borrowed a hundred roubles from
Litvinov and never repaid the debt even though he won four
hundred roubles with the money. One quiet guest, Potugin,
visited Litvinov the next day, and they both expressed their
displeasure with their compatriots who had condemned Russia.
They felt that their country could advance through hard work.
Potugin left to take care of a small girl who had no parents and
was his charge. After a short walk, Litvinov returned to his room
and found a letter from Tat'iana as well as a bouquet of heliotrope.
A servant admitted that a lady had bribed him into letting her into
Litvinov's room. The gift brought back many memories. Ten years
before in Moscow when Litvinov was a student, he had fallen in
love with Irina Osinina, a member of a noble but impoverished
family. At first she gave him little attention, but gradually her
haughtiness disappeared and she accepted him as her suitor. Her
father, Prince Osinin, received an invitation to a court ball, and
Litvinov urged Irina to attend. He gave her a bouquet of heliotrope for the occasion. The next day Irina refused to see Litvinov,
and he learned two days later that she had gone to St. Petersburg

with Count Reisenback, a cousin of her mother. Irina's success at
the court ball had caused her to seek a brilliant match in the
capital. Litvinov was saddened by his loss but eventually found love
in Tat'iana. Potugin came to Litvinov with an invitation to visit
the home of General Ratmirov, a vain aristocrat. Irina was married
to the general and entertained a set of frivolous society members.
Litvinov was repelled by a séance and the empty conversation.
Irina would not leave Litvinov alone and begged him to love her
again. He finally admitted his love and broke his engagement to
Tat'iana. Potugin urged Litvinov to abandon Irina. He confessed
that his own love for her had caused him to agree to marry a friend
of hers who was to bear an illegitimate child. The marriage never
took place, but he had to support the little girl. To prove that
Irina was not shallow and heartless, Litvinov told her that he would
not become her lover unless she went away with him. He named
the train he would be on with a seat for her. She was not at the
station when he took his seat. When he saw her through a window,
he motioned for her to come. She refused. She could not give up
her position in society for her love. Litvinov returned to his father's
estate, which he inherited after his parent's death. The young
landowner spent three years in solitude while trying to improve
the estate. When an uncle visited and told of meeting Tat'iana,
Litvinov wrote and asked her forgiveness. Tat'iana was embarrassed by his penitence and invited him to visit. Their love was
renewed, and they were soon married. Irina continued to have
many admirers in St. Petersburg, but she was considered cold and
indifferent. After Potugin's young charge passed away, he too
severed ties with his former love. Irina was still in society, but
very much alone.

About, Alcibiades, Aleksandr Feodorovich, Annette, Avvakum,
Babette, Rostislav Bambaev, Barnaulov, Bastia, Batzov,
Belskaia, Bichat, Tit Bindasov, Blazenkampf, Matilda Bona-
parte, Brohan, Buckle, Vaska Buslaev, Catullus, Chopin,
Chukcheulidze, Cleopatrinka, Cora, Kirsha Danilov, Duchess
of Devonshire, Nikanor Dmitriev, Dolskii, Draper, Egorovna,
Elistratov, Evseev, Finikov, Fourier, Fox, Furstin, Garibaldi,
Glinka, Gneist, Greene, Gubarev, Haydn, Hegel, Heliogabalus,
Helmholtz, Homer, Horatio, Hume, Iazykov, Isabella, Ize-
dinov, Kock, Kokhanovskaia, Koko, Kulibin, Lassalle, Leda,
Gregorii Mikhailovich Litvinov, Litvinova, Liza, Lukin,

Luzhin, M____, Macaulay, Murat, Marks, Matilda, Matrena Kuzmichevna, Meyerbeer, Mikhnev, Milanovskii, Mozart, Muller, Napoleon III, Nash, Natal'ia Nikitishna, O____, Onatas, Pavel Vasil'evich Osinin, Praskovia Danilovna Osinina, Pachette, Patti, Peel, Pelikanov, Tsar Petr I, Phidias, Pirogov, Pishchalkin, Plenkovich, Pleskachev, Irinarkh Potugin, Sozont Ivanovich Potugin, Praskovia Iakovlevna, The Queen of the Wasps, R____ R____, Rappeau, Valerian Vladimirovich Ratmirov, Irina Osinina Ratmirova, Reisenbakh, Renan, Reumont, Riehl, Riurik, Robespierre, Saint-Simon, Sardou, Sarkisov, Sauerbrengel, Schulze-Delitzsch, Sh____, Shakespeare, Shchapov, Shelgunov, Kapitolina Markovna Shestova, Tat'iana Petrovna Shestova, Smith, Solomon, Solon, Boleslav Stadnitskii, Stahr, Stowe, Strauss, Stur, Subbotin, Sukhanchikov, Taine, Telushkin, Tenteleev, Vakhrushkin, Varlamov, Verdier, Veuillot, Viktorinka, Virchow, Semen Iakovlevich Voroshilov, Vorotinskaia, X____, Y____, Z____, Zizi, Zluitenkhov, Zozo.

Spring Freshets, I. S. Turgenev, 1872.

Returning to Russia from Italy, Dmitrii Sanin stopped in Frankfurt. In a confectionary shop he helped revive a young man from a fainting spell. The sister of the ailing man, Gemma, was a classical beauty, and Sanin fell in love. She was betrothed to Kluber, a German merchant. At a picnic, a German officer, von Dönhov, was fresh with Gemma and Kluber insisted that they leave quickly. Sanin returned and challenged the officer to a duel. The dueling parties settled their affair amiably. Sanin proposed marriage to Gemma, and she accepted, breaking with Kluber. Sanin decided to sell his estate in Russia and went to an old friend, Polozov, in Wiesbaden. Maria, Polozov's wife, was very wealthy. She bet her husband that she could captivate Sanin. Her charms were overwhelming, and Sanin went with the couple to Paris, forgetting Gemma. Back in Russia after many years, Sanin found a garnet cross which Gemma had given him after his proposal. He was overcome with emotion. He returned to Frankfurt, but Gemma had moved to New York, where she lived with her husband and five children. He wrote her a letter and asked her forgiveness. She answered that she did not think ill of him. She actually thanked him for stopping her marriage to Kluber. She was now very happy and wealthy. Her daughter was soon to be married. Sanin sent her the garnet cross mounted on a magnificent pearl necklace. He decided to sell his estate and move to New York.

Aeneid, Alexander of Macedon, Allori, Almaviva, Benediktov, Bernadotte, Chrysothemis, Panteleone Cippatola, Correggio, Danneker, Dante, Devrient, Dido, Don Giovanni, von Dönhov, Garcia, Gaston, Glinka, Goethe, Tat'iana Iurevna Gromoboeva, Gromoboi, Hoffman, Karl Kliuber, Knallerbsen, Kolyshkina, Kovrizhikin, La Fontaine, Lasunskaia, Lenore, Lenskii, Lizst, Luisa, Malts, Merope, Mikhail Pavlovich, Principessa di Monaco, Natal'ia Kirilovna Naryshkina, P____, Patti, Ippolit Sidorovich Polozov, Maria Nikolaevna Polozova, Pushkin, Raphael, Retz, Rikher, Rinaldini, Robert le Diable, Emilio Roselli, Gemma Roselli, Giovanni Battista Roselli, Lenore Roselli, Dmitrii Pavlovich Sanin, Jeremiah Slocum, Tarbuskii, Tshibadola, Weber.

Virgin Soil, I. S. Turgenev, 1877.

During the revolutionary activity of the 1870s, the student Nezhdanov held meetings in his St. Petersburg apartment with his cohorts Fekla Mashurina, Pakhlin and Astrodumov. The latter received a letter from Vasilii Nikolaich, the head of the Socialist Revolutionary Movement, which ordered Miss Mashurina and Astrodumov to report in another city. The conspirators went to Nezhdanov to obtain money for their trip. During their talk, the landowner Sipiagin came and hired Nezhdanov as a tutor for his nine-year-old son on his country estate. Nezhdanov accepted the position to earn money for the cause, but he found life in the country boring. He liked the lady of the household, Valentina, but was repulsed by a frequent visitor, the conservative landowner Kallomeitzev. Mariana, the Sipiagins' niece, was attractive but distant. When Valentina's brother Markelov came to visit, he and the tutor became friends and discovered that they were both revolutionaries. As relations between Mariana and Nezhdanov strengthened, he confessed his liberal views and she admitted her dissatisfaction with her dependency on the Sipiagins. They parted after declaring their love for each other and agreeing to support revolutionary activity. Nezhdanov received a letter from the head of the socialist movement requesting that he go with Markelov to visit Solomin, a factory manager, and Golushkin, a merchant. While Nezhdanov was talking with

Markelov and Solomin in a park about their contribution to the revolutionary movement, Pakhlin suddenly appeared. He escorted his acquaintances to his old relatives, the Subotchevs, who were eccentric and lived in the past. Solomin received an invitation to Sipiagin's estate, and Nezhdanov encouraged him to accept. After showing Solomin his factory, Sipiagin offered him the managership; but he refused. Nezhdanov and Mariana told Solomin of their desire to leave the Sipiagin household and start some definite action for the cause. Solomin offered them rooms in his factory as a temporary refuge. They moved there and began explaining their cause to lower-class people. Mariana was satisfied with her efforts, but Nezhdanov became depressed. When news came of an uprising in the area where Markelov was working, Nezhdanov went to help, but soon joined some workers in a dram shop and became drunk. Pavel Egorich, a fellow revolutionary, took him home as Pakhlin arrived with astounding news: the peasants had turned on Markelov, and he was captured; and Golushkin had been betrayed and was therefore betraying everybody. Pakhlin suggested they ask Sipiagin for help since Markelov was his brother-in-law and Mariana his niece. Mariana declined the idea for herself but said Pakhlin could try helping Markelov. Pakhlin went to Sipiagin, who went to the governor's house, where Markelov was held. Sipiagin tricked Pakhlin, in an indirect way, into telling where Nezhdanov and Mariana were staying. Markelov met with Sipiagin, but refused to repent and humble himself. During an inquest, Markelov's honesty and sympathy for the lower classes aroused compassion among the judges and accusers. Sipiagin left his relative to await trial. Arrangements were made for the arrest of the other conspirators. Nezhdanov informed Mariana that he no longer believed in their cause. Solomin urged them to protect themselves by marrying and leaving the factory. Nezhdanov meekly consented; but as they prepared to leave, he slipped outside and shot himself. Dying, he asked Solomin to marry Mariana. An inquest of the suicide revealed nothing. Mariana and Solomin were suspected, but there was no evidence. They had left and married. After nine months, Markelov was tried and sentenced. Miss Mashurin went into hiding. Ostrodumov was murdered by a petty burger he was inciting to riot. Golushkin, becuase of his confessions, received a light punishment. No special attention was paid to Pakhlin. Sipiagin eventually became a privy councillor and ceased looking

for his niece. Kallomeitsev acquired a reputation as a very trustworthy official. Years later Pakhlin met Miss Machurina. He
asked if she still took orders from Vasilii Nikolaich or from some
anonymous individual. She answered that perhaps it was from the
latter. Pakhlin said, "Anonymous Russia."

Agafon, Agrematskii, Aleksandr Pavlovich, Alesha, Anna Zak-
harovna, Aristarchus, Basanov, Binder, Bismarck, Boria,
Börne, Candide, Cato, Chateaubriand, Cicero, Dandin, Danton,
Darwin, Dmitrii the Pretender, Dobroliubov, Don Juan,
Empress Ekaterina II, Elizar, Empress Elizaveta, Euler,
Faleev, Fedor, Feodosii, Fimushka, Fitiuev, Fomushka,
Fourier, G____, Gallemeyer, Garasia, Gauss, Gavrila, Goethe,
Gogol', Golopletskii, Kapiton Andreich Golushkin, Gregorii,
Hamlet, Heine, Ivan, John the Forerunner, Quentin Johnson,
Barde de Kabylina, Kalliopich, Semen Petrovich Kallomeitsev,
Kant, Karageorgevich, Karelius, Katkov, Khemnitzer, Father
Kiprian, Kiril, Kisliakov, Klim, Konopatin, Kovrizhkin,
Kukol'nik, Ladislas, Laplace, Lenskii, Lukeria, Sergei Mik-
hailovich Markelov, Fekla Mashurina, Mendelei, Mendels-
sohn, Mikheich, Moller, Moloch, Mozart, Napoleon III,
Nebuchadnezzar, Neptune, Aleksei Dmitrievich Nezhdanov,
Nogent, Obrenovich, Pimen Ostrodumov, Ostrovskii, Sila
Samsonich Paklin, Pavel Egorich, Peel, Perepentev, Perfishka,
Philaret, Polly, Porpoise, Proudhon, Khavronia Pryshchova,
Pufka, Pugachev, Pushkin, Rachel, Raphael, Rinaldinin,
Sadovskii, Samuel, Santo-Fiume, Vladimir Silin, Silushka,
Mariana Vekentevna Sinetskaia, Boris Andreich Sipiagin,
Kolia Sipiagin, Valentina Mikhailovna Sipiagina, Skoropikhin,
Snadulia, Snapochka, Vasilii Feodotich Solomin, Spielhagen,
Stephenson, Foma Lavrentevich Subochev, Evfenia Pavlovna
Subocheva, Sully-Prudhomme, Sverlitskii, Talleyrand, Tat'iana
Osipovna, Teacher, Thiers, Aleksei Ivanich Tveritinov,
Ul'iashevich, Valia, Vasia, Vasil'evna, Vasilii Nikolaich,
Vikhorev, Virgil, Voldemar, Voltaire, Father Zosima.

War and Peace, L. N. Tolstoi, 1866.

Book One.

In July, 1805, Anna Sherer, a lady-in-waiting to the Dowager
Empress, held a soirée for the elite of St. Petersburg. Prince
Vasilii Kuragin, an old government official, discussed Napoleon
as the "anti-Christ" and Tsar Aleksandr I as the savior of civiliza-

tion. The prince complained about his foolish son, Ippolit, and asked the hostess to help him find a wealthy wife for his other son, the dissolute but dashing Anatol'. Princess Anna Drubetskaia, an impoverished aristocrat from a good family, came and begged Prince Vasilii for help in furthering her son Boris's career. The handsome and proud Prince Andrei Bolkonskii, an admirer of Napoleon, arrived with his beautiful wife, Lise, who complained that her husband was leaving her at their country estate, Bald Hills, while he went off to military service. The arrival of Pierre Bezukhov, the illegitimate son of a wealthy and gravely ill count, caused the hostess great concern since she did not approve of his aimless life and manners. Pierre promised his friend, Prince Andrei, to cease his bacchanalian life, but soon left for a boisterous party at Anatol's which ended with the strapping of a policeman and a bear together, and throwing them into a river. Pierre and the gambler Dolokhov were ordered out of the city because of their conduct.

Princess Anna Drubetskaia carried the news of the incident to Moscow, where she visited her friend, the Countess Rostova. The Rostovs were celebrating the name day of their youngest daughter, Natasha. During the festivities, the young girl saw her brother Nikolai kiss their cousin, Sonia, and pledge his love. The oldest Rostov daughter, Vera, admonished Sonia for expecting Nikolai to marry her when she had no dowry. The impetuous Natasha cornered Boris Drubetskoi and kissed him, securing a promise of marriage in four years. Princess Anna left the Rostovs to visit the ailing Count Bezukhov in hopes of obtaining money. Forcing herself into the private quarters of the count by claiming a distant relationship, the princess surmised that the naive Pierre might be cheated out of his inheritance by Prince Vasilii, who had also come from St. Petersburg in hopes of an inheritance. In an indecorous scuffle, Princess Anna protected a portfolio which contained the letter legitimizing Pierre as the count's heir. Only the death of the count brought an end to the intrigues over the will. Pierre became one of the richest men in Russia; yet he was generous to everyone.

Meanwhile, at Bald Hills, Prince Nikolai Bolkonskii, a follower of Voltaire and an example of the universal man of the eighteenth century, welcomed the arrival of his son Andrei and daughter-in-law Lise, who was pregnant. The old prince's daughter, Mar'ia, was homely and religious, and lived by the dictates of her demanding father. Her friend, Julie Karagina, an heiress, wrote her from Moscow that Nikolai Rostov had joined the service. She also hinted that a marriage was being planned for Mar'ia, a reference to the scheme Prince Vasilii mentioned to Anna Sherer about his son Anatol'. Prince Andrei soon left Lise in the country and entered military service.

In the War of 1805, Russia combatted Napoleon's forces in Austria. When the Austrian army of General Mack was defeated, the general himself managed to reach the headquarters of the Russian commander, General Kutuzov, whom Prince Andrei served as an adjutant. Mack's defeat forced the Russians to retreat toward Vienna across the Enns River. At Krems, the Russians had a small victory; and Prince Andrei hastened with the news to Brum, the Austrian capital in exile. He was greatly disappointed at the weak reception he received. Bilibin, a Russian diplomat at the Austrian court, introduced Andrei to the Russian social set, where he met Ipollit Kuragin. Andrei was displeased with the superficiality of the diplomatic set and soon returned to Kutuzov. Life among the officers in the field was portrayed in the activities of the enthusiastic Nikolai Rostov. Wounded in battle, he was helped by Captain Tushin, whose heroic deeds were witnessed by Prince Andrei as the Russian forces gathered for the decisive Battle of Austerlitz.

In St. Petersburg, Prince Vasilii used his influence to have Pierre made a gentleman-of-the-bedchamber of the tsar. Obligated, Pierre succumbed to Vasilii's clever schemes and married the prince's daughter, the incredibly beautiful Hélène Kuragina. Having matched his daughter with a man of wealth, Prince Vasilii journeyed with his son Anatol' to Bald Hills in hopes of arranging an engagement with the heiress Mar'ia. Old Prince Bolkonskii detested the Kuragins and insulted his daughter when he saw that she favored the match. He suggested that Anatol' would be more interested in Mlle. Bourienne, Mar'ia's companion, and Mar'ia did accidentally come upon the French girl in an embrace with Anatol'. Mar'ia quickly refused the proposal.

During the battle of Austerlitz, Prince Andrei was wounded and was left dying on the field. Napoleon and his retinue passed and saw the distinguished-looking Russian officer. Looking at the blue sky and reflecting on his ebbing life, Prince Andrei sensed the pettiness of his former hero's ambition. Napoleon ordered that Prince Andrei be taken to his own French physicians.

Book Two.

In 1806, Nikolai Rostov returned to Moscow with a military comrade, Denisov, who carried on a flirtation with the carefree Natasha. She attended her first formal ball and was delighted with adult life. Nikolai lost 43,000 roubles while playing cards with Dolokhov. Old Count Rostov paid the debt, but his financial position was no longer secure. The count gave a splendid dinner in honor of General Bagration. During the dinner, Pierre challenged Dolokhov to a duel because of an alleged affair the rake was having with Pierre's wife. While he wounded his opponent in the encounter, Pierre was disheartened by the incident. He separated from Hélène and left for his estates near Kiev. In despair, Pierre eagerly accepted Freemasonry when he accidentally met a Mason at a posting station. Pierre tried to adapt the principles of the Masons to the running of his properties. His kindness was abused, and he was deceived by his administrators. At Bald Hills, Prince Andrei suddenly returned from his long recuperation just when Lise was expecting her child. She died in childbirth, but left Andrei a son and heir. Pierre came to the Bolkonskii estate, and he and Andrei found inspiration in each other's company.

Back at the front in Poland, Nikolai Rostov's regiment suffered from hunger and disgusting living conditions. During a visit to a squalid hospital, he met Captain Tushin, who had lost an arm. Nikolai's wounded friend, Denisov, was in a typhus ward, a place of incredible misery and horror. Nikolai went to Tilsit for the famous meeting of the two Emperors, Napoleon and Aleksandr I.

Prince Andrei visited the country estate of the Rostovs and was delighted with Natasha. Feeling that his life was not over, he went to St. Petersburg, and became involved in high social and governmental circles. Pierre returned to the capital city and accepted a reconciliation'with Hélène. The event did not cease his spiritual turmoil. The Rostovs visited in St. Petersburg, and their eldest daughter was married to a Captain Berg with a dowry the family could not afford. The major characters came together at a grand ball attended by the Emperor. Pierre asked Andrei to dance with Natasha, and she was thrilled. Andrei decided to propose marriage, and the Rostov family approved. However, old Prince Bolkonskii was reticent and asked his son to wait a year. Natasha sadly accepted the prince's desire, and Andrei went abroad. Because of the Rostovs' precarious financial position, the countess urged Nikolai to leave the military service and manage their estates.

Nikolai regretfully accepted his family duty but was not able to untangle their domestic affairs. The countess urged Nikolai to marry the heiress Julie Karagina, but he managed to postpone his decision and returned to his regiment.

Pierre, disillusioned, returned to Moscow, and renewed his drinking and aimless living. Old Prince Bolkonskii and Mar'ia returned to their city palace for the winter season. Boris Drubetskoi visited in hopes of marrying an heiress and succeeded in winning Julie Karagina. Count Rostov left the ailing countess in the country, and went to Moscow with Natasha and Sonia. In order to avoid the expense of opening their city mansion, they stayed with Maria Dmitrievna, known as "the terrible dragon" in society. When the count and Natasha called on the Bolkonskiis, the old prince behaved rudely, and embarrassed Natasha and Mar'ia. They parted on unfriendly terms. Saddened, Natasha became easy prey for the desires of Anatol' Kuragin. With Hélène's help, he convinced Natasha of his love and persuaded her to run away with him. Sonia discovered the plot and helped stop the elopement. Pierre forced Anatol' to leave the city and informed Natasha that the rake was already married. With her engagement to Andrei dissolved, Natasha felt that her life was over. Pierre tried to calm her and realized that he himself was in love. Driving home, Pierre saw a comet and interpreted it as a sign of a new life in the future.

Book Three.

In 1812, Napoleon's forces invaded Russia and Nikolai Rostov was again in battle. His younger brother, Petia, wanted to join the service, but his parents forbade him. Natasha was ill after her scandalous behavior but slowly recovered. Because of the war, Moscow became filled with patriotic meetings. Pierre offered to equip and maintain a thousand men at the front. Prince Andrei commanded a regiment. When he knew that the French forces were advancing on his father's estate, he sent Mar'ia word to evacuate. Retreating from Smolensk, Andrei went to Bald Hills and found the family had indeed departed. He thought they were safe in Moscow, but actually Mar'ia had taken their ailing father to a smaller estate still in the danger zone. Old Prince Bolkonskii died, and Mar'ia was stranded because the peasants were in revolt. Nikolai Rostov came by, and helped her pack and leave for Voronezh. They parted as good friends.

Moscow prepared for Napoleon's onslaught. Pierre went to Borodino and witnessed one of the greatest military battles in history. Andrei was seriously wounded and taken to a hospital. He saw Anatol' Kuragin, but his hatred dissolved as he saw the amputation of his enemy's leg. Andrei realized that his love for mankind had come too late. After the Battle of Borodino, the inhabitants of Moscow began to leave the city. The Rostovs, at Natasha's insistance, abandoned their possessions and carried wounded soldiers in their horse carts. Natasha did not know that Prince Andrei was among those she helped save. Pierre remained in Moscow in hopes of assassinating Napoleon. When the French entered, the fires from their kitchens and campfires set the city afire. The Rostovs viewed the conflagration from a distant village.

Book Four.

During a soirée at Anna Sherer's in St. Petersburg, the sudden death of the beautiful Hélène from a strange malady surprised everyone. Pierre, in Moscow, was accused of arson by the French and was taken to prison. He was ordered shot but was spared at the last minute. In prison, he met Platon Karataev, a truly simple and honest man. Pierre was greatly inspired by the peasant's kindness and acceptance of the unfathomable world. Nikolai Rostov was sent to Voronezh for procurement of horses. There he again met Mar'ia Bolkonskaia, and they both sensed their mutual attraction. Mar'ia, learning that Andrei was with the Rostovs, went to them and helped Natasha care for her wounded brother. Andrei succumbed to death peacefully.

Napoleon, realizing that his forces could not winter in Moscow, withdrew from the city toward Smolensk. Russian partisans began attacking the retreating army. Petia Rostov, who had finally entered the service, was killed in an attack. Pierre was rescued by Dolokhov and Denisov. He recounted how the French had shot his peasant friend, Platon, because he was ill and could not walk. Back in Moscow, Pierre visited Mar'ia Bolkonskaia and found Natasha there. Events brought them together, and they both confessed to Mar'ia their love for each other.

Epilogue One

Tolstoi presented his thought about the forces which act in history and their connection with the roles of Napoleon and Aleksandr I.

Old Count Rostov died after Pierre and Natasha married. Nikolai retired from the service and married Mar'ia Bolkonskaia. He
became an excellent overseer of their estates. Sonia lived with
Nikolai and Mar'ia as a governess for their children. By 1820,
Natasha had three daughters and a son. Pierre and Natasha
visited Nikolai and Mar'ia at Bald Hills. Pierre told of new groups
of men who were interested in changing the government. Nikolai
defended loyalty to the monarchy. Prince Andrei's adolescent son,
young Nikolai Bolkonskii, overheard the political argument of
his elders and swore that he would someday make a career for himself that would make his deceased father proud.

Epilogue Two
Tolstoi gave general reflections about the study of mankind
among historians. He stated that two honored propositions lie
at the base of the works of modern historians: (1) that nations are
guided by individuals and (2) that a goal exists toward which nations
are moving. Tolstoi presented the difficulty of determining the
forces which act on peoples of all nations. A major problem was
finding the causes of historical events in the light of contemporary
understanding.
Brother A___, Achilles, Adam, Adele, Adonai, Maria Dmitrievna Akhrasimova, Akinfii, Tsar Aleksandr Pavlovich, Alenina,
Alesha, Alexander of Macedon, Alfons Karlovich, Alkid, Iakov
Alpatich, Amalek, Amelie, Andrei Sevastionich, Andreich,
Andriushka, Anferov, Anisia Fedorovna, Aniska, Annette,
Anton, Antonov, Stepan Stepanovich Apraksin, Apraksina,
Arakcheev, Arinka, Arkharov, Armfeldts, Asch, Aubert-Chalme,
Auersperg von Mautern, Avgustin, Brother B___, Prince of
Baden, Baggovut, Bagration, Baikov, Balaga, Balashev, Ban-
darchuk, Barclay de Tolly, Barthélemy, Duke of Bassano,
Iosif Alekseevich Bazdeev, Makar Alekseevich Bazdeev, Sofia
Danilovna Bazdeeva, Bazov, Beauche, Beauharnais, Beau-
marchais, Beausset, Bekleshov, Agrafena Ivanovna Belova,
Belliard, Bennigsen, Adolf Berg, Bernadotte, Berthier, Bes-
sieres, Kiril Vladimirovich Bezukhov, Petr Kirilovich Bezuk-
hov, Petia Bezukhov, Elena Vasil'evna Bezukhova, Lise
Bezukhova, Bilibin, Bismarck, Bitskii, Bogdanich, Bogdanovich, Bolkovitinov, Lise Bolkonskaia, Mar'ia Nikolaevna
Bolkonskaia, Andrei Nikolaevich Bolkonskii, Nikolai Andreevich Bolkonskii (Nikolenka), Nikolai Andreevich Bolkonskii,

Napoleon Bonaparte, Bondarenko, Boria, Borenka, Borzozowska, Vincent Bosse, Bourbon, Bourienne, Branitski, Broussier, Brozin, Buxhöwden, Bykov, Caesar, Caroline the Hungarian, Castres, Caulaincourt, Chalme, King Charles IX of France, King Charles X of France, King Charles IX of Sweden, King Charles XII of Sweden, Chateaubriand, Charon, Chartorizhskii, Chatrov, Semen Chekmar, Chernyshev, Cherubini, Chichagov, Chigirin, Claparède, Clausewitz, Clement, Compans, Condé, Cossack, Crosart, Crow, Czartorizhski, Ivan Vasil'evich D——, Dandin, Danilo, Danilo Terentich, David, Davout, Davydov, Davydov, Demian, Demosthenes, Kiril Andreevich Denisov, Vasilii Dmitrich Denisov, Dessaix, Dessalles, Diana, Diderot, Eduard Karlich Dimmler, Dmitriev-Mamonov, Dmitrii Vasil'evich, Dokhturov, Dolgorukov, Fedor Ivanovich Dolokhov, Maria Ivanovna Dolokhova, Don Juan, Dorokhov, Dron Zakharich, Dronushka, Anna Mikhailovna Drubetskaia, Boris Drubetskoi, Duchesnois, Duniasha, Duport, Duroc, Durosnel, Dussek, Echartschausen, Eckmühl, Efim, Fedor Iakovlevich Eiken, Tsarina Ekaterina I, Empress Ekaterina II, Ekaterina Pavlovna, Ekonomov, Elchingen, Elizabeth de France, Elizaveta Alekseevna, Ellen Lelia, Elohim, Duke of Enghien, Ermiskin, Ermolov, Essen, Evstafievich, Fabvier, Fain, Fedeshou, Fedia, Fedor, Fedosiushka, Fedotov, Feller, Feoktist, Ferapontov, Archduke Ferdinand, Fichte, Field, Figner, Filipp, Fishova, Foka, Fouche, Franz, Emperor Franz Joseph, Emperor Frederick II, Emperor Frederick Wilhelm III, Friant, Friez, Fritz, Saint Frola, Frolova-Bagreeva, Funke, Brother G——, Gavrila, Gavrilo Ivanich, Genlis, King George III, Georges, Gerakov, Gérard, Gérard, Gérard, Gerasim, Gervais, Gervinus, Gibbon, Gideon, Girchik, Glinka, Godfrey, Golenishchev-Kutuzov, Goliath, Golitsyn, Golukhovskii, Gorchakov, Gossner, Grekov, Grishka, Gruzinskii, Gudovich, Gur'ev, Haine, Hardenberg, Haugwitz, Hélène, Heloise, Hercules, Herder, Hohenlohe, Hover, Iakov, Iakovlev, Ignashka, Ignat, Ilagin, Il'ia Ivanovich, Il'ia Mitrofanich, Il'in, Il'iusha, Tsar Ioann Vasil'evich IV, Ipatka, Irina Vasil'evna, Iusupova, Ivan, Ivan the Terrible, Ivan Sidorich, Ivanushka, Jacquot, Jeanne d'Arc, Saint John, Joseph, Josephine, Joshua, Jovert, Julner, Junot, Kaisarov, Kamenskii, Julie Karagina, Varia L'vovna Karagina, Karamzin, Platon Karataev, Karl Ivanich, Archduke Karl Ludwig,

Karp, Karpushka, Katerina Petrovna, Katia, Katish, Kempiiskii, Kepler, Khandrikov, Khovtikov, Kikin, King of Hearts, King of Naples, King of Rome, Kiril Matveich, Kiriusha, Kirsten, Kiselev, Kliucharev, Kochubei, Koko, Kolia, Komarov, Kondratevna, Konovnitsyn, Konstantin Pavlovich, Kourakine, Kozlovskii, Kroug, Krudener, Anatolii Vasil'evich Kuragin, Ipolit Vasil'evich Kuragin, Vasilii Sergeevich Kuragin, Aline Kuragina, Kurbskii, Kutuzov, Lanfrey, Langeron, Lannes, Lanskoi, Laocoön, Larrey, Lauriston, Lavater, Saint Lavra, Lavrushka, Lazarchuk, Lazarev, Lelorgme, Lemarrois, Leppich, Lichtenfels, Lichtenstein, Likhachev, Lili, Ligne, Liubomirski, Lopukhin, Lorrain, King Louis XI, King Louis XIV, King Louis XV, King Louis XVI, King Louis XVIII, Lovaiskii, Luther, Mack, Magnitskii, Maistre, Makar Alekseevich, Makarin, Makarka, Makeev, Maksim, Malasha, Malbroug, Malvina, Anna Ignatevna Malvintseva, Katerina Semenovna Mamontova, Ol'ga Mamontova, Sophia Mamontova, Marat, Maria Bogdanovna, Empress Maria Fedorovna, Maria Genrikhovna, Maria Nikolaevna, Queen Maria Theresa, Maria Viktorovna, Marie, Empress Marie Louise, Marin, Markov, Masha, Matilda, Matrena Matrevna, Matrena Timofeevna, Matrioshka, Mausfield, Mavra Kuzminishna, Mavrusha, Medvedev, Meinen, Pelageia Danilovna Meliukova, Sasha Meliukova, Merivier, Meshcherskii, Meshkov, Metternich, Michaud-de-Bogetur, Midian, Mikhail, Mikhail Ivanovich, Mikhail Kirilich, Mikhail Mitrich, Mikhail Sidorich, Mikhailo, Mikhelson, Mikolka, Miloradovich, Mironov, Misha, Mishka, Mitenka, Mitka, Mitrich, Molière, Montmorency, Montesquieu, Morand, Moreau, Morel, Morio, Morkov, Mortemort, Mortier, Moses, Mouton-Duvernet, Mudrov, Murat, N____ N____, Napoleon I, Napoleon II, Napoleon III, Naryshkin, Naryshkina, Nastasia Ivanovna, Natasha, Natalie, Nesvitskii, Neverovskii, Ney, Nikolai, Nikita, Nikita Ivanich, Saint Nikola, Nikolai Ivanovich, Nikolenka, Nikolev, Nikolushka, Nikulin, Nostitz, Novosiltsev, Brother O____, Fedia Obolenskii, Kitty Odyntsova, Oldenburg, Orlov, Orlov-Denisov, Onufrick, Ostermann-Tolstoi, Oudinot, Palen, Panin, Paris, Saint Paul, Pauliicci, Pavel Petrovich, Pavel Timofeich, Pelageiushka, Pernetti, Maria Ignateevna Peronskaia, Saint Peter, Peter of Amiens, Petin'ka, Petia, Tsar Petr I, Tsar Petr III, Petrov, Petrushka Pfühl,

Photius, Pierre, Pitt, Pius VII, Platoche, Platon, Platosha, Platov, Plutarch, Polia, Poniatowski, Potemkin, Potier, Potocka, Pozniakov, Praskovia Savishna, Prianichnikov, Prokofii, Prozorovskii, Przazdzieska, Przhibyshevskii, Ptolemy, Pugachev, Pushkin, Queen of St. Petersburg, Queen of Spain, Raevskii, Ramballe, Rameau, Rapp, Rastopchin, Razumovskii, Repnin, Rhipheus, Riurik, Robespierre, Rohans, Andriusha Rostov, Il'ia Andreevich Rostov, Mitia Rostov, Nikolai Il'ich Rostov, Petr Il'ich Rostov, Natalia Rostova, Natalia Il'inichna Rostova, Natasha Nikolaievna Rostova, Vera Il'inichna Rostova, Rousseau, Rovigo, Rumiantsev, S____ S____, Saint-Thomas, Saltykov, Samson, Savary, Savostianov, Savel'ich, Scaevola, Schelling, Anna Pavlovna Scherer, Schmidt, Schneider, Schoss, Schubert, Schwartzenberg, Sebastiani, Sedmoretskii, Selivanov, Semen, Semenova, Sergei, Shapovalov, Shcherbatii, Shcherbatov, Shcherbinin, Shinshin, Shinshina, Shishkov, Shittov, Shlosser, Shtaps, Sidorov, Sismondi, Sistine Madonna, Smolianiknov, Sofia Aleksandrovna, Sokolov, Il'ia Osipovich Sokolov, Solomon, Sonia, Soniushka, Sophie, Sorbier, Souza-Botelho, Speranskaia, Speranskii, Staël, Stein, Stepan Stepanich, Streshka, Stevens, Stolypin, Straunch, Stroganov, Strongman Andreich, Sukhtelen, Super-Sham, Suvorov, Talleyrand-Perigord, Talma, Taras, Tatar, Tatarinova, Telianin, Terentii, Thomas a Kempis, Tiers, Tikhon, Timokhin, Tishka, Tit, Titus, Toll, Tolstoi, Topcheenko, Tormasov, Tuchkov, Turenne, Tushin, Tutolmin, Uncle, Urusov, Uvarko, Uvarov, Brother V____, Valuev, Vasil'chikov, Vasil'ev, Vasil'ich, Vasilii Ignatich, Vasilisa, Vaska, Veimars, Vereshchagin, Vessenii, Viazemskii, Viazmitinov, Viceroy, Villeneuve, Vinesse, Vlas, Vogel', Volkinskii, Vrbna, Weirother, Willarski, Wintzengerode, Wittgenstein, Wlocki, Wolzogen, Wurttemberg, Zakhar, Zakharchinko, Zakharich, Zalataev, Zdrzhinski, Zhilinski, Zinaida Dmitrievna, Zikin, Zubov, Zubova.

CHARACTERS

A____, Brother. *War and Peace*. A member of a Masonic lodge whom Pierre Bezukhov knew when he was studying to be a Mason.

Abbé, Monsieur 1'. *Evgenii Onegin* (1,3). Onegin's teacher who taught him playfully so as not to wear him out.

About, Edmond François Valentin (1828-2885). *Smoke* (XV). When Litvinov went to Irina Ratmirova's party, the guests talked about the notorieties of the Parisian demi-mode and mentioned a novel by About, who was known for his wit and fancy.

Achilles. *A Gentry Nest* (25). The hero of Homer's *Iliad* who was invulnerable except in the heel. Paris hit his heel with an arrow and killed him. When Mikhailevich talked with Lavretskii, he said that his friend knew the Achilles' heel of the Germans. *War and Peace* (3, 3, 1). Tolstoi referred to the Greek sophism about Achilles and the tortoise which was based on the division of motion into separate units rather than on continuity.

Adam. *Anna Karenina* (5, 6). The Biblical figure recalled during Kitty Shcherbatskaia's wedding to Konstantin Levin. The creation of women from Adam's rib was stated in the ceremony. *War and Peace* (2, 2, 2). Adam was mentioned when Pierre Bezukhov talked with a Mason during a wait at the Torzhok post station.

Adele. *War and Peace* (E, 1, 12). An acquaintance who urged Pierre Bezukhov to buy a gold comb set for his wife, Natasha (née Rostova).

Adonai. *War and Peace* (2, 3, 10). In Masonic writings, Adonai is the name of the creator of the world.

Aeneas. "Lebedian'," in *A Hunter's Sketches*. The hero of Virgil's epic *Aeneid*. Remembering a dinner that was most unpleasant, the narrator recalled Aeneas as another who knew how disagreeable it is to recall past grief.

Aeneid. Spring Freshets (39). An epic poem by Virgil which Polozova read in Latin and mentioned during a theater performance when she was bored.

Aesop. *Fathers and Sons* (5). The Kirsanovs' steward called a laborer Aesop after the famous storyteller.

Afanasii Nefedych. "L'gov," in *A Hunter's Sketches*. The uncle of Sergei Sergeich.

Agaf'ia. *Anna Karenina*. The old nurse and housekeeper at the Levin estate. "Dubrovskii." Troekurov's poultry woman. "Tat'iana Borisovna and Her Nephew," in *A Hunter's Sketches*. A housekeeper and nurse.

Agaf'ia Vlas'evna. *A Gentry Nest*. Liza Kalitina's nurse.

Agafon. *Evgenii Onegin* (5, 9). The Russian version of Agathonicus which was mentioned when Tat'iana indulged in fortune-telling. *Virgin Soil*, A footman of the Sipiagins.

Agatha, *On the Eve* (12). See "Max."

Agrafena, "The Office," in *A Hunter's Sketches*. The woman in charge of poultry to whom the narrator was advised to go for tea. "Living Holy Relics," in *A Hunter's Sketches*. Vasilii's wife.

Agrafena Petrovna. *The Resurrection*. A former maid of Nekhliudov's mother. She had the appearance and manners of a lady.

Agremantskii, Slavianskii (1834-1908). *Virgin Soil* (38). The singer and director Paklin referred to while conversing with Miss Mashurina.

Aibulat. *Rudin* (8). The alias for K. M. Rosen. Volyntsev did not like poetry but quoted the poem "Two Questions" by Aibulat.

Akhrasimova, Maria Dmitrievna. *War and Peace*. The grande dame who was known in St. Petersburg and Moscow society as "the terrible dragon" because of her straightforward speech. The Rostovs spent one winter with her.

Akim. "Bezhin Meadow," in *A Hunter's Sketches*. The forester who drowned.

Akinfii, Father. *War and Peace*. Princess Maria Bolkonskaia's confessor.

Aksin'ia. "Death," in *A Hunter's Sketches*. The wife of a dying peasant.

Aksin'ia Nikitishna. "The Office," in *A Hunter's Sketches*. A guest of Losniakova. "Raspberry Spring," in *A Hunter's Sketches*. Mitrofan's wife.

Akulina. "The Country Doctor," in *A Hunter's Sketches*. The doctor's wife. "The Meeting," in *A Hunter's Sketches*. The peasant girl who loses her boyfriend in the meeting overheard by the narrator. "Raspberry Spring," in *A Hunter's Sketches*. Petr Il'ich's mistress.

Akulina Pamfilovna. *The Captain's Daughter*. Father Gerasim's wife.

Akul'ka. *The Captain's Daughter*. The one-eyed cow woman seduced by Beaupré. *Evgenii Onegin*. The girl Mme. Larina called Selena for a while.

Albano, Francesco Abani (1578-1660). *Evgenii Onegin* (5, 40). The Italian painter in whose style Pushkin wanted to describe a ball in St. Petersburg.

Alcibiades (450-404 B.C.). *Smoke* (14). The brilliant Athenian general who Plutarch said captivated everyone around him. Potugin called Churilo Plenkovich, a Russian hero from the ancient *bylinni*, the Russian Alcibiades.

Alcides. *A Gentry Nest* (15). One of the names of Hercules which Turgenev used in referring to Lavretskii.

Aleko. "First Love" (17). The fictional hero of Pushkin's poem "The Gypsies" (1824). Jealousy from his sweetheart's relations with another gypsy drove Aleko to murder. Vladimir B____ thought of Aleko when he was jealous of Zinaida Zasekina's relations with her other admirers.

Aleksandr. *Anna Karenina*. The grandson of Countess Vronskii.

Aleksandr I (1777-1825). *A Gentry Nest* (8). The Russian tsar who reigned when the Lavretskii family was cheated out of the Princess Kubenskaia's money. *Fathers and Sons* (12). Matvei Kaliazin was mentioned as a statesman during the reign of Aleksandr I. *Virgin Soil* (7). In a conversation with Kallomeitsev, Sipiagin mentioned that Aleksandr I conferred the Order of St. Andrew on Chateaubriand. *War and Peace*. The Russian Emperor during the Napoleonic Wars.

Aleksandr II (1818-1881). *Anna Karenina*. The tsar during the time of the novel.

Aleksandr III (1845-1894). *Resurrection* (1, 3). Nekhliudov received a letter from an aristocrat who opposed Aleksandr III's policies against students and progressives.

Aleksandr Aleksandrovich. See Aleksandr III.

Aleksandr Feodorovich, Prince. *Smoke*. The aristocrat who said Irina reminded him of the Duchess of Devonshire at a ball.

Aleksandr Nikolaevich. See Aleksandr II.

Aleksandr Pavlovich. See Aleksandr I.

Aleksandra Andreevna. "The Country Doctor," in *A Hunter's Sketches*. The widow's daughter who was dying but fell in love with the doctor.

Alekseev. "The Death of Ivan Il'ich." The man who might receive the post held by Ivan before his death.

Aleksei, Father. "Living Holy Relics," in *A Hunter's Sketches*. A village priest.

Aleksei Romanych. "Raspberry Spring," in *A Hunter's Sketches*. The late master of Shumikino.

Alena Timofeevna. "L'gov," in *A Hunter's Sketches*. The mistress who designated the coachman Suchok as her fisherman.

Alenina. *War and Peace*. An acquaintance the Rostovs saw at the opera.

Alesha. A diminutive of Aleksei. *Anna Karenina*. Vronskii was sometimes called Alesha. *Virgin Soil*. Mariana's name for Nezhdanov.

Alesha the Trickster. *War and Peace* (2, 2, 15). A subject of tales told by soldiers.

Aleshka. *Anna Karenina*. The village idiot near Levin's estate.

Alexander of Macedon (356-323 B.C.). *Spring Freshets* (21). Pantaleone woke Sanin on the morning of his duel with the words "He sleeps like Alexander of Macedon on the eve of the Battle of Babylon." *War and Peace* (3, 1, 2). The Greek Emperor whom Napoleon remembered when he ordered his troops to cross the Niemen and invade Russia in 1812.

Alexisa (1788). *Fathers and Sons* (20). The only book Arina Bazarova read was *Alexisa or the Hunt in the Forest* by Ducré-Duminile (1761-1819).

Alfons Karlovich. *War and Peace* (1, 3, 7). The Dutchman whom Nikolai Rostov knew at Olmutz.

Alfredo. *On the Eve* (33). The hero of the opera *La Traviata* (1853), by Giuseppe Verdi (1813-1901) which Insarov heard in Venice.

Alina, Princess. *Evgenii Onegin* (2, 30). Larina's maiden cousin who praised the English writer Samuel Richardson (1689-1761).

Aline. *Resurrection*. A friend of Charskaia.

Alkid. *War and Peace* (2, 1, 3). See Hercules.

Alliluev. "Khor' and Kalinych," in *A Hunter's Sketches*. The merchant to whom Polutykin sold several acres of land profitably.

Allori, Chrisophano (1577-1621). *Spring Freshets* (3). The noted Italian painter. Sanin thought Gemma Roselli's hair was like Judith's in Allori's painting by that name.

Almaviva. *Spring Freshets*. Sanin was compared to the flighty lover Almaviva from the opera *The Barber of Seville* (1816), by Gioacchino A. Rossini (1792-1868).

Alpatich, Iakov. *War and Peace*. The servant whom Count Nikolai Bolkonskii sent to Smolensk to inquire about the advance of the French.

Amalek. *War and Peace* (3, 1, 18). The Biblical hero mentioned in a prayer by Natasha Rostova as the French were approaching Moscow.

Ambodik. *A Gentry Nest*. The author of a mysterious work Fedor Lavretskii found in his Aunt Glafira's things after her death.

Amelie. *War and Peace*. The girl suggested for Prince Andrei Bolkonskii while he was stationed at Brunn.

Anatolii Petrovich. *Resurrection*. The assistant inspector who led condemned prisoners to the gallows.

Andrei. *War and Peace*. See Bolkonskii, Prince Andrei Nikolaivich.

Andrei Sevastionich. *War and Peace*. The captain of Nikolai Rostov's squadron near the town of Ostrovna who accepted Rostov's suggestion to attack.

Andreich. *War and Peace*. A diminutive for the patronymic of Prince Nikolai Andreevich Bolkonskii.

Andriusha. A diminutive for Andrei. "The Kreutzer Sonata." Pozdnyshev's son. *On the Eve*. See Bersenev, Andrei.

Andriushka. A diminutive for Andrei. *The Captain's Daughter* (omitted chapter). The servant who bound and shackled Petr Grinev's family. *Evgenii Onegin*. A coachman of Onegin. *War and Peace* See Andrei Bolkonskii.

Anferov. *War and Peace*. A family a priest mentioned when Pierre Bezukhov was looking for the parents of the girl he saved during the burning of Moscow.

Anfisushka. *Fathers and Sons*. A servant of the Bazarovs.

Anichkin, Count. *Anna Karenina*. The head of Stepan Oblonskii's department.

Anisia. *Evgenii Onegin*. A housekeeper for Onegin. *Resurrection*. A peasant woman in Nekhliudov's village.

Anisia Fedorovna. *War and Peace*. The housemaid and mistress of the Rostovs'"uncle," Count Mikhail Nikanorych.

Aniska. A diminutive for Anisia. *War and Peace*. The woman who led Pierre Bezukhov to the home where the child was trapped in a fire during the burning of Moscow.

Aniutka. "Bezhin Meadow," in *A Hunter's Sketches*. Vania's sister.

Anna. See Karenina Anna.

Anna Fedotovna, Countess. "Queen of Spades." The grandmother of Tomskii. She knew the three winning cards which so fascinated Hermann and which led to her own death.

Anna Ivanovna. "First Love." The wife of the host at the party where the men spoke of their first loves.

Anna Pavlovna. *War and Peace*. See Anna Pavlovna Scherer.

Anna Vasil'evna. *Resurrection*. The wife of the governor of Siberia. She was a grand dame of the old school, and spoke French naturally and Russian unnaturally.

Anna Vlasev'na. *The Captain's Daughter*. The wife of the postmaster in Tsarskoe Selo who informed Masha of the Empress's schedule.

Anna Zakharovna. *Virgin Soil*. Sipiagin's aunt who took care of Kolia.

Annette. *Smoke*. The Princess who resembled a stout washerwoman. *War and Peace*. A pet name for Anna Pavlovna Scherer. Also a diminutive for Princess Anna Drubetskaia.

Annie. *Anna Karenina*. A diminutive Anna Karenina used for her daughter.

Annuskha. *Anna Karenina*. Anna's maid on the train. "Kassian from Fair Strath," in *A Hunter's Sketches*. A peasant girl who was a relative of Kassian. *On the Eve*. Shubin was walking with Bersenev, lamenting the fact that Elena did not love him. He stated that "Annushkas" were for him, indicating girls on a lower social level.

Anpadist. "The Steward," in *A Hunter's Sketches*. A peasant who accompanied the narrator.

Antip. "The Steward," in *A Hunter's Sketches*. The peasant who complained against the tyranny of Saphron Iakovlich, the steward.

Anton. "Dubrovskii." An old coachman for Dubrovskii. Also Father Anton was a priest at Kistenevka, the Dubrovskii estate. *A Gentry Nest*. A steward at Lavretskii's estate, Vasil'evskoe. *War and Peace*. An old servant of Prince Andrei Bolkonskii.

Anton Pafnutich. "Dubrovskii." A landowner and neighbor of Troekurov.

Antonov. *War and Peace*. The soldier Tushin asked to put a coat over the wounded Nikolai Rostov during the fighting near Schöngraben.

Antony, Mark (83-31 B.C.). "First Love" (11). The Roman general mentioned by Zinaida Zasekina.

Antropka. "The Singers," in *A Hunter's Sketches*. The boy being called by his brother at the end of the story when the narrator was leaving the village.

Apfelbaum. "Princess Mary," in *The Hero of Our Time*. The conjurer, acrobat and chemist who was to perform in a restaurant.

Apollo's grandsons. *Evgenii Onegin* (1, 49). The ancients considered poets the grandsons of Apollo, the god of the sun and patron of the arts. In the seventeenth century they were nephews.

Apraksia. *A Gentry Nest*. A servant at the Lavretskii estate, Vasil'-evskoe, and a nurse of Liza Kalitina as a child.

Apraksin, Stepan Stepanovich. *War and Peace*. The aristocrat who attacked Pierre's speech at the Moscow Assembly of Nobles during Napoleon's approach.

Apraksin, Victor. *The Resurrection*. A gentleman who was discussed at a party at the Maslinnikovs'.

Apraksina, Countess. *Anna Karenina*. Prince L'vov discussed her sudden death. *War and Peace*. A noble lady mentioned at the Rostovs' name-day party for Natasha.

Apukhtin, Evgenii Ivanovich. *Anna Karenina*. A captain of cavalry who declined candidacy for the Marshal of the Nobility.

Apuleius, Lucius (b. 114 A.D.). *Evgenii Onegin* (8, 1). The Roman poet and author of *The Golden Ass*. Pushkin read Apuleius as a student in the lyceum.

Arago, Dominique François Jean (1786-1853). *Resurrection* (3, 12). The French physicist whose fame was in the field of magnetism and optics. His books, translated into Russian, were very popular. He emigrated to America and became a general in the Mexican army. Tolstoi wrote that Nabatov accepted God as did Arago, as a hypothesis.

Arakcheev, Count Aleksei Andreevich (1769-1834). *War and Peace* (1, 3, 11). The Russian statesman who was in Aleksandr I's suite at Austerlitz in 1805. From 1808 to 1825 he was the minister of war. During that time he founded several military settlements which were known for their poor management.

Archimedes (287-212 B.C.). *Rudin* (3). The Greek mathematician who discovered that a body loses weight in water. Rudin mentioned his name in connection with self-love which he said was a lever of Archimedes.

Ardalion Mikhailich. "Death," in *A Hunter's Sketches*. The narrator's neighbor who had a large forest.

Arina Timofeevna. "Ermolai and the Miller's Wife," in *A Hunter's Sketches*. The miller's wife who was formerly a servant in Zverkov's household.

Arinka. *War and Peace*. A woman serf at the estate of Count Mikhail Nikanorych, an "uncle" of the Rostovs.

Arinuskha. *The Captain's Daughter*. The woman Zurin led Grinev to when the latter became drunk.

Aristarchus (d. 156 B.C.) *Virgin Soil*. Paklin called the art critic Skoropikhin a Russian Aristarchus after the famous Greek critic who was noted for his work on Homer's *Iliad* and *Odyssey*.

Aristophanes (c. 450-380 B.C.). *Rudin* (4). The Greek dramatist of comedy best known for the *Clouds, Birds*, and *Frogs*. Lezhnev thought of Aristophanes when his friend Shchitov performed in student assemblies.

Arkadii. *Fathers and Sons*. See Kirsanov, Arkadii.

Arkharov. *War and Peace*. A rich, noble Moscow family which was known for its hospitality.

Arkhip. "Dubrovskii." The Dubrovskiis' blacksmith who wanted to kill the clerks who came to take possession of the estate. "Death," in *A Hunter's Sketches*. The village constable.

Armfeldts, Gustav-Moritz (1757-1814). *War and Peace* (3, 1, 6). A Swedish General who was accused of treason in 1794 and went to Russia. He returned to Sweden and served in various governmental positions before returning to Russia in 1811. He then entered Russian service and escorted Aleksandr I during his stay in the army in 1812.

Armida. *Evgenii Onegin* (1, 33). The heroine of *Liberated Jerusalem*, by Torquato Tasso (1544-1595). Armida was an enchantress and sorceress.

Arnim, Countess Elisabeth Bretano von (1785-1859). *Rudin* (7), See Bettina von Arnim.

Asch, Baron Kazimir Ivanovich. *War and Peace* (3, 2, 4). The governor of Smolensk from 1807 to 1822.

Aubert-Chalme. *War and Peace*. A French woman who was allowed to remain in Moscow after French residents had been expelled during the War of 1812.

Auersperg von Mautern, Prince Karl (1740-1822). *War and Peace* (1, 2, 10). An Austrian field marshal during the War of 1805.

Aurora. *Evgenii Onegin* (5, 21). The mythological goddess of dawn. Ol'ga Larina, rosier than Aurora, asked her sister about her dream.

Automedon. *Anna Karenina* (6, 9). In Homer's *Iliad*, Automedon was the skilled coachman for Achilles. When Veslovskii drove a carriage into a marsh, he refused Levin's pleas to let the coachman drive, saying that he, Veslovskii, was Automedon. *Evgenii Onegin* (7, 35). Pushkin referred to Russian coachmen as Automedons.

Avdiusha. "Bezhin Meadow," in *A Hunter's Sketches*. A brother of
Il'iusha, one of the boys in the woods at night.

Avdotia. "Two Landowners," in *A Hunter's Sketches*. Stregonov's
housekeeper.

Aveneva. *Anna Karenina*. The woman mentioned as the mistress of
Biriuzovskii.

Avgustin, Aleksei Vasil'evich Vinogradskii (1766-1819). *War and
Peace* (3, 1, 19). The bishop mentioned at the ceremony in
the Cathedral of the Assumption which the tsar attended.
Later (3, 3, 5), Avgustin was forbidden by Count Rostopchin
to take holy relics out of Moscow during the approach of
Napoleon's army.

Avgustina Kristianovna. *On the Eve*. A widow of German origin who
was Nikolai Artemevich Stakhov's mistress.

Avvakum (1620-1682). *Smoke* (5). The seventeenth-century religious
leader who fanatically held to the old beliefs of the Russian
church, refusing to adhere to the reforms adopted by the
Patriarch Nikon. After years of suffering and imprisonment
for his obstinacy, he was burned at the stake for his beliefs.
Potugin referred to Avvakum as "my colleague."

Azamat. "Bela," in *A Hero of Our Time*. The hotheaded son of an
Asiatic prince. Azamat stole his sister, Bela, for Pechorin.

B____, Brother. *War and Peace*. An acquaintance of Pierre Bezukhov
in the Masons when he was studying their doctrine.

B____, Count. *On the Eve*. The owner of estates managed by the
father of Kurnatovskii.

B____, Prince. *The Captain's Daughter*. The major of the guards who
enlisted Grinev in the Semenov regiment before the young
hero was even born.

B____, Maria Nikolaevna. "First Love." An embittered woman and
the mother of Vladimir. She knew that her husband had
married her for money.

B____, Petr Vasilich. "First Love." Vladimir's father, who dis-
played indifference to his son. He loved Zinaida Zasekina.

B____, Vladimir Petrovich (Volodia). "First Love." The young man
who was very much in love with Zinaida Zasekina but found
out that she was having a secret affair with his father.

Babette, Princess. *Smoke*. A lady mentioned as a companion of Chopin.

Bach, Johann Sebastian (1685-1750). *Anna Karenina* (7, 5). The

German composer whose works were played at a matinee
concert Konstantin Levin attended. *A Gentry Nest.* Lemm
preferred the music of Bach.

Baden. *War and Peace* (3, 1, 7). The German family from the Principality of Baden mentioned by Napoleon at dinner with
Balashev.

Baden, Prince of. *War and Peace* (3, 1, 6). Napoleon sarcastically
referred to a Prince of Baden, indicating an insignificant
prince.

Baggovut, Karl Fedorovich (1761-1812). *War and Peace* (4, 1, 6). The
Russian General who was in the Turkish War of 1806 and
who was killed in 1812 in the Battle of Tarutina when he
commanded the Second Infantry Corps.

Bagration, Prince Petr Ivanovich (1765-1812). *War and Peace* (1, 2,
13). The Russian General of noble Georgian descent who
participated in almost all engagements during the campaigns
from 1805 to 1807. In 1809, he was Russian Supreme Commander against the Turks. In 1812, he commanded the
Second Western Army and died from wounds during the
Battle of Borodino.

Baikov, Il'ia Ivanovich. *War and Peace* (1, 3, 18). The driver of Tsar
Aleksandr's horses.

Baklaga. "Lebedian'," in *A Hunter's Sketches.* The favorite companion
and servant of Prince N——.

Baklashov, Petr. *The Resurrection.* A merchant on the jury at Katiusha
Maslova's trial.

Balaga. *War and Peace* (2, 5, 16). A notorious troika driver who drove
for Anatol' Kuragin and Dolokhov.

Balakirev, Milii Alekseevich (1836-1910). *Anna Karenina* (7, 5).
The musical composer who greatly influenced Russian music
of the nineteenth century. Levin heard his fantasia "King
Lear on the Heath" at a matinee concert.

Balashev, Aleksandr D. (1770-1837). *War and Peace* (3, 1, 3). The
Adjutant General who informed Aleksandr I that Napoleon
had crossed the Niemen. Balashev also served as War
General of St. Petersburg (1809-1810) and as Minister of
Police (1810-1816).

Balzac, Honoré de (1799-1850). *A Gentry Nest* (40). The noted
French novelist whom Varvara Lavretskaia found boring.

Bambaev, Rostislav Ardalionich (Roston). *Smoke.* A Moscow acquaintance who introduced Gregorii Litvinov to a set of
boring intellectuals in Baden.

Bandarchuk. *War and Peace*. The hussar who rode past Rostov after his horse was shot during an engagement near Schöngraben.

Baratynskii, Evgenii Abromovich (1800-1844). *Evgenii Onegin*. The Epigraph to Chapter Seven is from Bartynskii's poem "Feasts" (1821). Also (4, 30). The poet, whose verses might "nimbly ornament" an album, was a worthy rival of Pushkin among his contemporaries.

Barbe. *A Gentry Nest*. The name used by Varvara Lavretskaia in her affair with her lover.

Barbier, Henri Auguste (1805-1882). "First Love" (16). A French poet. Zinaida Zasekina said that Maidanov would write a poem à la Barbier if he knew whom she loved.

Barclay de Tolly, Michael Andreas (1761-1818). *War and Peace* (3, 1, 6). The Russian general who commanded the First Russian Army in the War of 1812.

Barnaulov, Prince. *Smoke*. The man who, according to Mme. Sukhanchikova, had ordered someone's ear bitten off.

Barthélemy, Auguste Marseille (1795-1867). *War and Peace* (4, 2, 17). In the War of 1812, he was sent by Napoleon to Kutuzov with a proposal for peace.

Bartnianskii. *Anna Karenina*. An acquaintance of Oblonskii in St. Petersburg.

Basanov. *Virgin Soil*. A revolutionary betrayed and arrested in the beginning of the novel. His lot was repeated when other revolutionaries met the same fate in the denouement of the story.

Basistov. *Rudin*. The young university graduate who taught Dar'ia Lasunskaia's sons and who became an admirer of Rudin.

Bassano, Duke of. *War and Peace* (3, 1, 3). Napoleon formed the Principality of Bassano in 1809. In 1811 his state secretary Mape was made minister and became known as the Duke of Bassano.

Bastia, Frederick (1801-1850). *Smoke* (3). The French economist called a "fool" by Voroshilov, who himself prized only the best in culture.

Batzov. *Smoke*. A friend of Litvinov who carried off a merchant's daughter after making her intoxicated.

Baudran, Madame. *A Gentry Nest*. A Parisian dressmaker.

Baush. "Ovsianikov, the Freeholder," in *A Hunter's Sketches*. The chief huntsman and whipper-in of Turgenev's grandfather.

Bayle, Pierre (1647-1706). *Evgenii Onegin* (8, 35). The French thinker who greatly influenced philosophy in the eighteenth century.

Onegin read the "skeptic Bayle" while trying to forget Tat'iana when she refused to answer his letters.

Bazarov, Evgenii Vasil'ich. *Fathers and Sons*. The nihilist hero who became a symbol of the progressive young people of the 1860s. His philosophy of life contrasted greatly with the conservative Russians of the period. He died before he was able to achieve his goals.

Bazarov, Vasilii Ivanich. *Fathers and Sons*. The retired surgeon and father of Evgenii. His great hopes for his son were shattered by the young man's death in a typhus epidemic.

Bazarova, Arina Vals'evna. *Fathers and Sons*. The superstitious and kind gentlewoman who was the mother of Evgenii.

Bazdeev, Iosif Alekseevich. *War and Peace* (2, 2, 2). The Mason whom Pierre Bezukhov met while traveling. He later became Pierre's teacher in Masonic writings.

Bazdeev, Makar Alekseevich. *War and Peace* (3, 3, 18). The half-mad brother of Pierre Bezukhov's deceased benefactor in Moscow.

Bazdeeva, Sofia Danilovna. *War and Peace* (3, 3, 18). The widow of Pierre Bezukhov's benefactor in Moscow.

Bazov. *War and Peace*. The major with whom Rostov danced the *trepak* in the military service.

Beauche. *War and Peace*. A French soldier at the crossing of the Niemen River when Napoleon invaded Russia.

Beauharnais, Eugène de (1781-1824). *War and Peace* (3, 2, 27). The stepson of Napoleon I who was adopted by the Emperor in 1806. He participated in many battles, including Borodino.

Beaumarchais (1732-1799). *War and Peace* (E, 2, 4). The nom de plume of Pierre Augustin Caron, the French dramatist.

Beaupré. *The Captain's Daughter*. The French tutor of Petr Grinev. He was a barber in France before coming to Russia.

Beausset, de. *War and Peace* (3, 2, 26). The prefect of Napoleon's palace who brought a picture of the Emperor's son to Borodino before the battle there.

Beethoven, Ludwig von (1770-1827). *Anna Karenina* (1, 33). The German composer whom Karenin liked to discuss to show that he kept up on things. *A Gentry Nest* (4). Liza Kalitina and Panchin played Beethoven's sonata for four hands on the piano. "Hamlet of the Shchigrovskii District," in *A Hunter's Sketches*. Sofia, the Russian Hamlet's dead wife, used to play Beethoven on the piano. "The Kreutzer Sonata" (23). Trukhachevskii and Pozdnysheva played a Beethoven sonata at an evening party. *Resurrection* (3, 24). Beethoven's Fifth

Symphony was played at a dinner which Nekhliudov attended and during which he envied the hostess for her family life and happiness. *Rudin* (1). Muffel talked about Beethoven with eloquence and rapture.

Beh. *Resurrection.* The senator who was described as a practical jurist and a liberal.

Beist, Friedrich Ferdinand (1813-1886). *Anna Karenina.* An Austrian statesman known for his opposition to Bismark's politics. He is mentioned as a society member who recently left St. Petersburg for Wiesbaden.

Belevolenskii, Petr Mikhailovich, "Tat'iana Borisovna and Her Nephew," in *A Hunter's Sketches,* The governmental administrator who took Tat'iana's nephew to St. Petersburg to study art.

Bekleshov, Aleksandr A. (1745-1808). *War and Peace* (1, 1, 21). Elected in 1806 to be commander in chief of the Second Regional Field Troops, he was a friend of Speranskii and Governor-General of Moscow.

Beliavskaia. *Resurrection.* A guest at the Maslinnikovs' party.

Bela. "Bela," in *A Hero of Our Time.* The daughter of an Asiatic prince who was abducted by her brother and killed by a bandit.

Belenitsyna. *A Gentry Nest.* A provincial gentlewoman who visited the Kalitins.

Belliard, Augustus (1769-1832). *War and Peace* (3, 2, 24). The officer who pleaded with Napoleon for more troops during the Battle of Borodino.

Bellini, Vincenzo (1802-1835). *A Gentry Nest* (40). The composer of "Son geloso" from his opera *La Sonnambula* (1831). Varvara Lavretskaia asked Panchin if he knew the song.

Beloborodov, Ivan Naumovich. *The Captain's Daughter* (11). The old man whom Pugachev made his field marshal. However, Pushkin erred with the historical facts. Beloborodov joined Pugachev's forces in 1774 and served in the area of Ekaterinburg, not in the outskirts of Berdskii where Pushkin placed him.

Belova, Agrafena Ivanovna. *War and Peace.* An elderly spinster who lived near the Rostovs' country estate.

Belovzorov, Viktor Egorych. "First Love." A hussar known for his jealousy.

Belozorov, Andriusha. "Tat'iana Borisovna and Her Nephew," in *A Hunter's Sketches.* The lazy, untalented nephew of the heroine.

Belskaia, Eliza. *Smoke*. The orphan friend of Irina Ratmirova. She died shortly before her prearranged marriage to Potugin.

Benediktov, Vladimir Grigorevich (1807-1873). *Spring Freshets* (6). The Russian poet whom Turgenev praised in his youth but later criticized in his novels.

Bennigsen, Count Leontii Leontevich (1745-1826). *War and Peace* (2, 2, 8). A general on the main staff of the army who participated in the Battle of Borodino.

Bentham, Jeremy (1748-1832). *Anna Karenina* (1, 3). The English philosopher of the Utilitarian school who preached "the greatest good for the greatest number." Oblonskii read an article in which Bentham was mentioned. *Evgenii Onegin* (1, 42). Pushkin wrote that capricious belles of society might read Bentham but that their conversation would still be trite.

Berg, Adolf. *War and Peace*. The pretentious husband of Princess Vera Rostova who used his wife's name and money for his own advancement.

Bernadotte, Juan Batiste (1763-1844). *Spring Freshets* (12). Pantaleone played Napoleon and made his poodle, Tartaglia, be Bernadotte in a playful game. *War and Peace* (3, 1, 6). Bernadotte was elected ruler of Sweden and served as a Marshal of France.

Bernhardt, Sarah (1844-1923). "The Death of Ivan Il'ich" (8). A famous French actress whom Fedor Petrovich saw on the stage.

Bernov. *Resurrection*. The soldier who conducted Nekhliudov to Maslova's cell in Siberia.

Bersenev, Andrei Petrovich (Andriusha). *On the Eve*. A student who wanted to be a professor of philosophy. He loved Elena Stakhova but did not confess his feelings.

Bertenev. *Anna Karenina*. The head of a political party working against the communists.

Bertha. *Anna Karenina*. A blind French lady at a German spa. *Resurrection*. One of the girls from Kitaeva's who visited Maslova in jail.

Berthier, Louis Alexander, Prince of Neuchatel (1753-1815). *War and Peace* (3, 1, 7). The French Marshal with whom Napoleon rode in a carriage part of the time during the retreat from Moscow. In 1813, he urged Napoleon to accept Austria's offer to mediate peace.

Bespandin. "Freeholder Ovsianikov," in *A Hunter's Sketches*. The landowner who plowed up ten acres of peasants' land for himself. Ovsianikov's nephew, Mitia, was helping them fight the illegal action.

Bessières, Jean Baptiste, Duc de Istria (1768-1813). *War and Peace* (3, 1, 7). The French Marshal who participated in many Napoleonic campaigns. In 1812, he commanded a cavalry corps, and in 1813, he was General in Chief of all cavalry forces.

Betsy. *Anna Karenina*. See Tverskaia, Betsy. *A Gentry Nest*. The name which Varvara Lavretskaia used for herself during her secret, adulterous affair in Paris.

Bettina von Arnim (1785-1859). *Rudin* (6). The name taken by Elizabeth Bretano, Countess von Arnim, in her publication "Letters to a Child" in 1835. The letters purported to be her correspondence with Goethe. "Tat'iana Borisovna and Her Nephew," in *A Hunter's Sketches*. An elderly maiden guest mentioned Bettina von Arnim.

Bezukov, Count Kiril Vladimirovich. *War and Peace*. A distinguished figure during the reign of Ekaterina II. At his death, his illegitimate son Pierre was made the legal heir to his fortune and title.

Bezukhov, Petia. *War and Peace*. The infant son of Pierre and Natasha Bezukhova (née Rostova).

Bezukhov, Count Pierre Kirilovich. *War and Peace*. The heir to the Bezukhov fortune who was coaxed into marrying Elena Kuragina. After the War of 1812 and the death of his wife, he married Natasha Rostova.

Bezukhova, Elena Vasil'evna Kuragina. *War and Peace*. The great beauty of St. Petersburg society, who married Pierre Bezukhov for his wealth. After many affairs, she died of a rare disease during the War of 1812.

Bezukhova, Lisa. *War and Peace*. The daughter of Pierre and Natasha Bezukhov.

Bezzubova, Countess. *Anna Karenina*. A woman cured by Landau, whom she later married.

Bibish. *Anna Karenina*. See Miakhii.

Bichat, Marie François Xavier (1771-1802). *Evgenii Onegin* (8, 35). The French anatomist and physiologist whom Onegin read while trying to forget Tat'iana. *Smoke* (4). Bichat was mentioned by Voroshilov when he was finally able to interrupt Madame Sukhanchikova.

Bikbaev, Fomka. *The Captain's Daughter*. The peasant who helped Pugachev with steam bathing.

Bilibin. *War and Peace*. The Russian diplomat in Vienna with whom Prince Andrei stayed during the War of 1805.

Bindasov, Tit. *Smoke*. The curmudgeon and crafty fellow who was always pestering Litvinov.

Binder. *Virgin Soil*. The French carriage maker from whom Kallomeitsev bought his calash.

Biriuzovskii. *Anna Karenina*. The man mentioned by the Princess Varvara as the lover of Mrs. Aveneva.

Birkopf. "Chertopkhanov and Nedopiuskin," in *A Hunter's Sketches*. The former soldier whom Pantelei's mother hired to teach her son, but the teacher drank and slept all day.

Birukov, Taras. *Resurrection*. The husband who allowed himself to be arrested so that he could follow his wife to Siberia.

Birukova, Feodosia. *Resurrection*. Maslova's friend in prison. She had tried to poison her husband, but in prison she discovered that she loved him and he loved her.

Bismarck, Otto, Prince von (1815-1898). *Virgin Soil* (14). The German statesman mentioned by Kallomeitsev in an argument with Nezhdanov. *War and Peace* (E. 2, 5). Tolstoi mentioned Bismarck in his comments on history.

Bitskii. *War and Peace*. A popular figure and newsmonger in St. Petersburg society.

Blangy, Theophile Henri, Viconte de (1737-1799). "L'gov," in *A Hunter's Sketches*. A French aristocrat who came to Russia after the revolution.

Blazenkampf, Count. *Smoke*. An aristocrat who declared that Irina Ratmirova was "la reine du bal."

Blind Boy. "Taman,'" in *A Hero of Our Time*. The boy who helped the smugglers rob Pechorin and who was deserted by them.

Blinker. "The Singers," in *A Hunter's Sketches*. An old house serf who robbed his mistress, paid for his crime and was freed.

Boboshin, Count. *On the Eve*. A well-known plutocrat who wanted to buy one of Shubin's sculptures but later changed his mind.

Bobrishchev. *Anna Karenina*. A Moscow family that gave joyous balls, in the opinion of Kitty Shcherbatskaia.

Bovrov, Sergei. "Petr Petrovich Karataev," in *A Hunter's Sketches*. A friend of Karataev.

Bochkova, Efimia Ivanovna. *Resurrection*. A chambermaid in the Hotel Mavretania.

Bogatyrev. *Resurrection.* An aide-de-camp to the Emperor who promised Nekhliudov that he would personally place Maslova's petition before the tsar.

Bogdanich. *War and Peace.* A regimental commander at Braunau during the War of 1805.

Bogdanova, Tat'iana Borisovna. "Tat'iana Borisovna and Her Nephew," in *A Hunter's Sketches.* A legendary old lady who was known for her kindness and hospitality.

Bogdanovich, Ippolit (1743-1803). *Evgenii Onegin* (3, 29). The Russian poet who wrote the comic work "Dushen'ka" (1783).

Bogdanovich, Modest Ivanovich (1805-1882). *War and Peace* (4, 4, 5). The Russian historian who wrote a history of the War of 1812 which Tolstoi quoted in referring to Kutuzov.

Bogodukhova, Vera Efremovna. *Resurrection.* A political prisoner in jail with Maslova.

Bohl, Petr Petrovich. *Anna Karenina.* An aristocrat who declined candidacy for the Marshal of the Nobility.

Bolgin. *On the Eve.* A senator and rich relative of Anna Stakhova.

Bolius. *A Gentry Nest.* The person Maria Kalitina wrote to for a French governess.

Bolkhovitinov. *War and Peace.* The officer who took the dispatch from Dokhturov to Kutuzov about the evacuation of the French from Moscow.

Bolkonskaia, Princess Liza. *War and Peace.* The beautiful wife of Prince Andrei who died in childbirth.

Bolkonskaia, Princess Mar'ia Nikolaevna. *War and Peace.* Known for her kindness, Mar'ia bowed to her father's will and did not marry. After the War of 1812 and her father's death, she married Nikolai Rostov, who saved her during the war.

Bolkonskii, Prince Andrei Nikolaevich. *War and Peace.* The handsome discontent who left his wife, Princess Liza, and went to war. After her death in childbirth, he proposed to Natasha. She accepted, but her scandalous behavior with Anatol' Kuragin prevented the marriage. When Andrei was wounded, Natasha nursed him before his death.

Bolkonskii, Prince Nikolai Andreevich. *War and Peace.* The eccentric old father of Mar'ia and Andrei who was nicknamed "The King of Prussia."

Bolkonskii, Nikolai Andreevich (Nikolenka, Nikolushka). *War and Peace.* Prince Andrei's son by the Princess Liza.

Bonaparte, Matilda (1820-1904). *Smoke* (1). The niece of Napoleon

I and cousin of Napoleon III whose salon was a famous meeting place for writers and artists.

Bonaparte, Napoleon. See Napoleon I.

Boncourt. *Rudin.* The sixty-year-old governess who watched after Natal'ia Lasunskaia. After forty years in Russia, she could still barely speak Russian.

Bondarenko. *War and Peace.* A hussar orderly at Braunau.

Borenka. *War and Peace.* A diminutive for Prince Boris Drubetskoi.

Boria. *Virgin Soil.* A diminutive for Boris Sipiagin. *War and Peace.* A diminutive for Boris Drubetskoi.

Börne, Ludwig (1786-1837). *Virgin Soil* (16). The German publicist and critic mentioned by Markelov in a conversation with Nezhdanov.

Borozdina. *Anna Karenina.* A woman who called on Landau for an appointment.

Borzozowska, Panna. *War and Peace.* The person for whom the Uhlans gave a ball when Nikolai Rostov was serving in the Palograd Regiment in 1807.

Bosse, Vincent. *War and Peace.* The French drummer boy taken prisoner by Denisov during Napoleon's retreat from Moscow.

Bourbon. *War and Peace* (1, 1, 4). The French royal dynasty.

Bourdaloue. *Fathers and Sons.* The nickname for the governor of the province. See Bourda Louis.

Bourienne. *War and Peace.* The companion to Mar'ia Bolkonskaia who flirted with Prince Kuragin when he came to ask for Mar'ia's hand in marriage.

Boutet, Mars Anna Francoise Hippolyte (1779-1847). *A Gentry Nest* (15). The noted French actress whom Varvara saw often on stage.

Bovina, Countess. *Anna Karenina.* A Moscow society lady whom Stepan Oblonskii saw when he went to choir practice.

Branitski, Vladislav Ksaverievich (1782-1843). *War and Peace* (3, 2, 1). An Aide-de-Camp of Aleksandr I. He demanded that Barclay de Tolly take a stand against the French as they advanced on Moscow. Barclay dispatched him to St. Petersburg.

Bredikhina, Maria. *On the Eve.* A name Insarov thought up when he was having trouble obtaining a passport.

Breve. *Resurrection.* The public prosecutor who was conservative and self-satisfied.

Brenteln. *Anna Karenina.* A gentleman Dolly predicted would marry Miss Shakhovskii, and he did.

Brianskii. *Anna Karenina*. A horse dealer near Peterhov.

Briantsev. *Anna Karenina*. An influential state dignitary whom Oblonskii knew.

Brohan, Madeline (1833-1900). *Smoke* (21). The French actress who performed in the Théâtre Français from 1850 to 1885.

Broussier, Jean Batiste (1766-1814). *War and Peace* (4, 2, 15). The French General in charge of the French detachment at Fominskoe.

Brown, John. (1735-1788). *Fathers and Sons* (20). The noted English doctor whom Vasilii Bazarov cited as being a "vitalist."

Brozin. *War and Peace*. An officer of the General Staff who was a victim of Kutuzov's rage when the Supreme Commander found out that his troops had not gathered for the battle that was planned at Tarutino.

Brühl, Heinrich (1700-1763). *Fathers and Sons* (28). The Austrian minister for whom a terrace in Dresden was named. Pavel Kirsanov could be seen on the Bruhl Terrace as a refined old gentleman after he moved from the family estate.

Brutus (85?-42 B.C.). *On the Eve* (30). Shubin remarked that Insarov's face would make a model for a statue of Brutus, the famous Roman who murdered Caesar.

Büchner, Fredrich Karl Christian Ludwig (1824-1899). *Fathers and Sons* (10). The German writer whose book *Stoff und Kraft* was suggested to Nikolai Kirsanov by Bazarov as material that would catch him up on the times.

Buckle, Henry Thomas (1821-1862). *Smoke* (3). The English historian, known for his theories on the influence of climate on history, whom Bambaev mentioned to Litvinov when they met in Baden.

Buddha. "The Kreutzer Sonata" (11). The title given to Prince Sidhartha or Gautama, the founder of Buddhism in the sixth century B.C.

Buianov. *Evgenii Onegin*. A neighbor of the Larins.

Bukshevden, Nadine. *Resurrection*. A pretty, young guest at the Maslinikovs' party.

Bulanin. *The Captain's Daughter* (omitted Chapter). The name Pushkin used for Grinev before he settled on the latter.

Bunsen, Robert (1811-1899). *Fathers and Sons* (13). The German chemist whom Madame Kukshina referred to, causing Bazarov to be at a loss for words.

Buslaev, Fedor Ivanovich (1818-1897). *Anna Karenina* (7, 4). The author of the noted grammar book which was mentioned in a conversation between the two brothers-in-law Levin and L'vov.

Buslaev, Vaska. *Smoke*. A folk hero of Novgorod whom Potugin likened to Litvinov, arousing the latter's impatience.

Bustrapa (1808-1873). *On the Eve* (34). A nickname of the French Emperor Napoleon III which Lupoiarov mentioned while speaking of Venice.

Butenop, Brothers. "Two Landowners," in *A Hunter's Sketches*. The brothers who had a factory for agricultural implements.

Buxhöwden, Fedor Fedrovich (1750-1811). *War and Peace* (1, 2, 14). A general of the Russian army during the War of 1812.

Buzovkin. *Resurrection*. A convict whose daughter was taken away during a march to Siberia.

Buzovkina, Aksutka. *Resurrection*. Buzovkin's daughter, who was taken from the march of convicts on the way to Siberia.

Buzulukov. *Anna Karenina*. An officer who refused to show his helmet to a Grand Duchess because it was filled with candy he had stolen.

Buzyreva, Orina Egorovna. "Dubrovskii." See Egorovna.

Bykov. *War and Peace*. The man Denisov played cards with and called "the rat."

Byron, George Noel Gordon, Lord (1788-1824). *Evgenii Onegin*. The epigraph to Chapter Eight is from his poem "Fare Thee Well" (1824). Also (3, 12). The English author was mentioned as being draped in woebegone Romanticism and hopeless egotism. *Fathers and Sons* (12). Matvei Kaliazin called Byron "out of date." "First Love" (11). Maidanov mentioned the Byronic style. *On the Eve* (34). Lupoiarov quoted Byron when describing the glories of Venice. "Princess Mary," in *A Hero of Our Time*. Princess Mary read Byron in English, according to her mother.

Caesar, Julius (110-44 B.C.). "First Love" (6). When Zinaida Zasekina did not notice Vladimir Petrovich B____ in the garden, he was so upset he could not concentrate while reading Caesar's works. "Princess Mary," in *A Hero of Our Time*. When Grushnitskii stumbled during the duel with Pechorin, the latter told him to be careful because Caesar had also stumbled on the way to the forum, where he was killed. *On the Eve* (25). After examining the ailing Insarov, the doctor quoted the lines "aut Caesar, aut nihil." *War and Peace* (1, 1, 5). Pierre picked up the first book that came to his hand while waiting for Prince Andrei Bolkonskii. The book was Caesar's *Commentaries.* (2, 1, 3). Prince Bagration was called a "Caesar in the fray" at the reception held by Count Il'ia Rostov. (E, 1, 3). Tolstoi commented that men excused their war crimes by saying that they acted like Caesar, as if that excused their behavior.

Caius. "The Death of Ivan Il'ich" (6). The Shakespearean character in the plays *King Lear* and *The Merry Wives of Windsor* who was mentioned by Kiezeweller.

Cambyses (529-522 B.C.). *Rudin* (5). Mlle. Boncourt was acquainted only with Cambyses, the King of Persia, among the great men of antiquity.

Canaletto, Antonio (1697-1768). *On the Eve* (33). The Italian painter noted for his scenes of Venice in mists and sunlight. Turgenev felt that the painter did not capture Venice on canvas.

Candide. *Virgin Soil* (19). The famous literary character created by Voltaire in the play *Candide, ou L'Optimisme* (1759). Fomushka Subochev read the work in translation.

Canning, George (1770-1827). *Rudin* (4). Lasunskaia said that her butler resembled the English statesman Canning, noted for his foreign policy based on "neutrality, but not indifference."

Canut. *Anna Karenina.* An acquaintance of the Shcherbatskiis at a German spa.

Captain of the Dragoons. "Princess Mary," in *A Hero of Our Time.* The officer who wanted to teach Pechorin a lesson for his behavior. He joined in a plot against his enemy and did not put a bullet in Pechorin's gun before the duel with Grushnitskii. Pechorin knew of the plot and, to the surprise of the captain, demanded a bullet in his gun before he fired. The captain objected, and Pechorin threatened to duel with him if he did not oblige. Grushnitskii, knowing it meant his death, told the captain to comply.

Card. *Anna Karenina.* The English caretaker of Vronskii's horse.

Carême, Marie Antoine (1784-1833). "The Steward," in *A Hunter's Sketches.* The French author of books on culinary art.

Caroline the Hungarian. *War and Peace.* The woman who owned a tavern at Olmutz where the Pavlograd Hussars celebrated their awards during the visit of the Emperors of Russia and Austria.

Casanova de Seingalt, Giovanni Jacopo (1725-1798). "The Queen of Spades." According to Tomskii, Casanova wrote in his memoirs that St. Germain was a spy.

Castor. *Father and Sons* (12). The mythological hero and son of Zeus whom Vasilii Bazarov was reminded of when he saw his son with Arkadii Kirsanov.

Castres. *War and Peace.* Marshal Davout's adjutant after the crossing of the Niemen River and the invasion of Russia.

Catherine. See Katerina or Ekaterina.

Cato, Mark Portius of Utica (95-46 B.C.). *Virgin Soil* (33). The Roman whose courage in the time of Julius Caesar inspired Paklin to call Mariana Sinetskaia a woman of the time of Cato.

Catullus, Gaius Valerius (c. 84-54 B.C.). *Smoke* (5). The Roman poet who Potugin claimed had expressed Romantic sentiment before Byron.

Caulaincourt, Armand Augustin Louis, Marquess de (1772-1827). *War and Peace* (2, 3, 9). The French ambassador to St. Petersburg during Napoleon's reign. Louis the XVIII pardoned him at the request of Aleksandr I.

Chaadaev, Petr Iakovlevich (1793-1836). *Evgenii Onegin* (1, 25). An influencial freethinker who was known as a foppish wit.

Chadskii. *Evgenii Onegin* (8, 13). The hero of Griboedov's play *Woe from Wit* (1822-23).

Chagin. *Anna Karenina.* The man who was remembered by Karenin as someone who was unfaithful to his wife.

Chalme. *War and Peace.* The seamstress at the shop where Natasha Rostova's trousseau was ordered.

Chamfort, Sebastian Roch Nicolas de (1741-94). *Evgenii Onegin* (8, 35). A French publicist at the time of the French revolution.

Chaplitskii. "The Queen of Spades." The man who died in poverty after squandering millions of roubles.

Charcot, Jean Martin (1825-1893). "The Kreutzer Sonata" (8). The French neurologist who was famed for his work on hypnotism. *Resurrection* (1, 21). The prosecutor at Maslova's trial mentioned him.

Charles IX (1550-1574). *War and Peace* (3, 2, 28). The King of France who Voltaire said allowed the Massacre of St. Bartholomew because he had an upset stomach.

Charles X, Phillipe (1757-1836). *War and Peace* (E, 2, 4). The King of France who was mentioned by Tolstoi in his interpretation of history.

Charles XII (1682-1718). *War and Peace* (3, 1, 7). The King of Sweden who lost the famous Battle of Poltava to Petr I.

Charles XIII (1748-1818). *War and Peace* (3, 1, 6). The King of Sweden whom Napoleon called a madman.

Charon. *War and Peace* (3, 2, 17). In Greek mythology, Charon was the son of Erebus and Night, who carried the shades of dead people across the River Styx. When foreigners were being evacuated from Moscow before the arrival of Napoleon's forces, Rostopchin told the people entering a boat not to let the vessel become one of Charon's.

Charskaia, Countess Ekaterina Ivanovna. *Resurrection*. The aunt of Nekhliudov who wrote letters to important people in regards to Maslova's appeal.

Charskii, Count Ivan Mikhailich. *Resurrection*. The relative of Nekhliudov who wrote letters to well-placed officials in support of Maslova's appeal.

Charskii, Prince. *Anna Karenina*. A guest at Kitty Shcherbatskaia's wedding.

Chateaubriand, Vicomte François René de (1768-1848). *Evgenii Onegin* (4, 26). The French writer who was a forerunner of the Romantic movement in France. Lenskii read Ol'ga a moral novel whose author knew nature "better than Chateaubriand." *Virgin Soil* (7). Sipiagin alluded to the French writer when answering Kallomeitsev's attack on literature. *War and Peace* (E, 1, 1). Tolstoi referred to Chateaubriand in his discussion of history.

Chatrov. *War and Peace*. An old comrade in arms of Prince Nikolai Bolkonskii who dined with him at Bald Hills.

Chechenskii, Prince. *Anna Karenina*. The man who was famous for playing billiards at Levin's club.

Chekmar, Semen. *War and Peace*. The valet of Count Il'ia Rostov.

Chelakhov. "Princess Mary," in *A Hero of Our Times*. The owner of the store where Pechorin outbid Princess Mary for the Persian rug he put on his horse.

Chepuzova, Elena Antonovna. *Rudin*. The neighbor of Dar'ia Lasunskaia who had tortured her own niece, according to Pigasov.

Cheralinskii. "Queen of Spades." The famous gambler with whom Hermann played for high stakes after he knew the secret cards.

Chernobei, Anastasii Ivanovich. "Lebedian'," in *A Hunter's Sketches*. The horse dealer who sold the narrator a lame horse.

Chernov, Mikhail Ivanovich. *Resurrection*. A guest at the Maslennikovs' manor.

Chernyshev, Aleksandr Ivanovich (1786-1857). *War and Peace* (3, 1, 10). A general in the Russian army in 1805 and 1812 who served as Minister of War from 1848 to 1852.

Chertopkhanov, Eremei Lukich. "Chertopkhanov and Nedopiuskin," in *A Hunter's Sketches*. The father of Pantelei who squandered the family fortune.

Chertopkhanov, Pantelei Eremeich (Pantiusha). "Chertopkhanov and Nedopiushkin," in *A Hunter's Sketches*. The proud, gruff landowner who befriended Nedopiushkin.

Cherubini, Luigi (1760-1842). *War and Peace* (2, 3, 13). The Italian composer of the song Natasha sang when she thought she was in love with Boris Drubetskoi.

Chervianskaia, Mariette. *Resurrection*. The married woman who made overtures toward Nekhliudov after agreeing to help him in his efforts for Katiusha Maslova.

Chervianskii. *Resurrection*. Mariette Chervianskaia's husband who was a general, and who smiled with his mouth but never with his eyes.

Chibisova, Masha. *Anna Karenina*. A ballerina under the patronage of Stepan Oblonskii.

Chichagov, Pavel Vasil'evich (1765-1849). *War and Peace* (4, 3, 19). The Russian Admiral who was Minister of Naval Affairs and a member of the State Council during Aleksandr I's reign. When he was ordered to help stop the French retreat and his slowness allowed the enemy to pass Berezin, Chichagov was accused of treason by many.

Chigirin, Karpushka. *War and Peace* (3, 2, 17). Tolstoi either made a mistake or deliberately changed the name. The person who did make observations in the official reports distributed in Moscow was Karniushka Chikhirin.

Chikurasov, Prince Arkadii. *On the Eve*. Anna Vasil'evna Stakhova's guardian who was rich and reared the girl in luxury.

Chikurasova, Princess. *On the Eve*. A rich relative of Anna Vasil'evna Stakhova.

Childe Harold. *Evgenii Onegin* (1, 38). The hero of Byron's poem (1812) by that name. He was known for his misspent youth and indifference to others. Onegin appeared in drawing rooms like Childe Harold, ill-humored, languid.

Chirikov. *Anna Karenina*. A Moscow magistrate, hunting companion and best man at Levin's wedding.

Chopin, Frederic François (1810-1849). *A Gentry Nest* (14). His mazurkas were played by Varvara Pavlova Lavretskaia. *Smoke* (1). He was supposed to have died in the arms of the Countess Babette.

Chtoppel, Rostislav Adamych. "Chertophkanov and Nedopiuskin," in *A Hunter's Sketches*. The relative of Pantelei who teased Nedopiushkin at the reading of the will.

Chumakov. *The Captain's Daughter*. The cossack who sang a dreary bargeman's chant on the eve of Pugachev's attack on Orenburg.

Chukcheulidze. *Smoke*. The Georgian Prince who shot his wife from a cannon, according to Madame Sukhanchikova.

Cicero, Marcus Tullius (106-43 B.C.). *Evgenii Onegin* (8, 1). Pushkin mentioned that he did not read Cicero in the lyceum. "Princess Mary," in *A Hero of Our Time*. Pechorin referred to Cicero in his arguments with Dr. Werner. *Virgin Soil* (19). An article about the Roman orator and statesman was in the Subochevs' album.

Cincinnatus (500-430 B.C.). *Fathers and Sons* (21). The legendary Roman dictator who tilled land. Vasilii Bazarov alluded to him while digging in the Bazarovs' garden and talking with Arkadii Kirsanov.

Cippatola, Panteleone. *Spring Freshets*. An old Italian man who worked for the Roselli family in a subservient role.

Circes. *Evgenii Onegin* (7, 27). In Homer's *Odyssey*, a sorceress who charmed travelers and bewitched them.

Claparède, Michel (1774-1841). *War and Peace* (3, 2, 34). A French divisional commander at Borodino in 1812.

Clara. See Klara.

Clarissa. *Evgenii Onegin* (3, 10). The heroine in Tat'iana Larina's favorite book, *Clarissa Harlowe* (1749), by Samuel Richardson (1689-1761), who furthered the development of the English novel. Pushkin read a 1777 edition when he was in exile at Mikhailovskoe.

Clausewitz, General Karl von (1780-1831). *War and Peace* (3, 2, 25).

The Prussian military theoretician who was in Russian service in the War of 1812, serving under Generals Uvarov, Pahlen and Wittgenstein. Tolstoi wrote that Prince Andrei Bolkonskii overheard Clausewitz's conversation with some military figures at the Battle of Borodino.

Clement. *War and Peace* (4, 3, 9). The name a French officer used when he mistook Dolokhov for someone else during Dolokhov's daring reconnaissance mission in territory occupied by the French.

Clementi, Mutsio (1752-1832). *Resurrection* (1, 51). When Nekhliudov went to see Katiusha Maslova, he heard someone playing Clementi's roulades. The inspector explained that his daughter wanted to be a concert pianist.

Cleopatra (69-30 B.C.). *Evgenii Onegin* (1, 17). The Egyptian Queen of the Ptolemaic dynasty who was the subject of a play Onegin saw. "First Love" (11). The queen mentioned by Zinaida Zasekina when she said that the clouds in the sky must have been in the same formation when Cleopatra met Antony on her barque.

Cleopatrinka. *Smoke*. The daughter of Prince Osinin was called by the diminutive of Cleopatra. She was not so vivacious as her sister Victorinka.

Clytemnestra. *Spring Freshets* (7). The wife of Agamemnon who killed her husband when he returned from Troy. Panteleone mentioned her when he commented on Gemma Roselli's reading.

Columbus, Christopher (1451-1506). *War and Peace* (3, 3, 6). The famous explorer. When Elena Bezukhova's spiritual advisor said that she presented her marital situation with the simplicity of "Columbus's egg," he referred to a legend: when asked how one could place an egg so it would stand, Columbus suggested it be broken.

Compans, General Jean Dominique (1769-1845). *War and Peace* (3, 2, 27). The French officer who proposed the leading of troops through the woods at Borodino. Napoleon approved the plan.

Comte, Auguste (1798-1857). *Resurrection* (2, 23). In his studies on the veracity of the Russian Orthodox Church, Selenin did not read the French philosopher Comte, the founder of Positivism, but instead turned to Hegel.

Condé. *War and Peace* (1, 1, 4). A titled French family. Louis Joseph (1736-1818) fought for Russia.

Condillac, Étienne Bonnot de (1715-1780). *Fathers and Sons* (12). The deist and sensualist writer who was read during the reign of Aleksandr I. His most famous works were *Traité des sensations* (1754) and *Traité des animaux* (1755).

Conegliano, Cima da (1459-1517). *On the Eve* (33). The artist of a picture which Elena (née Stakhova) and Insarov liked in Venice.

Conrad. "Dubrovskii" (2, 14). The hero of the poem "Conrad Valenrod" (1824) by Adam Mickiewicz (1798-1855). Conrad's sweetheart embroidered, in her distress, a green rose with red leaves. Pushkin stated that Mar'ia Troekurova did not make the same mistake when she was worried.

Cooper, James Fenimore (1789-1851). *Fathers and Sons* (13). The noted American author of The *Pathfinder* (1840) whom Mme. Kukshina compared to her steward Erofei.

Copernicus, Nicolaus (1473-1543). *Rudin* (3). Rudin asked Pigasov whether he believed in Copernicus's theories on astronomy.

Cora. *Smoke.* An upperclass Parisian lady.

Corday, Charlotte (1758-1793). *Anna Karenina* (5, 9). The French patriot who stabbed to death Marat, a leader of the Terrorists. She was guillotined July 17, 1793. In a conversation with Anna and Vronskii, Golenishchev suggested the fanatic French revolutionary Corday as a subject for a painting instead of Christ, indicating that artists should turn to historical subjects instead of Biblical ones.

Cordelia. *Anna Karenina* (7, 5). The youngest of King Lear's daughters in Shakespeare's *King Lear* and the only one who loved him. Levin forgot her name while discussing M. A. Balakirev's (1837-1910) operetta "King Lear on the Heath" with Pestsov.

Correggio, Antonio (1494-1534). *Spring Freshets* (4). The Italian painter known for his classical landscapes with their effects of color and light. He painted a magnificent dome in Parma, the native town of Mme. Roselli. "Tat'iana Borisovna and Her Nephew," in *A Hunter's Sketches*. Mentioned by the narrator in his comments on self-styled art critics.

Corsair. *Evgenii Onegin* (3, 12). The sea-pirate hero of Byron's poem by that name (1813).

Cossack. *War and Peace*. A nickname for Natasha Rostova by Maria Akhrosimova.

Croesus (560-546 B.C.). *Fathers and Sons* (20). The wealthy King of Lydia whom Bazarov named when he told his father not to apologize to Arkadii Kirsanov for their modest homestead.

Crooks. *Resurrection*. A good tennis player.

Crosart. *War and Peace* (3, 3, 3). A French officer who had participated in Napoleon's Spanish campaign and who offered Rostopchin a plan for the defense of Moscow based on the siege of Saragossa.

Crow. *War and Peace*. A soldier in the Eighth Company during the French retreat.

Cypris. *Evgenii Onegin* (4, 27). The goddess of love and beauty whose temple was in Ol'ga Larina's album.

Czartoryski, Prince Adam Jerzy (1770-1861). *War and Peace* (1, 3, 9). The governmental figure and close friend of Aleksandr I who was minister of interior from 1804 to 1806.

D____, Ivan Vasil'evich. *War and Peace*. An acquaintance of Pierre Bezukhov in society and in the Masons.

Dalai Lama. "Hamlet of the Shchigrovskii District," in *A Hunter's Sketches*. Turgenev commented that the Russian Hamlet would ask the Grand Lama of Tibet for a pinch of tobacco if he confronted him.

Damian, Saint. "Raspberry Spring," in *A Hunter's Sketches*. The saint in whose name the church was built near the village Shumikhino.

Danchenko, Iurii Dmitrich. *Resurrection*. A juryman at Katiusha Maslova's trial.

Dandin, Georges. *Virgin Soil* (25). The hero of the play *Georges Dandin* by Molière. Kallomeitsev quoted from the play to inform Valentina Sipiagina in a clever way that her failure to carry off her conversation with Solomin was her own fault. *War and Peace* (3, 3, 5). Kliucharov mentioned Dandin in a verse he wrote after abandoning Moscow.

Danilo. *War and Peace*. A huntsman and whipper-in at the Rostov estate.

Danilo Terentich. *War and Peace*. Count Il'ia Rostov's valet.

Danilov, Kirsha. *Smoke*. The "Collection of Kirsha Danilov" contains the folk legends about Buslaev. See Buslaev.

Danneker, Henrich (1758-1841). *Spring Freshets* (1). The German sculptor whose statue of Ariadne attracted Sanin in Frankfurt.

Dantan, Jean Pierre (1800-1896). *On the Eve* (1). The French portraitist, noted for his caricatures, whom Shubin said he imitated when doing a bust of Avgustina Khristianovna.

Dante Alighieri (1265-1321). "The Queen of Spades" (2). The Italian poet was quoted in the lines "The bread of charity is bitter, and the steps to a stranger's house are steep." The lines referred to Lisaveta Ivanovna's humiliating position at the Countess Anna Fedotovna's. *Spring Freshets* (6). Pantaleone refused to leave Italy, the land of Dante, to go to Russia with Prince Tarbusskii.

Dar'ia. *On the Eve*. A servant of the Strakhovs. *Rudin*. See Lasunskaia, Dar'ia.

Dar'ia Petrovna, Princess. "The Queen of Spades." An old acquaintance of Countess Anna Fedotovna. She had been dead seven years, but the Countess did not know it.

Darialov. *Anna Karenina*. Karenin remembered him as a man who had been unfaithful to his wife.

Darwin, Charles (1809-1882). *Resurrection* (1, 27). In a conversation between Nekhliudov and Kolossov, the latter stated that there was much truth in Darwin's theory of evolution but that he exaggerated. *Virgin Soil* (38). Paklin referred to Darwin's theory as, perhaps, the answer for the thing the Russians are always waiting for to explain life's meaning.

Dasha. "Death," in *A Hunter's Sketches*. A friend of the author. She was one of Sorokoumov's loves in his youth.

Daudet, Alfonse (1840-1897). *Anna Karenina* (7, 10). The French writer Anna mentioned in a conversation with Vorkuev and Levin. The latter greatly appreciated the pleasure his remarks gave Anna.

David. *War and Peace* (3, 1, 18). The Biblical figure mentioned in a prayer by Natasha Rostova when the French attacked Smolensk.

Davout, Louis Nicoles, Duke of Auerstast and Prince of Eckmuhl (1770-1823). *War and Peace* (3, 1, 4). One of Napoleon's ablest generals who was known for his cruelty with his subordinates.

Davydov. *War and Peace* (3, 2, 39). The family that owned the land where part of the Battle of Borodino was fought.

Davydov, Denis Vasil'evich (1784-1839). *War and Peace* (4, 3, 3).

The Russian poet and military writer who commanded guerrilla detachments during the retreat of the French from Moscow.

Debrett, John (1752-1822). *Fathers and Sons* (21). The English compiler of the Peerage of England. Vasilii Bazarov stated that he was of simple background, not out of Debrett, like his wife.

Deforge, Monsieur. "Dubrovskii." The name which Dubrovskii used when he disguised himself as a French tutor.

Delaunay, Marie Amélie (Dorval) (1798-1849). *A Gentry Nest* (15). A noted French actress who caused Varvara to cry when she saw her on stage.

Delphine. *Evgenii Onegin* (3, 10). The name of a favorite heroine of Tat'iana in the novel *Delphine* (1802), by Madame de Staël.

Del'vig, Anton Antonovich (1798-1831). *Evgenii Onegin* (6, 20). Pushkin's childhood friend who became a poet of note.

Demian. *War and Peace.* A butler at the Bolkonskii estate, Bald Hills.

Demin, Colonel. *Anna Karenina.* The officer who gave a party for Vronskii's regiment at his large country estate.

Demon. *Evgenii Onegin* (8, 12). Pushkin wrote a poem "Demon" (1823), in which the mythological creature was pictured as a spirit of negation and doubt.

Demosthenes (384-322 B.C.). *A Gentry Nest* (25). Lavretskii called his friend Mikhailevich "a Poltavan Demosthenes." *Rudin* (6). Lezhnev said that Rudin talked like Demosthenes before the roaring sea. *War and Peace* (1, 2, 11). Bibilin mentioned the Attic orator in a discussion with Prince Bolkonskii.

Denisov, Kiril Andreevich. *War and Peace.* The uncle of Vaska Denisov and an acquaintance of Kutuzov.

Denisov, Vasilii Dmitrich (Vaska). *War and Peace* (1, 2, 4). The squadron commander of the Pavlograd Hussars at Braunau with whom Nikolai Rostov shared quarters. Denisov had a speech impediment which made his language colorful.

Depré. *A Gentry Nest* (14). A wine store merchant from whom a general's footman bought Lafitte wine for Lavretskii.

Derzhavin, Gavrila Romanovich (1743-1806). "Chertopkhanov and Nedopiuskin," in *A Hunter's Sketches.* Pantelei greatly esteemed the famous Russian poet. *Evgenii Onegin* (8, 2). Pushkin was lauded by the noted poet while he was still a student.

Dessaix, Comte Joseph Marie (1764-1834). *War and Peace* (3, 2, 27). The commander of a French division at Borodino in 1812.

Dessalles, Monsieur. *War and Peace*. The French tutor for Prince Andrei Bolkonskii's son.

Devkin, Makar. *Resurrection*. The peasant who risked his life to give Nekhliudov information about prison matters.

Devonshire, Duchess of. *Smoke*. An English aristocrat who was said to resemble Irina at a court ball.

Devrient, Philip Edward (1801-1871). *Spring Freshets* (39). The director of the Royal Troup of Karlsruhe. Sanin and Polozov watched performances of the group in Wiesbaden.

Diana. *Evgenii Onegin* (1, 32). The ancient Roman goddess of the moon and the hunt. *War and Peace* (2, 4, 6). Ilagin called Natasha "Diana" during the hunt at "uncle's" estate.

Dickens, Charles (1812-1870). *Anna Karenina* (1, 11). The English writer Oblonskii mentioned to Levin at lunch when he referred to the Dickensian character who avoided all embarrassing questions by throwing them over his right shoulder with his left hand. The character referred to was Mr. Podsnap from the novel *Our Mutual Friend* (1864).

Didelot, Charles Louie (1767-1837). *Evgenii Onegin* (1, 18). A famous ballet master.

Diderot, Denis (1713-1784). *A Gentry Nest* (8). The French encyclopedist whose works Lavretskii's father studied in his youth. *War and Peace* (E, 2, 4). Tolstoi named the encyclopedist in a discussion on the interpretation of history.

Dido. *Spring Freshets* (39). The famous heroine from the *Aeneid* who burned herself to death on a pyre when she lost Aeneas's love. Polozova mentioned her to Sanin during a boring theater performance.

Dimmler, Eduard Karlich. *War and Peace*. A musician at the Rostov estate.

Diogenes (c. 412-323 B.C.). *Rudin* (4). Lasunskaia compared Lezhnev with Diogenes, the noted Greek cynic who, according to Seneca, lived in a tub.

Dmitriev, Ivan Ivanovich (1760-1837). *Evgenii Onegin*. The epigraph to Chapter Seven is from his poem "The Liberation of Moscow" (1795).

Dmitriev, Nikanor. *Smoke*. In a letter from his father, Litvinov read about a coachman, Nikanor Dmitriev, who had been bewitched but survived.

Dmitriev-Mamonov, Matvei Aleksandrovich (1790-1863). *War and Peace* (3, 1, 23). The Mason and son of a favorite of Ekaterina II. He furnished a regiment at his own expense during the War of 1812.

Dmitrii. "The Death of Ivan Il'ich." Ivan Il'ich's faithful servant.

Dmitrii the Pretender (Lzhedmitrii) (d. 1610). *Virgin Soil* (34). The pretender who claimed to be the son of Ivan the Terrible. Paklin maintained that the Russian peasants needed a legend to be moved to action. See Otrep'ev, G. B.

Dmitrii Alekseich (Mitia). "Freeholder Ovsianikov," in *A Hunter's Sketches*. Ovsianikov's nephew who was continually in trouble.

Dmitrii Vasil'evich. *War and Peace*. A nobleman who looked after the financial affairs of the Rostovs.

Dobroliubov, Nikolai Aleksandrovich (1836-1861). *Virgin Soil* (28). The liberal poet whose poem Mariana quoted after she and Nezhdanov had run away from the Sipiagin household.

Doche, Maria Carlotta Evgenia (1821-1900). *A Gentry Nest* (Epilogue). The French actress whom Varvara Lavretskaia greatly admired.

Dockmaned Filly. "The Singers," in *A Hunter's Sketches*. The nickname of a landed proprietress known for her spirited nature.

Dokhturov, General Dmitrii Sergeevich (1756-1816). *War and Peace* (1, 2, 9). A Russian officer in the campaigns of 1805 and 1812.

Dolgorukov, Iurii Vladimirovich (1740-1830). *War and Peace* (2, 1, 2). The Russian general who was selected the Chief of Troops of the Seventh District in 1806.

Dolgorukov, Mikhail Petrovich (1770-1808). *War and Peace* (1, 3, 9). The Russian colonel who was in Paris in 1800 on the commission to exchange prisoners between the French and Russians.

Dolgorukov, Petr Petrovich (1777-1806). *War and Peace* (1, 3, 9). The Russian general who was one of Aleksandr I's closest aides.

Dolgovushin. *Anna Karenina*. An acquaintance of Stepan Oblonskii.

Dolly. *Anna Karenina*. The family name for Dar'ia Oblonskaia (née Shcherbatskaia).

Dolokhov, Fedor Ivanovich. *War and Peace*. The carouser and gambler whom Pierre Bezukhov wounded in a duel over his wife. Dolokhov, the "bully," cried, thinking of his mother.

Dolokhova, Maria Ivanovna. *War and Peace*. The kind mother of Dolokhov who nursed him after his duel with Pierre Bezukhov.

Dol'skaia, Zinaida Aleksandrovna. "First Love." See Z. A. Zasekina.

Dol'skii. "First Love." The man Zinaida Zasekina married after her affair with Petr Vasilich B____. *Smoke.* An upperclass family name Turgenev used when implying that scandalous activities took place in society.

Don Giovanni. *Spring Freshets* (22). The hero of a Mozart opera (1787) by that name. Pantaleone called Sanin a hero of the Don Giovanni type, "a son of snow and granite."

Don Jaun (14th Cent.). *Evgenii Onegin* (7, 22). The son of a leading family of Seville who killed the commandant of Ulloa after seducing his daughter. Byron's poem "Don Juan" (1819-1824) created a hero who influenced romantic literature. Evgenii Onegin was described as a "singer of Don Juan." *Fathers and Sons* (4). The hero Arkadii mentioned when describing Pavel's youth to Bazarov. "The Kreutzer Sonata" (5). Pozdnyshev stated that each man is a Don Juan before he marries. *Virgin Soil* (21). Markelov called Nezhdanov a Don Juan, but Nezhdanov did not know that Markelov knew of his feelings for Mariana. *War and Peace* (1, 2, 11). Bilibin referred to Ippolit Kuragin as a Russian Don Juan.

Don Quizote. *Rudin* (11). Rudin quoted the famous Cervantes hero on the virtue of liberty.

Dönhov, Baron von. *Spring Freshets.* The drunk officer who made advances toward Gemma and was consequently challenged to a duel by Sanin.

Donizetti, Gaetano (1797-1848). *A Gentry Nest* (39). The composer of *Lucia di Lammermoor* (1835), from which Varvara Lavretskaia played some excerpts on the piano.

Dorofeich. "Bezhin Meadow," in *A Hunter's Sketches.* Kuzka's father.

Dorokhov, Ivan Semenovich (1762-1815), *War and Peace* (4, 2, 15). The Russian General who headed a guerrilla detachment near Tarutino with amazing élan.

Dorval. See Delaunay, Marie.

Dostoevskii, Fedor Mihailovich (1821-1881). *Resurrection* (1, 7). One of the Russian writers whose works Nekhliudov gave Katiusha Maslova to read when he first met her at his aunt's.

Dram. *Anna Karenina.* Mentioned by Karenin as a man whose wife was unfaithful.

Draper, John (1811-1882). *Smoke* (4). The historian of culture and apologist of bourgeois industry who was mentioned by Voroshilov when he finally interrupted Madame Sukhanchikova.

Dron Zakharich. *War and Peace.* A village elder at the Bolkonskii estate.

Dronuskha. *War and Peace.* A diminutive for Dron.

Drubetskaia, Princess Anna Mikhailovna. *War and Peace.* An impoverished member of an ancient aristocratic family who arranged a military position for her son, Boris, through Prince Vasilii Kuragin.

Drubetskoi, Boris. *War and Peace.* The handsome young aristocrat whose mother secured him a high military position through family ties. He later married the heiress Julie Karagina.

Dubois. *Anna Karenina.* A name thought up by Tolstoi to designate one of the writers Levin thought about when he studied how to improve his lands and the lot of his peasants (3, 29).

Dubrovskii, Andrei Gavrilovich. "Dubrovskii." The retired officer whose friend Troekurov cheated him out of his estate.

Dubrovskii, Vladimir Andreevich (Volodia). "Dubrovskii." The young officer who returned to his father's estate and became the Russian Robin Hood, robbing the rich and giving to the poor.

Duchesnois, Catherine Josephine Rafin (1777-1835). *War and Peace* (3, 3, 29). The noted French actress who Napoleon said was plain of face but perfect in form. She was mentioned in a conversation about Paris when Pierre was imprisoned in Moscow during the French occupation.

Dufar. *Resurrection.* A French wigmaker who made a fortune and bought a large estate, but would not rent land to peasants.

Dumas, Alexandre, *fils* (1824-1895). *A Gentry Nest* (40). The writer Varvara Lavretskaia adored. *Rudin* (5). Lasunskaia did not allow her daughter to read him.

Duniasha. *Anna Karenina.* Kitty's maid. "First Love." Zasekin's maid. *Fathers and Sons.* A servant to Paul Kirsanov. *War and Peace.* A maid at the Rostov country estate.

Duport, Louis (1782-1853). *War and Peace* (2, 5, 9). The Parisian ballet master who migrated to Russia in 1830 and became an orchestra conductor.

Duport, Pierre (1765-1840). *War and Peace* (2, 1, 1). The French general who actively engaged in Napoleonic campaigns.

Durdoleosova, Princess. *Fathers and Sons.* The wife of Sitnikov. He had to be subservient to her in spite of his contempt for women.

Duroc, Gerard Chistophe Jean Auguste (1772-1813). *War and Peace* (3, 1, 6). The French Marshal who was very close to Napoleon and accompanied him on all marches from 1805 to 1813.

Durosnel, Antoine Jean Auguste (1771-1849). *War and Peace* (3, 3, 34). The French general who was designated commandant of Moscow when the French occupied the city.

Dussek, Johann Ladislas (1760-1812). *War and Peace* (1, 1, 26). The composer of the sonata which Mar'ia Bolkonskaia played one evening at Bald Hills.

E____. *On the Eve*. The person in whose home in Moscow Insarov met Lupoiarov.

Eagle. "Khor' and Kalinych," in *A Huntsman's Sketches*. The merchant who sold scythes each mowing season.

Echartschausen, Karl (1752-1803). *War and Peace* (E, 1, 13). The German writer and mystic mentioned by Denisov in conversation.

Eckmühl, Prince of. *War and Peace* (3, 2, 27). A title given to Davout. See Davout.

Edwards, Miss. *Anna Karenina*. An English governess at Anna's.

Efim. "Death," in *A Hunter's Sketches*. The man from whom Maxim bought a horse for his wife. *War and Peace*. An old coachman at the Rostov household when they were evacuating Moscow.

Efimich. "Fatalist," in *Hero of Our Time*. The Cossack who killed Vulich while in a drunken stupor.

Efremova, Vera. *Resurrection*. A political prisoner in love with Novodvorov.

Egor. *Anna Karenina*. A waiter in the hotel where Levin stayed. "The Kreutzer Sonata." Pozdnyshev's footman.

Egor Dmitrich. "The Steward," in *A Hunter's Sketches*. The man who reported a land deal to Arkadii Pavlych Penochkin.

Egorov. *Anna Karenina*. Vronskii's steward.

Egorovna. "Dubrovskii." A woman who looked after Vladimir Dubrovskii when he was young and after Andrei Dubrovskii when he became ill. *Fathers and Sons*. The deceased nanny of Arkadii Kirsanov. *Smoke*. A servant in the Osinin mansion.

Eikhen, Fedor Iakovlevich. *War and Peace*. An officer of the general staff who was a victim of Kutuzov's rage when the supreme commander found out that his troops had not gathered for the battle that was planned at Tarutino.

Ekaterina I (1683-1727). *War and Peace*. The widow of Petr I who was Empress of Russian from 1824 to 1827.

Ekaterina II (1729-1796). *Anna Karenina* (3, 27). The Russian Empress was mentioned by a landowner in conversation with Levin to show that he was learned. *The Captain's Daughter* (14). Masha managed to meet the Empress and save Grinev. *Fathers and Sons* (3). When Arkadii Kirsanov drove around the family estate, he was reminded of maps drawn up in the Empress's reign. *A Gentry Nest* (19). Ekaterina II reigned from 1762 to 1796. *Virgin Soil* (18). The customs of the Empress's reign were still alive in the household of Paklin's relatives, the Subochevs. *War and Peace* (1, 1, 2). Ekaterina II was in charge of the education of her grandson, Aleksandr I.

Ekaterina Pavlovna (1788-1819). *War and Peace* (2, 3, 1). The sister of Aleksandr I who, it was rumored, might become the wife of Napoleon I.

Ekonomov. *War and Peace* (1, 2, 20). The major to whom Dolokhov gave a captured French sword.

Elchingen, Duke of. *War and Peace* (3, 2, 27). A title belonging to Marshal Ney. See Michel Ney.

Elena. *Evgenii Onegin*. The princess who was Tat'iana Larina's aunt and who wore a particular style of bonnet. *On the Eve*. See Stakhova, Elena.

Eletskaia. "The Queen of Spades." A woman Tomskii described as being "exquisite" at a ball.

Eletskii. *Anna Karenina*. An aristocratic girl who was mentioned for having made a poor marriage contract.

Elisevich, G. Z. *Fathers and Sons* (13). A writer on *The Contemporary* who according to Madame Kukshina, had written an article on embryology.

Elistratov, Stepan Nikolaevich. *Smoke*. A man mentioned in conversation.

Elizabeth de France, Philippine Marie Hélène (1764-1794). *War and Peace* (1, 1, 5). The sister of Louis XVI who refused to abandon her brother during the French Revolution. She was beheaded after her brother and Marie Antoinette were executed.

Elizar. *Virgin Soil*. A peasant whom Nezhdanov considered bright, but with whom he had trouble communicating.

Elizaveta, Empress (1709-1761). *Virgin Soil* (19). The material that lined the Subachevs' coach was woven during the reign of Elizaveta, 1741-1761.

Elizaveta Alekseevna, Empress (1779-1826). *War and Peace* (4, 1, 1). The wife of Aleksandr I.

Ellen Lelia. *War and Peace*. A name for Princess Elena Vasil'evna Kuragina (Bezukhova).

Elohim. *War and Peace* (2, 3, 10). In Masonic writings, Elohim is the name for the ruler of all.

El'vina. *Evgenii Onegin* (1, 32). A girl Pushkin mentioned as a beloved one. She has never been identified.

Emerson, Ralph Waldo (1803-1882). *Fathers and Sons* (8). The American idealist whom Madame Kukshina greatly admired.

Emma. *Resurrection*. A prostitute mentioned by an officer.

Engeni, Mme. "The Office," in *A Hunter's Sketches*. A French governess.

Enghien, Duc Louis Antoine Henri (1772-1804). *War and Peace* (1, 1, 5). A member of the French royal family who lived in Baden after the French revolution of 1789. He had no part in the plot to assassinate Napoleon in 1804. However, Napoleon wanted revenge on the Bourbons, and therefore had the prince arrested and shot.

Eniusha. *Fathers and Sons*. Evgenii Bazarov's mother called her son by this diminutive.

Enoch. *Anna Karenina* (5, 27). A Biblical patriarch recalled by Anna's son Serezha, when Karenin questioned him on religion.

Eol. *Evgenii Onegin* (1, 20). The god of the wind. Pushkin wrote that Istomina flew on stage like a fluff from Eol's lips.

Eremeich. "Fatalist," in *A Hero of Our Time*. One of the cossacks who were looking for a drunken comrade.

Ermak. "First Love" (14). The hero of a tragedy by Khomiakov. See Aleksei Stepanovich Khomiakov.

Ermil. *Anna Karenina*. A field laborer at Levin's estate. "Bezhin Meadow," in *A Hunter's Sketches*. A dog keeper. "Two Landowners," in *A Hunter's Sketches*. The coachman of Stegunov.

Ermilin, Prokhor. *Anna Karenina*. A worker at Levin's estate.

Ermiskin, Matvei. *War and Peace*. A prosperous peasant whom Nikolai Rostov admired.

Ermolai. *A Hunter's Sketches*. The huntsman who accompanied the narrator in "Chertopkhanov and Nedopiuskin," "Ermolai and the Miller's Wife," "L'gov," "Living Holy Relics," "Biriuk, The Morose One," "My Neighbor Radilov," and "Rattling Wheels."

Ermolov, "Princess Mary," in *A Hero of Our Time*. The owner of the bathhouse where Ligovskaia took baths at 11 A.M. sharp.

Ermolov, Aleksei Petrovich (1772-1861). "Bela," in *A Hero of Our*

Time. The commander in the Caucasus under whom Maxim Maksimovich once served. *Fathers and Sons* (8). A picture of the noted general was hanging in Fenichka's room. *War and Peace* (3, 1, 9). The Russian general who participated in the campaigns of 1805-1807. In 1812, he was head of the First Army Headquarters. In 1817, he became the Supreme Commander of the Caucasus.

Ernest. *A Gentry Nest*. The name signed on the note which revealed Varvara Lavretskaia's infidelity.

Ernst, Heinrich Wilhelm (1814-1865). "The Kreutzer Sonata." The German composer whose music was played by Trukhachevskii and Pozdnysheva.

Erofei. *Fathers and Sons*. The steward of Eudoxie Kukshina who reminded her of *The Pathfinder* by James Fenimore Cooper. "Kassian from Fair Strath," in *A Hunter's Sketches*. The narrator's coachman.

Essen, Ivan Ivanovich (1759-1813). *War and Peace* (1, 3, 8). The general of the Russian army who commanded a corps in 1805 which was designated to fight together with the Austrians. In November, 1805, his corps joined the Austrians, but they were sixty miles from Austerlitz during the famous battle there.

Euler, Leonard (1707-1783). *Virgin Soil* (2). The mathematician whom Paklin cited in conversation with Ostrodumov.

Eve, *Anna Karenina* (3, 4). Anna teased Vronskii about his passion and said that he enjoyed seeing his former mistress as nude as Eve. *Evgenii Onegin* (8, 27). Eve was called the mother of us all.

Evseev. *Smoke*. The man who sent to the Gubarevs and was called a scoundrel by Madame Sukhanchikova.

Evstafievich. *War and Peace*. The head coachman for Pierre Bezukhov in Moscow.

Fabvier, Charles Nicolas (1782-1855). *War and Peace* (3, 2, 26). The French officer who came to Napoleon at Borodino with the news that his troops had been defeated at Salamanca, Spain.

Fain, Agaton Jean François (1778-1837). *War and Peace* (4, 2, 10). Napoleon's secretary and historian.

Faleev. *Virgin Soil*. A merchant who owned the spinning factory where Solomin lived.

Falieri, Marino (1273-1355). *On the Eve* (34). The Venetian doge who was decapitated for treason. Lupoiarov was impressed with the doge's palace.

Fanarin, Anatolii Petrovich. *Resurrection*. The advocate to whom Nekhliudov went to try to appeal Maslova's case.

Faublas. *Evgenii Onegin* (1, 12). A noted fictional lover who was the hero of many novels by Jean Baptiste Louvet de Couvrai (1760-1797).

Fedeshou. *War and Peace*. A soldier in the parade at Braunau.

Fedia. "Bezhin Meadow," in *A Hunter's Sketches*. The oldest of the peasant children the narrator met in the meadow. *A Gentry Nest*. A diminutive for Fedor Lavretskii. "Khor' and Kalinych," in *A Hunter's Sketches*. A sportsman who was Khor's son. *War and Peace*. A diminutive for Fedor Dolokhov.

Fediushka. "The Office," in *A Hunter's Sketches*. A clerk on duty in the office. *On the Eve*. A page in the Stakhovs' home.

Fedka. *Fathers and Sons*. A servant of the Bazarovs. *Resurrection*. A peasant boy in Nekhliudov's village. Also, a blind prisoner.

Fedor. *Anna Karenina*. A worker at Levin's estate. "First Love." Vladimir Petrovich's footman. "The Steward," in *A Hunter's Sketches*. The name of the steward. *Virgin Soil*. A footman on the Sipiagin estate. *War and Peace*. The peasant who helped carry Andrei Bolkonskii off the battlefield at Borodino. Also, a servant boy at the Rostov estate.

Fedor. Prince, *War and Peace*. The aristocrat who called Pierre Bezukhov from Bald Hills to St. Petersburg on business when Pierre was visiting the Rostovs.

Fedor Avksent'evich. *A Gentry Nest*. A priest of the Holy Trinity Church who gave Saltykova a relief for chest ailments.

Fedor Mikheich. "My Neighbor Radilov," in *A Hunter's Sketches*, The ruined landed proprietor who lived with Radilov.

Fedor Petrovich. "The Death of Ivan Il'ich." The fiancé of Lisa Golovina.

Fedor Vasil'evich. "The Death of Ivan Il'ich." A member of the court who studied law with Ivan Il'ich Golovin and was considered to be under obligation to Ivan.

Fedorov. *Resurrection*. A handsome, gifted prisoner.

Fedoseich. "The Steward," in *A Hunter's Sketches*. The village constable.

Fedos'ia Mikhailovna. "Freeholder Ovsianikov," in *A Hunter's Sketches*. A Moscow seamstress.

Fedos'ia Nikolaevna. *Fathers and Sons*. The mistress of Nikolai Kirsanov after his wife's death. She bore his son Mitia.

Fedosiev, Ivashka. "Bezhin Meadow," in *A Hunter's Sketches*. The boy who was prophesied to die.

Fedosiushka. *War and Peace*. A pock-marked pilgrim who visited the Bolkonskii estate.

Fedot. *Anna Karenina*. The son of a peasant near Levin's estate. *Fathers and Sons*. The keeper of a posting station at the Khokhlovskii settlement.

Fedotov. *Resurrection*. The jailer where Maslova was imprisoned. *War and Peace*. A soldier whose trivial conversation was reported as the Russians retreated near Braunau.

Fedotovna. "Dubrovskii." The wife of Father Anton.

Feklista. "Bezhin Meadow," in *A Hunter's Sketches*. The mother of Aniutka's lover, Vasia.

Feller. *War and Peace*. The doctor who treated Natasha after her scandalous behavior with Anatol' Kuragina.

Fenichka. *Fathers and Sons*. A diminutive for Fedos'ia.

Fentinkov. *Anna Karenina*. A person mentioned as the one whom a certain Laura had stopped seeing.

Feodosii. See Vasiliev, Feodosii.

Feoktist. *War and Peace*. The club chef who arranged Count Rostov's reception for General Bagration.

Ferapontov. *War and Peace*. The keeper of an inn in Smolensk where Alpatich stayed.

Ferdinand, Archduke Karl Joseph (1781-1850). *War and Peace* (1, 2, 1). The Commanding General of the Austrian Army during the War of 1805.

Ferry, Henrico (1856-1929). *Resurrection* (2, 30). The Italian criminologist whom Nekhliudov studied in trying to understand why the persecuted in criminal courts were the same kind of people as the judges who judged them.

Féval, Paul Henri Corentin (1817-1887). *A Gentry Nest* (40). The French novelist and playwright whom Varvara adored.

Fichte, Johann Gottlieb (1762-1814). *War and Peace* (E, 1, 1). The German philosopher and idealist mentioned by Tolstoi in his interpretation of history.

Field, John, (1782-1837). *War and Peace* (2, 4, 10). The famous pianist and composer who gave concerts in St. Petersburg.

Figner, Aleksandr Samoilovich (1787-1813). *War and Peace* (4, 2, 15). A famous partisan fighter in 1812.

Filatevna. *Evgenii Onegin*. Tat'iana's nurse in the 1837 edition. In earlier editions, she was called Fadeevna and Filipevna.

Filipovich. "Hamlet of the Shchigrovskii District," in *A Hunter's Sketches*. A former tutor of the Russian Hamlet.

Filipp. *Anna Karenina*. A coachman at the Vronskii summer estate. Also a gardener at Levin's estate, Pokrovsk. "First Love." The butler in the Petrovich household who was fond of poetry. *Fathers and Sons*. The bailiff of the village near the Bazarov homestead. "Raspberry Spring," in *A Hunter's Sketches*. Vlas's son who was a coachman in Moscow. *Resurrection*. The Korchagin's strong and silent footman. *War and Peace*. A footman at the Bolkonskii estate.

Filipp Stepanich. *Rudin*. The landowner who was a Mason and who was trying to become a banker.

Filofei. "Rattling Wheels," in *A Hunter's Sketches*. The guide the narrator hired to drive him to Tula. His fear of the noisy gang who chased them also caused the narrator considerable consternation.

Fimushka. *Virgin Soil*. The diminutive for Evfemia Subocheva.

Finashka. *Resurrection*. A boy in the prison with Katiusha Maslova.

Finikov. *Smoke*. A gentleman at Irina Ratmirova's party who was known for his wealth and good looks.

Finmush. *Evgenii Onegin*. An old friend of Pelageia Nikolaevna.

Finogen. *Anna Karenina*. A worker on a peasant farm near Levin's estate.

Fishov, Baron. *War and Peace*. The aristocrat who wanted to talk with Prince Andrei Bolksonskii about the first meeting of the Council of State, but Pierre Bezukov interrupted them and asked Andrei to dance with Natasha Rostova at her first ball.

Fitiuev. *Virgin Soil*. An energetic peasant who would not work, thus causing Nezhdanov concern.

Flerov. *Anna Karenina*. A name not admitted to the first election for the Marshal of the Nobility because he was under trial.

Fleury, Désiré. "Death," in *A Hunter's Sketches*. The narrator's French tutor.

Flianov. *Evgenii Onegin*. The retired neighbor of the Larins who was an old rogue, glutton and buffoon.

Flora. *Evgenii Onegin* (1, 32). The goddess of flowers, youth and pleasures. Pushkin felt that Flora's cheeks were charming but preferred Terpsichore's feet. "The End of Chertopk-

hanov," in *A Hunter's Sketches*. The goddess whose statue was
put on the grave of Nedopiuskin instead of a statue of an
angel.

Fog. See Mikhailo Savel'ich.

Foka. *War and Peace*. A cook at the Bolkonskii estate.

Fokanych, Uncle. *Anna Karenina*. The peasant Fedor's name for the
peasant Platon.

Foma (Thomas in Russian). "Chertopkhanov and Nedopiuskin"
A Hunter's Sketches. Pantelei's servant. *Fathers and Sons*. A
laborer at the Kirsanov estate. *Virgin Soil*. See Subochev, Foma.

Foma Kuzmich. "Biriuk, The Morose One," in *A Hunter's Sketches*.
The forester who met the narrator in the woods and escorted
him to his hut.

Fomich. *Anna Karenina*. A laborer at Levin's country estate.

Fomin. *Anna Karenina*. A man in a court case in Oblonskii's department.

Fomushka. *Virgin Soil*. A diminutive of Foma. See Subochev, Foma.

Fontenelle, Bernard le Bovier de (1657-1757). *Evgenii Onegin* (8, 35).
The French writer whom Onegin read while trying to distract himself from thinking about Tat'iana.

Fonvizin, Denis Ivanovich (1745-1792). *Evgenii Onegin* (1, 18).
Pushkin referred to the writer as a friend of liberty.

Fortuna. *Evgenii Onegin* (1, 45). The goddess of fate from whom
Pushkin and Onegin expected misfortune.

Fouche, General Joseph (1759-1820). *War and Peace* (3, 2, 27). A
commander of artillery in the French Third Corps who
was the head of French political intelligence and spying.

Fourier, Charles (1772-1837). *Smoke* (14). The founder of a com-
munistic social system who was recalled by Potugin in
conversation. *Virgin Soil* (17). Kisliakov referred to the French
socialist-utopian writer in the letters which Nezhdanov
read.

Fox, Monsieur. *Smoke*. The medium whose experiments with a live
crab failed at Irina's party.

Franklin, Benjamin (1706-1790). *Anna Karenina* (5, 9). In a conversation with Anna and Vronskii, Golenishchev mentioned that
artists would do better to quit depicting Christ and turn
to history for subjects such as Franklin.

Franz. *War and Peace*. Bilibin's servant in Vienna.

Franz, Emperor Joseph Karl (1768-1835). *War and Peace* (1, 2, 3).
The German Emperor who became the ruler of Austria in
1806.

Frederick II, the Great (1712-1786). *Anna Karenina* (3, 28). The Prussian ruler who was mentioned in a conversation between Levin and Sviazhskii at the latter's residence. "Chertopkhanov and Nedopiuskin," in *A Hunter's Sketches*. Pantelei knew that the Prussian ruler was a distinguished person. *War and Peace* (1, 1, 27). The ruler noted for his diplomacy and military ability.

Frederick Wilhelm III (1770-1840). *War and Peace* (1, 1, 1). The Prussian ruler mentioned in conversation at Anna Pavlovna's.

Freischütz, Der. Evgenii Onegin (3, 31). An opera by Karl Maria von Weber (1786-1826), based on a legendary German marksman in league with the Devil.

Freitag. "First Love" (13). The man who vouched for the gentleness of a saddle horse, but Belovzorov was afraid the animal was too wild for Zinaida Zasekina.

Frémy, Edmond (1814-1894). *Fathers and Sons* (17). The French chemist whose book *Notions générales de Chimie* was recommended to Madame Odintsova by Bazarov when she wanted him to stay and give her lessons in chemistry.

Friant, Louis (1758-1829). *War and Peace* (3, 2, 27). A French general who commanded a division at Borodino.

Fridolin. *A Gentry Nest* (22). The hero of a ballad by Schiller. Lemm wrote a musical score based on the poem.

Friez. *War and Peace*. One of the doctors who treated Natasha after her scandalous behavior with Anatol' Kuragin.

Fritz. *War and Peace*. A name a soldier mentioned near the River Enns during the Russian retreat in 1805.

Frola, St. *War and Peace* (4, 1, 12). The saint mentioned by Platon Karataev in prayer.

Frolova-Bagreeva, Elizveta Milhailovna (b. 1799). *War and Peace* (2, 3, 28). See Speranskaia.

Funke, Baron. *War and Peace*. The man whom Prince Vasilii Kuragin called a poor choice for the position of first secretary in Vienna.

Funtikov, Anton Parfenich. "Freeholder Ovsianikov," in *A Hunter's Sketches*. The man who invited Ovsianikov to Sunday dinner.

Furstin, Frau. *Smoke*. The proprietress of one of the best hotels in Baden.

G____, Brother. *War and Peace*. One of Pierre Bezukhov's brothers in the Masons when Pierre was studying their doctrine.

G____, Prince. *Virgin Soil.* An imperial adjutant whose son Nezhdanov was illegitimate.

G____, Aleksandr Mikhailovich. "Hamlet of the Shchigrovskii District," in *A Hunter's Sketches.* The wealthy landowner who did not like women and gave only bachelor parties. The narrator did not like to attend such parties but was sometimes forced to.

G____v, Semen Vasil'evich. "Princess Mary," in *A Hero of Our Time.* Vera G____va's second husband, whom she respected but deceived.

G____va, Vera. "Princess Mary," in *A Hero of Our Time.* The woman who loved Pechorin but left him rather than renew an old affair.

Gagarin, Prince. *Rudin.* Lasunskaia met Muffel at Gagarin's.

Gagin. *Anna Karenina.* A well-dispositioned army officer from St. Petersburg.

Galignani, A. G. *Fathers and Sons* (4). The founder of a liberal newspaper published after 1804 in Paris in English. Pavel Kirsanov had a copy of the paper when Bazarov visited the Kirsanov estate.

Gallemeyer, Baron. *Virgin Soil.* A titled person who Kallomeitsev's grandfather liked to hint was part of his family.

Galtsin. *Anna Karenina.* One of Vronskii's rival racers in the horse race in which Vronskii fell from his horse, thus causing Anna to cry.

Gamba, Jacques François (1763-1833). "Bela," in *A Hero of Our Time.* The allusion about the Mountain of the Cross referred to a mistake in translation made by Gamba, the French consul in Tiflis, who in his book *Voyage dans la Russie méridionale et particulièrement dans les provinces situées au-dela du Caucase, fait depuis 1820 jusqu'au 1824* (2 vols., 1826), translated "Krestovaia" as "of Christopher" instead of "of the cross."

Garasia. *Virgin Soil.* A student in the country school near the Sipiagin estate.

Garcia, Manuel (1775-1832). *Spring Freshets.* A famous opera singer of Spanish descent. Pantaleone considered him a wonderful singer.

Garibaldi, Giuseppe (1807-1882). *Smoke* (4). The Italian patriot mentioned by Madame Sukhanchikova in a conversation with Voroshilov.

Garpenchenko. "Ovsianikov, the Freeholder," in *A Hunter's Sketches*. Fedos'ia Mikhailovna's master.

Garshin, Vsevolod Mikhailovich (1855-1888). *Resurrection* (1, 45). The Russian author who was to be discussed at the literary matinee of Madame Fanarin which Nikhliudov refused to attend.

Gaston. *Spring Freshets*. Polozova's French tutor, whom the woman loved in her youth.

Gauss, Karl Friedrich (1777-1855). *Virgin Soil* (2). The astronomer Paklin cited in conversation with Ostrodumov.

Gautier, Vladimir Ivanovich (1813-1887). *Anna Karenina* (6, 25). The book merchant in Moscow whom Anna stated as her source for books during her stay in the country.

Gavrila. "Bezhin Meadow," in *A Hunter's Sketches*. The village carpenter. *Virgin Soil*. A factory workman. *War and Peace*. A servant of Nikolai Rostov when he was stationed near Olmutz.

Gavrila Antonich. "The Office," in *A Hunter's Sketches*. The merchant who completed a bargain with the fat clerk, Nikolai Khvostov.

Gavrilo Ivanich. *War and Peace*. The man who investigated a proclamation that circulated in Moscow before the Russians left the city.

Gedenovskii, Sergei Petrovich. *A Gentry Nest*. A town gossip who posed as a model of propriety and respectability.

Gemma. See Roselli, Gemma.

Genlis, Madame de. *War and Peace* (1, 1, 11). A nickname for Countess Vera by her brother Count Nikolai Rostov. The real Madame Stephanie Felisita de Genlis (1746-1830) was a French novelist whose moralistic books were popular in her lifetime.

George III (1738-1820). *War and Peace* (1, 1, 5). The English King from 1760 to 1811 who was referred to at Anna Pavlovna's reception as a monarch who had offended dignity by sending an ambassador to Napoleon's court.

George, Henry (1839-1897). *Resurrection* (1, 4). The American economist whose single-tax theory was accepted by Nekhliudov and applied to his estates.

Georges, Mlle. (Margarita Josephine Veimar) (1786-1867). *War and Peace* (1, 1, 3). A French dramatic actress who was reported as the mistress of both Napoleon and the Duke of Enghien. She played in St. Petersburg and Moscow from 1808 to 1812.

Gerakov, Gavriel Vasil'evich (1775-1838). *War and Peace* (3, 2, 22). The author of many unsuccessful works written in an ultrapatriotic style. He was often satirized. At Borodino, Kutuzov asked to hear a poem by Marin which was based on a work of Gerakov. See S. N. Marin.

Gérard. *War and Peace*. The name Dolokhov used as a guise when he went reconnoitering among the French during their retreat from Moscow.

Gérard, Étienne Maurice (1773-1852). *War and Peace* (3, 1, 2). The French marshal who commanded a brigade at Borodino. Tolstoi reported his jocular remarks on Napoleon's invasion of Russia.

Gérard, François Pascalle Simon (1770-1837). *War and Peace* (3, 2, 26). The painter of the picture of Napoleon's son which was brought to the Emperor on the eve of the Battle of Borodino.

Gerasim. *The Captain's Daughter*. A priest. "The Death of Ivan Il'ich." The butler who nursed Ivan and gave him great comfort. "Raspberry Spring," in *A Hunter's Sketches*, The deaf church warden. *War and Peace*. A servant in the Bazdeev household in Moscow.

Gerasimova, Nastas'ia. *The Captain's Daughter*. Petr Grinev's great-aunt who went blind the year Petr was born.

Gervais, Andrei Andreevich (1773-1832). *War and Peace* (2, 3, 18). A relative of Speranskii's who served in the ministry of foreign affairs.

Gervinus, Georg Gottfried (1805-1871). *War and Peace* (E, 2, 1). A German historian and Shakespearean commentator. His *Geschichte der deutschen Dichtung* (5th edition, 1871-1874) was the first comprehensive and scholarly history of German literature. Tolstoi mentioned Gervinus in a discussion of the forces which play a role in history.

Giaour. *Evgenii Onegin* (7, 22). A non-Moslem. Byron wrote a poem by that name in 1813.

Gibbon, Edward (1737-1794). *Evgenii Onegin* (8, 35). The English historian, famous for his *Decline and Fall of the Roman Empire* (1776-1788). Onegin read Gibbon while trying not to think of Tat'iana. *War and Peace* (E, 2, 1). Tolstoi referred to Gibbon in a discussion on the difficulties of historical interpretation.

Gideon. *War and Peace* (3, 1, 18). The Biblical Israelite judge mentioned in a prayer by Natasha Rostova.

Girchik. *War and Peace* (2, 4, 4). A servant of Uncle Mikhail Nikanorych.

Girofalo, Baron Rafaelle (b. 1852). *Resurrection* (2, 30). The Italian criminologist who was a representative of the anthropological school. Nekhliudov read his book on crime to find out why the persecuted are the same sort of people as those who judge them.

Gladstone, William Edward (1809-1898). *Resurrection* (3, 24). A discussion about the English statesman arose during a dinner when Nekhliudov was a guest of the Governor of Siberia.

Glinka, Mikhail Ivanovich (1803-1857). *Smoke* (14). The Russian composer of the opera *A Life for the Tsar*. Potugin alluded to him in conversation. *Spring Freshets* (5). Sanin declaimed Pushkin's poem "I Remember a Wondrous Moment" to the Rossini family. Glinka set the poem to music.

Glinka, Sergei Nikolaevich (1776-1847). *War and Peace* (3, 1, 22). The editor of the *Russian Herald* in Moscow before the fall of the city.

Globov, Ivan Andreevich. "Dubrovskii." Globova's deceased husband.

Globov, Vanusha. "Dubrovskii." Globova's son.

Globova, Anna Savishna. "Dubrovskii." The landowner whose steward appropriated money which she had sent to her son by saying that Dubrovskii had robbed him. The steward was caught in his lie.

Gneist, Rudolph Henry (1816-1895). *Smoke* (3). The German statesman mentioned by Voroshilov in a conversation with Litvinov.

Godfrey Bulonskii (1060-1100). *War and Peace* (E, 2, 4). The ruler of Lower Lotharingia who was the leader of the First Crusade.

Goethe, Johann Wolfgang (1749-1838). *Anna Karenina*. The German writer whose works were mentioned. See Gretchen and Werther. *Evgenii Onegin* (2, 9). Lenskii was inspired by Goethe. *Fathers and Sons* (6). Pavel denounced Goethe in a conversation with Bazarov. *Rudin* (6). Rudin read aloud Goethe's *Faust* to Natalia. *Spring Freshets* (1). Sanin visited Goethe's house in Frankfort. "Tat'iana Borisovna and Her Nephew," in *A Hunter's Sketches*. A guest of Tat'iana's mentioned the German writer. *Virgin Soil* (35). Sipiagin quoted Goethe, not knowing that he was stating a line from *Goetz von Berlichingen* (1771).

Gogol', Nikolai Vasil'evich (1809-1852). *Anna Karenina* (5, 2). The Russian writer whose works were mentioned as follows: "The Writings of a Madman" (4, 14) and "The Marriage" (5, 2). *Fathers and Sons* (25). Arkadii read Gogol's letters while staying at Madame Odintsova's. *Virgin Soil* (19). Paklin liked to quote Gogol' in order to make an impression on his relatives, the Subochevs.

Golenishchev. *Anna Karenina.* A comrade of Vronskii in the Corps of Pages. They met accidentally abroad.

Golenishchev-Kutuzov, Pavel Ivanovich (1767-1829). *War and Peace* (2, 1, 3). The composer of solemn odes who became rector of Moscow University in 1810. He composed the song which was sung at Rostov's banquet for General Bagration.

Goliath. *War and Peace* (3, 1, 18). The Philistine giant slain by David. Natasha mentioned the giant in her prayer when the French were approaching Moscow.

Golitsyn, Aleksandr Mihailovich (1718-1783). *The Captain's Daughter.* The Russian officer who drove Pugachev from the Tatishchev Fortress and saved the city of Orenburg.

Golitsyn, Aleksandr Nikolaevich (1773-1844). *War and Peace* (1, 1, 5). The Russian statesman who was procurator of the senate and from 1816 to 1824 was the Minister of Education.

Golopletskii, Eremei. *Virgin Soil.* A villager whom Markelov praised as a reliable worker, but he betrayed Markelov.

Golovin, Il'ia Efimorvich. "The Death of Ivan Il'ich." Ivan's father, who was a member of various superfluous organizations.

Golovin, Ivan Il'ich. "The Death of Ivan Il'ich." The member of the Court of Justice who developed cancer and slowly died.

Golovina, Liza. "The Death of Ivan Il'ich." Ivan's daughter.

Golovina, Praskov'ia Fedorovna. "The Death of Ivan Il'ich." Ivan's wife, who acted as if Ivan were not dying, thus causing her husband great anxiety. Her maiden name was Mikhel.

Golukhovskii, Count. *War and Peace.* The Polish aristocrat who bargained for Rostov's horses when Rostov left the service in 1807 to help his parents run their estates.

Golushkin, Kapiton Andreich. *Virgin Soil.* A merchant who professed to be for the socialist cause but who really was more talk than action.

Gorchakova, Princess. *War and Peace.* Two princesses of the

Gorchakov family were mentioned for having found suitors at one of Vogel's balls.

Gornostaev, Pantelei. "Petr Petrovich Karataev," in *A Hunter's Sketches*. A friend of Karataev.

Gossner, Johann (1773-1858). *War and Peace* (E, 1, 13). The German mystic who traveled to St. Petersburg in 1820 on the invitation of the Biblical Society. In 1824, he was ordered out of Russia after the publication of his book *The Spirit of the Life and Teaching of Christ*.

Governor of Siberia. *Resurrection*. A general who believed that military officers should be cultured and spent his life trying to set an example. He became an alcoholic.

Grabets. *Resurrection*. A pretty political prisoner whom Novodvorov loved.

Grabovskii. *Anna Karenina*. The owner of a well-known stud horse.

Grandison. *Evgenii Onegin* (2, 20). The hero of the novel *The History of Sir Charles Grandison* (1753) by Samuel Richardson. Tat'iana prefered Grandison to Lovelace, another hero by Richardson.

Granovskii, Timofei Nikolaevich (1813-1855). *On the Eve* (4). The professor of history at Moscow University whom Turgenev knew. Bersenev stated that he would like to follow in the professor's footsteps.

Greene, Robert (1560-1592). *Smoke* (4). The English dramatist and contemporary of Shakespeare mentioned by Voroshilov when he managed to interrupt Madame Sukhanchikova.

Gregorii. *Virgin Soil*. A worker in Sipiagin's factory.

Grekov, Timofei Dmitrievich (b. 1780). *War and Peace* (4, 1, 6). The Russian major-general who was in the Turkish Wars of 1788 and 1793 and in the war with France, 1812-1815.

Gretchen. *Anna Karenina* (2, 18). The heroine of Goethe's *Faust*, whom Veslovskii mentioned to Oblonskii and Levin when he described a girl who appealed to him.

Grev, Baron. "The Death of Ivan Il'ich." The husband of Ivan's sister.

Griboedov, Aleksandr Sergeevich (1795-1829). *Evgenii Onegin*. An epigraph to Chapter Seven is from his play *Woe from Wit* (1824). *Rudin* (2). Dar'ia Mikhailovna Lasunskaia misquoted Griboedov's verses.

Grimm, Friedrich Melchior (1723-1807). *Evgenii Onegin* (1, 24). The writer who was supposed to have cleaned his nails in front of Rousseau, to the latter's disgust.

Grimm, Iakov (1785-1863). *Anna Karenina* (2, 6). The famous writer whose fable "The Man Without a Shadow" was mentioned by a woman while gossiping about Anna and Vronskii.

Grinev, Andrei Petrovich. *The Captain's Daughter.* Petr Grinev's father, who had served under Count Minikh before he retired to his Simbirsk estate.

Grinev, Petr Andreevich (Petrusha). *The Captain's Daughter.* The proud, young adventurous officer whose sense of honor caused him many problems; however, he maintained it throughout his many exciting escapades.

Grineva, Avdotia Vasil'evna. *The Captain's Daughter.* The mother of Petr Grinev.

Grisha. *Anna Karenina.* The youngest boy of Dolly and Stepan Oblonskii. Also Kitty and Konstantin Levin's son. "Dubrovskii." Vladimir Dubrovskii's valet. *Resurrection.* Nekhliudov remembered aspects of his Uncle Grisha's life in order to justify his own conduct toward Katiusha Maslova.

Grishin. *Resurrection.* The owner of a first-rate racing stable.

Grishka. *War and Peace.* A servant of the Rostovs in Moscow.

Gritskii. *Anna Karenina.* The name which the officers of Vronskii's regiment called their colonel.

Gromoboi, Prince. *Spring Freshets.* A deceased friend of Polozova. He once decorated her room with camellias, but she considered him a man of little stature.

Gromoboeva, Tat'iana Iur'evna. *Spring Freshets.* Gromoboi's wife.

Grote, George (1794-1871). *On the Eve* (25). The English historian who is noted for his *History of Greece* (8 vols., 1846-56). Bersenev read Grote after finishing Raumer.

Grushnitskii. "Princess Mary," in *A Hero of Our Time.* The pretentious young cadet who loved Princess Mary. Losing her affection to Pechorin, Grushnitskii sought revenge and joined in a ruse to humiliate his adversary. In a subsequent duel, Pechorin gave his opponent a choice between life and death. Grushnitskii chose the latter to avoid the shame he would otherwise have had to face in life. Pechorin shot him, and he fell into a canyon.

Gruzinskii, Prince. *War and Peace.* An aristocrat whose home was along the route Pierre Bezukhov took during the burning of Moscow.

Guardi, Francesco (1712-1793). *On the Eve* (33). The famed Italian painter who, according to Turgenev, could never capture the real Venice on canvas.

Gubarev. *Smoke.* An intellectual in Baden who was known for his leading of discussions.

Gudovich, Ivan Vasil'evich (1741-1820). *War and Peace* (2, 5, 11). The Governor-General of Moscow from 1809 to 1812. Prince Vasilii Kuragin agreed to pay half of Anatol' Kuragin's debts if he would go to Moscow and serve in a position he had arranged with Gudovich.

Guillot. *Evenii Onegin.* Onegin's French valet.

Guizot, François Pierre Guillaume (1787-1874). *Fathers and Sons* (12). The French bourgeois historian whom Matvei Koliazin once greatly appreciated.

Gulnare. *Evgenii Onegin* (4, 37). The heroine of Byron's poem *The Corsair* (1814). She released Conrad from a dungeon.

Gur'ev, Mikhail Vasil'evich. *War and Peace* (1, 3, 13). Tolstoi made a mistake when he wrote that Nikolai Rostov drove past Gur'ev's house in Moscow because the house did not belong to that family until 1850.

Gurkevich. *Resurrection.* A man imprisoned because he had worked for a constitutional government.

Gvozdin. *Evgenii Onegin.* A neighbor of the Larins whose serfs were kept in poor conditions.

Haine. *War and Peace.* The groom for the tsar's horse at Auster-litz and Tilsit.

Hamlet. "A Hamlet of the Shchigrovskii District," in *A Hunter's Sketches.* The Russian gentleman who claimed that he was the Russian version of Shakespeare's famous hero. *Virgin Soil* (2). Ostrodumov called Nezh-danov the Russian Hamlet.

Handel, Georg Friedrich (1685-1759). *A Gentry Nest* (5). The composer whom Lemm preferred after Bach.

Hannah. *Anna Karenina.* Anna's little girl protégée.

Happe. "The Death of Ivan Il'ich." The man who obtained the appointment which Ivan Il'ich Golovin wanted very much.

Hardenburg, Friedrich Leopold von. *Rudin* (6). See Novalis.

Hardenburg, Prince Karl August von (1750-1822). *War and Peace* (1, 1, 1). The aristocrat who served as Prussian Minister of Foreign Affairs from 1802 to 1806.

Harold, Childe. See Childe Harold.

Hartmann, Eduard von (1842-1906). "The Kreutzer Sonata" (11). A German philosopher cited by Pozhnyshev when he discussed the absence of meaning in life.

Haugwitz, Christian Avgust (1752-1831). *War and Peace* (1, 1, 1). The Prussian Minister of Foreign Affairs in 1802.

Haydn, Joseph (1732-1809). *Smoke* (14). The Austrian composer whom Potugin mentioned while talking with Litvinov.

Hegel, Georg Wilhelm Friedrich (1770-1831). *Anna Karenina* (8, 9). The German philosopher whom Levin read in his search for meaning in life. He concluded that Hegel's philosophy was constructed on a pattern of words remote from real life. "Death," in *A Hunter's Sketches*. The narrator mentioned Hegel while telling Sorokoumov about German philosophy. *Fathers and Sons* (5). Pavel considered Hegel the corruptor of minds in the generation before the nihilists. *Rudin* (2). Pigasov quoted Hegel on a question of truth. *Smoke* (5). Potugin claimed he could translate any page from Hegel's works without making use of a single non-Slavic word. *Resurrection* (2, 23). When Selenin studied the veracity of the Russian Orthodox Church, he read Hegel to clarify his mind on questions of religion and humanity.

Heine, Heinrich (1797-1856). *Anna Karenina* (1, 11). The German poet whose line "Himmlisch ist's, wenn ich bezwungen" was quoted by Oblonskii while having lunch with Levin. *Fathers and Sons* (25). Katia was reading Heine in the garden when Arkadii visited. *Virgin Soil* (16). Nezhdanov cited Heine when talking with Solomin.

Helena. "The Death of Ivan Il'ich." A friend of the Golovin family who went with them to see Sara Bernhardt.

"Hélène, La Belle." *Anna Karenina* (3, 13). The title of the operetta by Ludwig Galevi (1834-1908), which Karenin remembered when he was thinking of his unfaithful wife Anna. *War and Peace* (1, 3, 1). Elena Kuragina was referred to as La belle Hélène after the famous Greek beauty.

Heliogabalus (204-222). *Smoke* (15). The depraved Roman Emperor whose soullessly brutal expression of countenance was used to describe Finikov's face. See Finikov.

Helmholtz, Hermann Ludwig Ferdinand (1821-1894). *Smoke* (4). The German physicist and mathematician mentioned by Voroshilov when he interrupted Madame Sukhanchikova.

Heloise. *War and Peace* (1, 1, 23). A name for Julie Karagina by Prince Bolkonskii.

Helvetius, Claude (1715-1771). *A Gentry Nest* (8). The philosophical writer whom Lavretskii's father studied in his youth.

Hercules. "The Singers," in *A Hunter's Sketches*. The Wild Squire's figure made one think of the son of Jupiter who was the personification of physical strength. *War and Peace* (2, 1, 3). Hercules was mentioned in the poem composed for General Bagration at the dinner given for him by Count Il'ia Rostov.

Herder, Johann Gottfried von (1744-1803). *Evgenii Onegin* (8, 35). Onegin read the German philosopher while trying to distract himself from thinking about Tat'iana. *War and Peace* (2, 2, 12). Herder was mentioned by Prince Andrei Bolkonskii in a discussion with Pierre Bezukhov on the meaning of life.

Hermann. "The Queen of Spades." The son of a Russianized German, Hermann was an engineer who became captivated by a story of cards that always win. His calculations and intrigues led him to insanity.

Hertzen, Aleksandr Ivanovich (1812-1870). *Resurrection* (3, 18). The Russian thinker who was famous for his journal *The Bell*, which was written in London and widely read in Russia. He was mentioned in a conversation between Kryltzov and Nekhliudov.

Herz, Henri (1806-1888). *A Gentry Nest* (39). The composer of the étude which Varvara Lavretskaia played on the piano.

Hoffman, Ernst Theodor Amadeus (1776-1822). *Rudin* (6). Rudin read the German romantic writer and discussed his works with Natalia. *Spring Freshets* (11). Gemma and Sanin discovered romanticism in Hoffman's works, which were popular at the time.

Hoffman, Friedrich (1660-1742). *Fathers and Sons* (20). The German scholar and mystic whom Vasilii Bazarov cited as a "humoralist."

Hohenlohe, Friedrich Ludwig (1746-1818). *War and Peace* (1, 3, 11). A Prussian general at Austerlitz who was wounded in 1806 at the Battle of Jena.

Home. See Hume.

Homer (9th Cent. B.C.). *Evgenii Onegin* (1, 7). Onegin reproved the author of the *Iliad* and the *Odyssey*, preferring to read Adam Smith. *On the Eve* (3). When Shubin's father died, he left his son a statue of the Greek poet. *Smoke* (14). Potugin referred to Homer in conversation.

Horace (65-8 B.C.). *Evgenii Onegin*. The epigraph to Chapter Two is from Horace. (*Satires*, II, vi). "O Rus" means "Oh, countryside." Also (6, 7). Zaretskii lived in the country, as did Horace. *Fathers and Sons* (20). Vasilii Bazarov planted acacia trees, a species loved by Horace.

Horatio. *On the Eve* (21). Shubin called Bersenev "my friend, Horatio" after the often-quoted line from Shakespeare's *Hamlet*. *Smoke* (11). Potugin said, "There are many things on the earth, my friend Horatio."

Hover, Lord (1773-1846). *War and Peace* (1, 1, 1). An English diplomat at the court of Aleksandr I in 1804.

Howard, John (1726-1790). *Resurrection* (2, 14). The English philanthropist mentioned by Countess Ekaterina Ivanovna Charskaia when Nekhliudov was staying with her in St. Petersburg.

Hufeland, Christoph Wilhelm (1762-1836). *Fathers and Sons* (20). The German medical scholar noted for his book *The Art of Prolonging Human Life* (1797). His portrait hung in the Bazarov home.

Hugo, Victor Marie (1802-1885). "First Love" (11). Maidanov praised the noted French writer. *On the Eve* (34). The author of *Les Châtiments*, which Lupoiarov recalled while visiting Insarov in Vienna.

Hull, Miss. *Anna Karenina*. An English governess for the Oblonskii children.

Hume (Home), Daniel Dunglas (1833-1886). *Smoke* (15). The Scottish medium who was the rage in St. Petersburg during the 1860s, even performing in the Winter Palace for Tsar Aleksandr II. At Irina Ratmirova's party, he was the subject of conversation.

Hymen. *Evgenii Onegin* (4, 14). The god of matrimony in mythology. Evgenii Onegin mentioned Hymen when he spoke of his not being a marriageable type. Also (4, 50). Evgenii accused Hymen of being the source of yawns and boredom, and called himself an enemy of the god.

Iagushkin. "The Office," in *A Hunter's Sketches*. The landlord who wanted to see Vasilii Nikolaevich about some business of a shady nature.

Iakov. "Hamlet of the Shchigrovskii District," in *A Hunter's Sketches*. The steward who robbed the Russian Hamlet. *War and Peace*. A servant in the Kuragin manor house.

Iakovlev, Ivan Alekseevich (1767-1846). *War and Peace* (4, 2, 9). A rich Moscow baron who wished to take his family and servants out of Moscow after the French occupied the city. Napoleon approved the move when Iakovlev agreed to take a letter to Tsar Aleksandr I. Iakovlev fathered A. I. Hertzen. For a description of Iakovlev's exasperating experiences in leaving Moscow, see: Hertzen's *My Past and Thoughts*, Part I, Ch. I.

Ianko. "Taman,'" in *A Hero of Our Time*. The smuggler who lived as a Byronic hero with free will and no concern for the feelings of others.

Iashka the Turk. "The Singers," in *A Hunter's Sketches*. A contestant in the singing competition who had a beautiful voice.

Iashvin. *Anna Karenina*. A tall, handsome cavalry captain who was a friend of Vronskii in the military service.

Iav. "The End of Chertopkhanov," in *A Hunter's Sketches*. Pantelei thought that Iav was the man with whom his gypsy girl friend eloped.

Iazykov, Nikolai Mikhailovich (1803-1846). *Evgenii Onegin* (4, 31). A major Russian poet of the 1820s. *Smoke* (5). Turgenev referred to a remark by the critic Belinskii on Iazykov's poetry: "Wine only foams and sizzles in his verses, but doesn't intoxicate."

Iegudiil. "L'gov," in *A Hunter's Sketches*. The coachman left on shore to watch the dogs when the hunter went boating.

Ignashka. *War and Peace* (2, 5, 17). A servant of Anatol' Kuragin.

Ignat. *Anna Karenina*. Levin's coachman. *War and Peace* (3, 2, 22). A yard porter left at the Rostov mansion during the French occupation.

Ilagin. *War and Peace*. A neighbor of the Rostovs in the country. He
  sold three families of house serfs for one bitch dog.
Il'ia Ivanovich. *War and Peace*. See Baikov, Il'ia Ivanovich.
Il'ia Mitrofanich. *War and Peace*. A steward on one of Nikolai Rostov's
  estates.
Il'in. *War and Peace*. The sixteen-year-old officer in the Pavlograd
  squadron who was a protégé of Nikolai Rostov.
Il'in, F. I. "The Death of Ivan Il'ich." An acquaintance whom Ivan
  met on a train to St. Petersburg. The man told Ivan about a
  change in the ministry and the possibility of an opening for
  him.
Il'iusha. "Bezhin Meadow," in *A Hunter's Sketches*. A small boy in
  the meadow. "Lebedian'," in *A Hunter's Sketches*. A gypsy
  singer. *War and Peace*. See Sokolov, I. O.
Insarov, Dmitrii Nikanorovich. *On the Eve*. The Bulgarin who studied
  in Russia but longed to return to his homeland. After marrying Elena Stakova, he set off with his wife for Bulgaria, but
  he died in Venice.
Ioann Vasil'evich IV (Ivan the Terrible) (1530-1584). *A Gentry Nest*
  (17). Three members of the Pestovs were killed by Tsar Ivan.
  "Lebedian'," in *A Hunter's Sketches*. The horse dealer said that
  the horse he was showing was good enough for Tsar Ivan
  in a procession. *War and Peace* (E, 2, 4). Tolstoi mentioned the
  cruel tsar in a discussion of the forces that affect history.
Ipatka. *War and Peace*. A coachman for the Rostov family.
Irina. *Smoke*. Née Osinina, she married Ratmirov. See Osinina, Irina.
Irina Vasil'evna, Princess. *War and Peace*. A visitor of Maria Dmitri-
  evna Akhrosimova.
Irinochka. *Smoke*. A diminutive for Irina.
Irtenev, Nikolenka. *Resurrection*. The childhood friend of Nekhliudov
  with whom he pledged to live a good life and make others
  happy.
Isaac. *Anna Karenina* (5, 6). The Biblical figure mentioned in a prayer
  at Kitty and Levin's marriage.
Isabella. *Smoke*. The famous flower girl of the Jockey Club.
Istomina, Duniasha (1799-1848). *Evgenii Onegin* (1, 20). A popular
  Russian pantomimic ballerina.
Iusupova, Princess. *War and Peace*. A name dropped by Berg at his
  dinner party, referring to a member of a very wealthy Rus-
  sian family.
Iushka. "Two Landowners," in *A Hunter's Sketches*. An old servant of
  Mardarii Apollonich.
Ivan. *Anna Karenina*. A coachman at Levin's estate. "The Office," in

A Hunter's Sketches. Petr's brother, who was a clerk. Also a second clerk. *Father's and Sons.* The person Princess K____asked about, but no one paid her any attention. Bazarov concluded that the old Princess was kept at the house only because she was from a princely family. *Virgin Soil.* A lackey at the Sipiagin country estate. *War and Peace.* A servant of Uncle Mikhail Nikanorych.

Ivan Danilovich. "Dubrovskii." Shabashkin was on his way to see Ivan Danilovich when Troekurov called him to plot against Dubrovskii.

Ivan Ignatevich. "Princess Mary," in *A Hero of Our Time.* A second for Grushnitskii in his duel with Pechorin.

Ivan Ignatich. *The Captain's Daughter.* The one-eyed friend of Mironov.

Ivan Il'ich. "The Queen of Spades." The man who told Tomskii the story about Chlitskii and his relationship to the three cards. "The Death of Ivan Il'ich." See Golovin, Ivan Il'ich.

Ivan Ivanovich. *Anna Karenina.* A person mentioned at a ball because he spoke French badly. *Resurrection.* Sofia Karchagina's doctor, with whom it was rumored the woman was very intimate.

Ivan Petrovich. *Anna Karenina.* An acquaintance Anna met at the train station. *Evgenii Onegin.* Tat'iana's relative who was very simple.

Ivan Semenovich. "The Death of Ivan Il'ich." The man who succeeded Petr Ivanovich.

Ivan Sidorich. *War and Peace.* The name of a merchant who was fearful for his store during the Russian evacuation of Moscow.

Ivan the Terrible. See Ioann Vasil'evich IV.

Ivan Zakharych. "The Kreutzer Sonata." The doctor who saved Maria Ivanovna's daughter.

Ivanenko. *Resurrection.* A name mentioned by Charskaia to illustrate a typical fool in the governmental senate.

Ivanov, Aleksandr Andreevich (1806-1858). *Anna Karenina* (5, 9). The artist Golenishchev criticized in a conversation with Anna and Vronskii for his artistic presentation of Christ.

Ivanov, Evgraf (Featherbrain). *The Singers,* in "A Hunter's Sketches." The old house serf who was a ninny.

Ivanov, Ivan Semenich. *Resurrection.* The retired colonel in Maslova's trial.

Ivanushka. *War and Peace.* One of Mar'ia Bolkonskaia's religious "God folk at Bald Hills.

Ivanushka from Red Knolls. "Bezhin Meadow," in *A Hunter's Sketches.* The man who spent the night in the paper mill.

Ivanushka Kosoi. "Bezhin Meadow," in *A Hunter's Sketches*. The man who spent the night in a rolling room of a paper factory.

Ivashenko. *Resurrection*. The lawyer who talked too much and bored the court.

Izedinov. *Smoke*. A colonel of Uhlans who was well known for his obesity.

Jacquot. *War and Peace*. The woman Pierre Bezukhov mentioned in conversation during the confusion preceding the death of Count Bezukhov.

Jean. "The Death of Ivan Il'ich." The name Praskov'ia Fedorovna Golovin called her husband when she tried to be endearing.

Jeanne d'Arc (1412-1431). "Living Holy Relics," in *A Hunter's Sketches*. Lukeria told Petr Petrovich the legend of Jeanne d'Arc. *Resurrection* (2, 19). The old German baron, who had the power to relieve the hardships of prisoners in St. Petersburg prisons, was communicating with the spirit of Jeanne d'Arc in a séance when Nekhliudov went to him for help. *Rudin* (7). Rudin expressed the opinion that only Jeanne d'Arc could have saved France. *War and Peace* (3, 2, 17). Julie Drubetskaia mentioned the French national heroine.

John, St. *Anna Karenina* (5, 11). The apostle whom Mikhailov painted in a picture with Christ and Pilate. The remarks which Anna and Vronskii made about the picture greatly agitated the artist. *Resurrection* (1, 1). The novel begins with four Biblical quotations, one of which is from St. John (8, 7). *War and Peace* (3, 1, 19). A mason revealed to Pierre a prophecy concerning Napoleon which was drawn from the Revelation of St. John.

John the Baptist ("Forerunner"). *Fathers and Sons* (20). Arina Bazarova ate no watermelon because a sliced melon reminded her of the beheaded John the Baptist. *Virgin Soil* (18). The religious figure to whom Nezhdanov compared Markelov.

John, Sir. *Anna Karenina*. A missionary in India mentioned at Princess Betsy Tverskoi's.

Johnson, Quentin. *Virgin Soil*. A journalist whose writings Kisliakov used as a guide during his revolutionary work with the factory workers.

Jones. *Anna Karenina*. A name thought up by Tolstoi to designate one of the writers Levin read when he studied on how to improve his lands and the lot of his peasants (3, 29).

Joseph. *Anna Karenina* (5, 6). Kitty mentioned the Biblical figure in a prayer. *War and Peace*. A valet for Anatolii Kuragin in Moscow.

Josephine, Maria Rose (1763-1814). *War and Peace* (3, 1, 2). The wife of the Viscomte Alexander Bogarne, who was executed during the French revolution. She became the wife of Napoleon and was crowned Empress of France in 1804. In 1809, the Emperor divorced her.

Joshua, son of Nun. War and Peace (E, 2, 12). The Biblical figure mentioned by Tolstoi in his interpretation of history.

Jouvin. *A Gentry Nest* (39). The head of a firm of glove makers at Grenoble.

Jovert, Monsieur. *War and Peace*. The man who became the "directeur de conscience" of Elena Kuragina Bezukhova.

Jules, Monsieur. *A Gentry Nest*. A Parisian journalist of scandalous reputation whom Varvara Lavretskaia courted in order to have favorable press reports.

Julie. *Evgenii Onegin* (3, 10). The name of a favorite heroine of Tat'-iana in the novel *Julie ou La Nouvelle Heloise* (1761), by J. J. Rousseau (1712-1778).

Julner. *War and Peace*. A French colonel who commanded a chain of advanced posts in the Napoleonic campaigns in 1812. He met Balashov when he went to Napoleon with a letter from Aleksandr I.

Junot, Andoche, Duc d'Abrantes (1771-1813). *War and Peace* (4, 3, 12). The French marshal whose wife, the Duchesse d'Abrantes, had an affair with Metternich, the famous Austrian statesman. Napoleon ended the danger of a duel by sending Junot to Spain in 1810. During the French retreat from Moscow, Junot headed a baggage train. Because of his unsuccessful military actions, Napoleon put him out of the army.

Justine. *A Gentry Nest*. Varvara Lavretskaia's Parisian maid.

Juvenal (Decimus Junius Juvenalis) (60?-140). *Evgenii Onegin* (1, 6). The Roman lawyer and satirist of Roman vices whom Onegin studied just enough to give a few interpretations.

K___, Mlle. "Tat'iana Borisovna and Her Nephew," in *A Hunter's Sketches*. The sister of Aleksei Nikolaevich K___ who forced herself on Tat'iana Borisovna Bogdanova and caused the latter to distrust her neighbors.

K___, Aleksei Nikolaevich. "Tat'iana Borisovna and her Nephew," in *A Hunter's Sketches*.   A friend of Tat'iana Borisnovna Bogdanova.

K___, Princess Avdotia Stepanovna. *Fathers and Sons*. The maternal aunt of Anna Odintsova who resided at the latter's country estate, Nikol'skoe.

Kabylina, Barbe de. *Virgin Soil*. The person who had once owned the Subachevs' old album, bound in red morocco.

Kaidanov, I. K. (1780-1843). "First Love" (1). A historian whose works were very successful. His *A Manual for an Understanding of General Political History* (1821) had thirteen editions. Vladimir B___ read Kaidanov's history books.

Kaisarov, Andrei Sereevich (1782-1813). *War and Peace* (3, 2, 22). The writer and professor who was the brother of Kutuzov's adjutant. He was killed in action during the War of 1812.

Kaisarov, Paisii Sergeevich (1783-1844). *War and Peace* (3, 2, 22). The Russian general who served as Kutuzov's adjutant and in 1813 commanded a guerrilla detachment.

Kalinych. "Khor' and Kalinych," in *A Hunter's Sketches*. An idealistic peasant who loved nature and animals. He was quite a contrast to his friend, the materialist Khor'.

Kalitin. *A Gentry Nest*. The deceased husband and father of the Kalitin family.

Kalitina, Elena Mikhailovna (Lenochka). *A Gentry Nest*. The younger daughter of Mar'ia who grew up and inherited the estate at the end of the novel.

Kalitina, Elizabeta Mikhailovna (Liza) (Lizochka). *A Gentry Nest*. The elder daughter of Mar'ia who entered a nunnery to avoid the scandal of loving a married man, Lavretskii.

Kalitina, Mar'ia Dmitrievna (nee Pestova). *A Gentry Nest*. A fifty-year-old superficial matron who was the mother of Liza and Lonochka.

Kalliopich. *Virgin Soil*. The Subochevs' aged servant.

Kalliopin. "The Country Doctor," in *A Hunter's Sketches*. The councilman who played cards with the doctor at the judge's house.

Kallomeitsev, Semen Petrovich. *Virgin Soil*. A snobbish landowner who was courteous but malicious. He was a neighbor and frequent visitor at the Sipiagin estate.

Kaluzhskii, Prince Mishka. *Anna Karenina*. An admirer of Lisa Merkalov.

Kamenskaia, Madame. *Resurrection*. Charskii's sick friend, whose son was killed in a duel.

Kamenskii, Mikhail Fedorovich (1738-1809). "Rattling Wheels," in

A Hunter's Sketches. A poem by Zhukovskii was based on Field
Marshal Kamenskii. *War and Peace* (1, 2, 1). During a war with
Turkey, soldiers created a song based on Father Kamenskii,
as the field marshal was called. He also served in the War of
1805.

Kamenskii, Count Nikolai Mikhailovich (1776-1811). *War and Peace*
(3, 1, 8). An infantry general at Austerlitz who was later
Supreme Commander of the Moldavian Army against the
Turks in 1810.

Kamerovskii. *Anna Karenina*. An acquaintance of Vronskii in the military service.

Kant, Immanuel (1724-1804). *Anna Karenina* (8, 9). The German
philosopher whom Levin read in his search for meaning in
life. Levin decided that Kant's philosophy was based only on
reason and that there was more to life than a rational pattern
of words. *Evgenii Onegin* (2, 6). Lenskii was a follower of Kant.
Rudin (2). Pigasov says that Hegel and Kant do not agree on
the term "truth." *Virgin Soil* (38). Paklin stated that Russians
like Kant because of their interest in science.

Kantagriukhin. "Hamlet of the Shchigrovskii District," in *A
Hunter's Sketches*. The man who snored loudly in the room
next to the bedroom occupied by the narrator and the Russian Hamlet.

Kapiton Timofeich. "Death," in *A Hunter's Sketches*. A rural doctor
with a six-bed hospital.

Kapitonich. *Anna Karenina*. A hall porter at the Karenin home.

Karageorgevich. *Virgin Soil* (14). A princely Serbian dynasty founded
by Georgii Petrovich Chernyi (1752-1817). The family
fought with the Obrenovich family for governmental power.

Karagina, Julie. *War and Peace*. A wealthy heiress who was a friend
of Mar'ia Bolkonskaia and who married Boris Drubetskoi.

Karagina, Varia L'vovna. *War and Peace*. A visitor of the Rostovs on
the name day of the two Natal'ias (mother and daughter).

Karamzin, Nikolai Mikhailovich (1766-1826). *War and Peace* (2, 5, 5).
The author of the sentimental *Poor Liza*, which Boris Drubetskoi read to Julie Karagina when he was courting her.

Karasikov, Anton. "Ovsianikov, the Freeholder," in *A Hunter's
Sketches*. Aleksandr Korol'ev's neighbor.

Karataev, Petr Petrovich. "Petr Petrovich Karataev," in *A Hunter's
Sketches*. The landowner who related the narrator a sad tale
of love and financial ruin.

Karataev, Platon (Little Falcon). *War and Peace*. The peasant philosopher with whom Pierre was imprisoned in Moscow and who was later shot along the road during the French retreat. His philosophy was based on a humble acceptance of life and a great love for humanity.

Karchagin. *Resurrection*. A retired general who had peasants flogged or hanged simply because he was wealthy and could avoid the laws. *Rudin*. The society lion who once courted Natal'ia Lasunskaia.

Kardon-Kitaeva. "Death," in *A Hunter's Sketches*. The aunt from whom Ardalion Mikhailich inherited an estate.

Karelius. *Virgin Soil*. A journalist whose writings Kisliakov used as a guide while spreading propaganda among workers.

Karenin, Aleksei Aleksandrovich. *Anna Karenina*. The aloof and condescending husband of Anna. He refused to grant her a divorce because of what the public might say about him. Anna noticed his large ears after she fell in love with Vronskii.

Karenin, Serezha. *Anna Karenina*. The son Anna deserted for Vronskii.

Karenina, Anna Arkad'evna. *Anna Karenina*. The beautiful matron who found love with a handsome page of the Emperor, Vronskii. Jealousy, fear and misunderstanding led her to suicide under a train.

Karenina, Anna (Annie). *Anna Karenina*. Anna's daughter by Vronskii.

Karibanov, Prince. *Anna Karenina*. The man whom Karenin mentioned as someone whose wife was unfaithful.

Karl Ivanich. *War and Peace*. The doctor for Prince Andrei Bolkonskii's son at Bald Hills. His advice was accepted by Princess Mar'ia Bolkonskaia but scorned by Prince Andrei.

Karl Ludwig, Archduke (1771-1841). *War and Peace* (1, 2, 10). The brother of Franz II who was a war minister in 1805 and Supreme Commander of the Austrian army in Italy during a Napoleonic war.

Karmanov. *Resurrection*. The convict who persuaded a lad to exchange names with him so that he, Karmanov, would be exiled instead of going to the mines.

Karolinka. *The Captain's Daughter*. The subject of pranks by Andrei Petrovich Grinev and Andrei Karlovich R____.

Karp. "Chertopkhanov and Nedopiuskin," in *A Hunter's Sketches*. Pantelei's servant. *War and Peace*. A peasant mentioned as a plunderer in Moscow during the French occupation. Also a peasant on Prince Andrei Bolkonskii's estate.

Karpushka. *War and Peace*. See Chigirin.

Karr, Alphonse (1808-1890). *Anna Karenina* (8, 16). The French writer noted for his epigrams who was mentioned by Prince Shcherbatskii in a discussion about a war with Turkey.

Kartasov. *Anna Karenina*. The family Anna knew that snubbed her at the opera when she dared to appear while living openly with Vronskii.

Kartinkin, Semen Petrov. *Resurrection*. The servant in the Hotel Mavretania who masterminded the plot to kill and rob Smelkov.

Kasatkin. "Death," in *A Hunter's Sketches*. The man who wrote about Sorokoumov's death to the author.

Kasatkina, "Death," in *A Hunter's Sketches*. The landowner's daughter who was kind to Sorokoumov when he was sick.

Kasatkina, Kleopatra Aleksandrovna. "Death," in *A Hunter's Sketches*. The wife of the landowner Kasatkin.

Kassian (Kasianushka) (The Flea). "Kassian of Fair Strath," in *A Hunter's Sketches*. An old dwarf who had the reputation of being a holy fool.

Katavasov. *Anna Karenina*. The professor who had been a schoolmate of Levin.

Katenin, Pavel Aleksandrovich (1792-1853). *Evgenii Onegin* (1, 18). The poet who early championed Romanticism and whose ballads had an influence on the ballads of Pushkin.

Katenka. "The Death of Ivan Il'ich." A beloved one from Ivan's youth.

Katerina Alekseevna. *Resurrection*. The woman friend of the Korchagins who was a Slavophile and liked to play with words.

Katerina Karpovna. "Petr Petrovich Karataev," in *A Hunter's Sketches* The companion of Maria Il'inichna.

Katerina Petrovna. *Anna Karenina*. The lady who reared Anna Karenina. *War and Peace*. The lady who played waltzes at the governor's party in Voronezh.

Katerina Semenovna. "The Kreutzer Sonata." The woman who lost two children because she did not call a doctor.

Katia. A diminutive for Katerina. *Fathers and Sons*. See Lokteva, Katerina. *On the Eve*. A beggar girl whom Elena Stakhova met. The child died after the chance acquaintance. *Resurrection*.

The two-year-old granddaughter of the governor of Siberia. *War and Peace*. The child Pierre Bezukhov saved from a fire in Moscow. Also a maid of Princess Mar'ia Bolkonskaia.

Katish. A diminutive for Katerina. *War and Peace*. See Mamontova, Princess Katerina Semenovna.

Katkov, Mikhail Nikiforovich (1818-1887). *Virgin Soil* (7). The noted critic whose name was submitted to a school in Moscow for a particular post. He did not serve in the position.

Katiusha. A diminutive for Katerina (Catherine). *Resurrection*. See Maslova, Katerina Mikhailovna.

Katrin. *A Gentry Nest*. Lemm's cook.

Kaufman. *Anna Karenina*. A name thought up by Tolstoi to designate one of the writers whom Levin thought about when he studied how to improve his lands and the lot of his peasants.

Kaulbach, Wilhelm (1805-1874). *Anna Karenina* (2, 6). A German painter noted for his sense of satire. He was mentioned in a gossipy conversation at a gathering at the Princess Betsy Tverskaia's in St. Petersburg.

Kaverin, Petr (1794-1855). *Evgenii Onegin* (1, 16). A hard-drinking swashbuckler and notable womanizer who was a friend of Pushkin and influenced the young poet.

Kazbich. "Bela," in *A Hero of Our Times*. The bandit whose beautiful horse was stolen and traded for Bela in an intrigue arranged by Pechorin. Kazbich later stabbed and killed the captive Bela.

Kedrov, Prince. *Anna Karenina*. A comrade and fellow officer of Vronskii.

Keiss. *Anna Karenina*. A name thought up by Tolstoi to designate an author who wrote on the subject of perception. Koznyshev discussed the subject with Levin (1, 7).

Kempiiskii, Foma. See Thomas a Kempis.

Kepler, Johann (1571-1630). *War and Peace* (E, 2, 11). The astronomer who is considered the father of physical astronomy. He was mentioned by Tolstoi in a discussion on the interpretation of history.

Khailikov, Panfil. *Evgenii Onegin*. A neighbor of the Larins.

Khaltiupkina. *Resurrection*. The one named by Charskaia as a person who wanted to teach everybody.

Khandrikov. *War and Peace*. A commander in Korchevo whom Prince Nikolai Bolkonskii mentioned in a letter to his son Andrei.

Khariton. "Dubrovskii." Dubrovskii's cook.

Kharlova, Lizaveta. *The Captain's Daughter*. In a letter to Petr Grinev, Mar'ia Mironova mentioned Lizaveta's treatment by Puga-chev's mob. Lizaveta, according to Pushkin's *History of Pugachev*, was shot holding her little brother in her arms. Their bodies were left together unburied for several days.

Khemnitzer, Ivan Ivanovich (1745-1784). *Virgin Soil* (9). A Russian poet known for his fables written in a vigorous, popular language. He was quoted by Kallomeitsev.

Khliustov. *Anna Karenina*. A Marshal of the Nobility in Kashin prov-ince.

Khomiakov, Aleksei Stepanovich (1804-1860). *Anna Karenina* (8, 9). The Russian poet and Slavophile whose works Levin read in his search for meaning in life. Although he was at first impressed with the writer's philosophy, he gradually became disappointed and quit reading. *A Gentry Nest* (33). Panshin cited the poet one evening at the Kalitins. "First Love" (14). Vladimir B____ recited from Khomiakov's historical tragedy *Ermak*. *Resurrection* (2, 23). Nekhliudov read Khomiakov when he was investigating the veracity of the Russian Orthodox Church.

Khlopakov, Victor. "Lebedian'," in *A Hunter's Sketches*. A former officer who lived solely at the expense of his friends, be-littling himself for any favor.

Khor' (The Polecat). "Khor' and Kalinych," in *A Hunter's Sketches*. A peasant who was a realist and a shrewd administrator. He contrasted greatly with his friend Kalinych, a romantic and poor peasant.

Khoroshavka. *Resurrection*. A cell mate of Katiusha Maslova. She was being tried for stealing and arson.

Khostatova, Lidia. *Fathers and Sons*. An acquaintance of Mme. Kukshina's.

Khovtikov. *War and Peace*. A petty official who was to be a witness at the mock marriage between Natasha Rostova and Anatol' Kuragin.

Khriaka-Khrupenskii. "Chertopkhanov and Nedopiuskin," in *A Hunter's Sketches*. The landowner who wrote the article about the benefits of morality in the life of the peasants.

Khrushchev, Andrei. *The Captain's Daughter* (14). Grinev's grand-father knew Khrushchev, a participant in the A. P. Volynskii plot in 1740. Volynskii plotted against the power of Count A. I. Ostermann in the court of Empress Anne of Courland. Khrushchev was executed in June, 1740.

Khvalynskii, Viacheslav Illarionovich. "Two Landowners," in *A Hunter's Sketches*. A neighbor of the narrator who had peculiar habits.

Khvostov, Nikolai Eremeich. "The Office," in *A Hunter's Sketches*. The fat, head-office clerk.

Kiesewetter. *Resurrection*. A German evangelistic revivalist who held meetings at the Charskiis'.

Kiezewetter, Johann Godfried Karl Christian (1766-1819). "The Death of Ivan Il'ich." The author of books on logic.

Kikin, General Petr Andreevich (1772-1834). *War and Peace* (4, 2, 4). The officer who gave a ball in his house at Echkino, where Ermolov and Miloradovich were guests when Kutuzov sent them orders to begin an attack on the retreating French.

King of Hearts. *War and Peace*. A nickname for a regimental commander at Braunau.

King of Naples. *War and Peace* (3, 1, 4). A reference to Murat, who was King of Naples from 1810 to 1815. See Murat.

King of Prussia. *War and Peace*. See N. A. Bolkonskii.

King of Rome. *War and Peace*. The name given to Napoleon's child by his second wife, Maria Louise of Austria. See Napoleon II.

Kintil'ian Semenych. "Raspberry Spring," in *A Hunter's Sketches*. The steward of Valerian Petrovich.

Kiprian. *Virgin Soil*. A priest in the church near Sipiagin's country estate.

Kiril. *Virgin Soil*. A pantry server at the Sipiagin estate who was known as a bitter drunkard.

Kiril Matveich. *War and Peace*. A cousin of the Countess Rostova.

Kiril Selifanych. "Hamlet of the Shchigrovskii District," in *A Hunter's Sketches*. The one-eyed friend of Lupikhin.

Kirilov. *Anna Karenina*. An innkeeper known for his avarice.

Kirimova. *Resurrection*. A visitor of Nekhliudov's mother. Nekhliudov once flirted with Kirimova when he was a young man.

Kiriusha. *War and Peace*. An acquaintance of one of Mar'ia Bolkonskaia's "God folk."

Kirsanov, Arkadii Nikolaevich. *Fathers and Sons*. The young student who brought his friend, Bazarov, to the Kirsanov estate. The progressive ideas of the young men greatly upset Arkadii's father and uncle, Pavel Kirsanov.

Kirsanov, Nikolai Petrovich. *Fathers and Sons.* The middle-aged landowner who lived openly with a servant girl, Fenichka. His
son Arkadii approved of his illicit affair.

Kirsanov, Pavel Petrovich. *Fathers and Sons.* Nikolai's brother, who
was educated in the Corps des Pages and played the role
of a disillusioned country gentleman.

Kirsanov, Petr. *Fathers and Sons.* The deceased father of Nikolai and
Pavel Kirsanov. He was a former general in the army.

Kirsanova, Agafakleia Kuzminishna. *Fathers and Sons.* The deceased
mother of Nikolai and Pavel Kirsanov.

Kirsanova, Masha Prepolovenskaia. *Fathers and Sons.* The mother of
Arkadii Kirsanov.

Kirsten. *War and Peace.* The officer at Braunau who felt Nikolai
Rostov should apologize to the colonel about his accusations against Telianin.

Kiselev. *War and Peace.* A soldier in the Eighth Company during the
French retreat.

Kisliakov. *Fathers and Sons.* A journalist who wrote an article on female
labor which Mme. Kukshina asked Arkadii Kirsanov about.
Virgin Soil. A revolutionary who wrote letters and pamphlets
expounding his cause.

Kitaeva, Karolina Albertovna. *Resurrection.* The fat mistress of the
brothel where Katiusha Maslova worked. She gave Maslova
some money when the girl was convicted.

Kitty. *Anna Karenina.* See Shcherbatskaia, Princess Katerina.

Klara Vasil'evna. *Resurrection.* The mistress of the president of the
court in which Katiusha Maslova's trial took place. During
the trial proceedings, he kept thinking of a tryst with his
mistress Klara.

Klim. *Virgin Soil.* The consumptive factory worker whose flat tones
were audible in the church which the Sipiagins attended.

Kliuber, Karl. *Spring Freshets.* The former fiancé of Gemma Roselli.

Kliucharev, Fedor Petrovich (1754-1820). *War and Peace* (3, 3, 5). A
postmaster of Moscow who was arrested and exiled by Count
Rostopchin as a suspect in the Vereshchagin scandal. Aleksandr I made Kliucharev a senator in 1815. See Vereshchagin.

Kliukhin, First. "Hamlet of the Shchigrovskii District," in *A
Hunter's Sketches.* A famous Moscow tailor.

Knallerbsen. *Spring Freshets* (15). The name in the book title mentioned
by Kliuber. The full title is *Knallerbsen, oder Du sollst und wirst
lachen,* by Ouedlinburg (1841).

Knaust. *Anna Karenina*. A name thought up by Tolstoi to designate an author who wrote on the subject of perception. Koznyshev discussed the subject with Levin (1, 7).

Kniazhnin, Iakov Borisovich (1742-1792). *The Captain's Daughter*. The epigraph to Chapter Four is from Kniazhnin's play *Eccentrics (Chudaki)* (1790). *Evgenii Onegin* (1, 18). A classical author of the age of Ekaterina II whom Pushkin called the "imitative one" because of his remaking of French tragedies.

Koch, Gottlieb von der. "Death," in *A Hunter's Sketches*. The police superintendent who went along on the hunt with the narrator.

Kochubei, Viktor Pavlovich (1768-1834). *War and Peace* (2, 3, 4). The diplomat and statesman who was Minister of Interior from 1802 to 1807. He was a close friend of Aleksandr I.

Kock, Paul de (1794-1871). *A Gentry Nest* (40). The French novelist noted for his portraiture of cheap dissipation in low and middle-class life in Paris. Varvara Lavretskaia liked to read his novels. *Smoke* (14). Potugin mentioned the writer in conversation.

Kokhanovskaia. *Smoke* (5). The pen name of Nadezhda Stepanovna Sokhanskaia (1825-1884). Turgenev wrote that when Potugin advised Gubarev to read her works, he had in mind the novel *Theodocii Savvrich at Rest* (1864).

Koko. *Smoke*. The prince who was a well-known figure in society. *War and Peace*. A nickname for Prince Andrei Bolksonskii's son Nikolai (Nikolenka).

Kolia. *Fathers and Sons*. The infant son of Katia and Arkadii Kirsanov. *Resurrection*. The boy prisoner looked after by Maria Pavlovna. *War and Peace*. A diminutive for Count Nikolai Rostov.

Koliazin, Il'ia. *Fathers and Sons*. The tutor of Nikolai and Pavel Kirsanov in St. Petersburg. He was their cousin on their mother's side.

Koliazin, Matvei Il'ich. *Fathers and Sons*. The contemptuous maternal uncle of Nikolai and Pavel Kirsanov.

Koliazina, Agafeia. *Fathers and Sons*. The maiden name of the deceased mother of Nikolai and Pavel Kirsanov.

Kolosov, Ivan Ivanich. *Resurrection*. The bank director friend of General Karchagin. Kolosov was known as a great conservative.

Kol'tsov, Aleksei Vasil'evich (1809-1842). "Death," in *A Hunter's Sketches*. The Russian poet quoted by Turgenev in the story. *Rudin* (Epilogue). Rudin quoted the poet to Lezhnev.

Koltun-Babura. "Hamlet of the Shchigrovskii District," in *A Hunter's Sketches*. An uncle of the Russian Hamlet.

Kolyshev, Mikhail Petrovich. *A Gentry Nest*. The person who was reported dead in the copy of the *Moscow News* which Lavretskii found among his Aunt Glafira Lavretskaia's things.

Kolyshev, Petr Vasil'evich. *A Gentry Nest*. The person who Lavretskii thought was the father of Mikhail Petrovich Kolyshev.

Kolyshkina. *Spring Freshets*. See Polozova.

Komarov. *War and Peace*. A cossack who accompanied Petia Rostov during a reconnaisance mission when the French retreated from Moscow.

Komisarov, Osip (1838-1892). *Anna Karenina* (5, 23). A peasant hatmaker from Kostroma who hindered Karakozov from assassinating Aleksandr II in 1866. Komisarov became "von Komisarov" by a royal decree of the tsar after the incident. Countess Lidia Ivanovna admired him because he had saved the tsar.

Komov, Stefan Niktopolenych. "Ovsianikov, the Freeholder," in *A Hunter's Sketches*. A neighbor who tormented Ovsianikov's father.

Kondachovy, Brothers. "Death," in *A Hunter's Sketches*. The young men Dasha began running around with.

Kondratev, Markel. *Resurrection*. A political prisoner and former factory hand who believed everything Novodvorov said.

Kondratevna. *War and Peace*. An old woman worker at the Rostovs'.

Konopatin. *Virgin Soil*. The name Sipiagin called Paklin when he came with news of Markelov's arrest. Sipiagin used a play on words: in Russian, "paklia" is oakum and "konoplia" is hemp. He derived the name from the words close in meaning and sound.

Konovnitsyn, Petr Petrovich (1764-1822). *War and Peace* (4, 2, 5). In 1812, he commanded a division and was Minister of War from 1815 to 1819.

Konstantin Narkizych. "The Office," in *A Hunter's Sketches*. The peasant who argued with Kupria.

Konstantin Pavlovich (1779-1831). *On the Eve* (19). The second son of Tsar Pavel I. His picture hung on a wall in the Stakhovs' home. *War and Peace* (1, 3, 6). The brother of Aleksandr I who was the inspector general of all cavalry troops. At Aleksandr's death, he refused the throne of Russia.

Konsunskaia. *Anna Karenina*. The lady who was concerned that a guest wore a lilac dress at Kitty Shcherbatskaia's wedding.

Korableva. *Resurrection.* Katiusha Maslova's cell mate who had killed her husband for making up to her daughter. She was able to procure vodka for Maslova.

Korchagin, Petia. *Resurrection.* A student in the sixth grade.

Korchagina, Princess Mary (Missy). *Resurrection.* Nekhliudov was expected to marry her before he became involved in Katiusha Maslova's trial.

Korchagina, Sofia Vasil'evna. *Resurrection.* The former beauty who secluded herself from everyone but a chosen few.

Kornei. *Anna Karenina.* The valet of Karenin who told Anna she would die in childbirth. *Resurrection.* Nekhliudov's servant.

Kornilova. *Resurrection.* The aunt of Lidia Shustova.

Korob'in, Pavel Petrovich. *A Gentry Nest.* Varvara Lavretskaia's father, who was involved in a financial scandal and forced to retire from governmental service.

Korob'ina, Kalliopa Karlovna. *A Gentry Nest.* Varvara Lavretskaia's thin, nervous mother.

Korob'ina, Varvara Pavlovna. *A Gentry Nest.* The maiden name of Varvara Lavretskaia.

Korolev, Aleksandr Vladimirovich. "Ovsianikov, the Freeholder," in *A Hunter's Sketches.* A member of the gentry.

Korsunskaia, Lidia. *Anna Karenina.* The beautiful wife of the master of ceremonies at a ball.

Korsunskii, Egor. *Anna Karenina.* The master of ceremonies who invited Kitty Shcherbatskaia to dance at a ball.

Korzinskaia, Princess. *Anna Karenina.* A lady mentioned by Prince L'vov.

Kostia. A diminutive of Konstantin. *Anna Karenina,* See Levin, Konstantin. Also a servant at Levin's country estate. "Bezhin Meadow," in *A Hunter's Sketches.* A thoughtful and melancholy boy.

Kourakine, Prince Aleksandr Borisovich (1752-1818). *War and Peace* (3, 2, 1). The Russian diplomat sent by Aleksandr I as ambassador to Vienna (1806-1808) and later to Paris (1808-1812).

Kovrizhkin, Prince. *Spring Freshets.* The poet who wrote the verses about Gromoboi's funeral which Polozova did not wish to hear. Turgenev ridiculed the poet Petr Andreevich Viazemskii (1792-1878) in the character Kovrizhkin. *Virgin Soil.* Nezdanov mentioned Kovrizhkin as a lackey-enthusiast, but Turgenev was again referring to Viazemskii.

Kozel'skii, Prince. "Hamlet of the Shchigrovskii District," in *A Hunter's Sketches*. A stupid aristocrat who only occasionally visited his estate.

Kozlovskii, Prince. *War and Peace*. The commander of the Preobrazhenskii Regiment at Tilsit who was a comrade of Prince Andrei Bolksonskii at Braunau.

Koz'ma, Saint. "Raspberry Spring," in *A Hunter's Sketches*. The saint in whose name the church was built near Shumikhino.

Koznyshev, Sergei Ivanovich. *Anna Karenina*. A famous writer and a half-brother of Levin.

Krasovskii. "The Death of Ivan Il'ich." The members of the court were discussing the case of Krasovskii when the news of the death of Ivan arrived.

Kreigsmuth, Baron. *Resurrection*. An old retired general who was unsympathetic to any pleas for Katiusha Maslova.

Kriltsov, Anatolii. *Resurrection*. A political prisoner who loved Maria Pavlovna and who became consumptive in prison.

Kritskii. *Anna Karenina*. Nikolai Levin's friend from Kiev.

Krivin. *Anna Karenina*. A society lion with a bald head.

Krivtsov, Count. *Anna Karenina*. An aristocrat who was deeply in debt but who still kept two mistresses.

Kroug, Monsieur. *War and Peace*. The chargé d'affaires of Copenhagen who was a guest at one of Anna Pavlovna's soirées.

Krudener, Baroness Varvara Julia (1764-1825). *War and Peace* (E, 1, 14). A spiritualist who had great influence on Aleksandr I in 1817. The tsar considered his meeting with her a "miracle."

Krum. *On the Eve* (11). A famous Bulgarian prince whose health was toasted by Shubin while drinking with Insarov and Bersenev.

Krupianikov, Fofa. "Death," in *A Hunter's Sketches*. A student of Sorokoumov and the son of Gur Krupianikov.

Krupianikov, Gur. "Death," in *A Hunter's Sketches*. The landowner who hired Sorokoumov to teach his children.

Krupianikova, Zeza. "Death," in *A Hunter's Sketches*. A student of Sorokoumov and the daughter of Gur Kuprianikov.

Krupov. *Anna Karenina*. The man mentioned by Serpukhovskoi as a person whose career was ruined by his amorous affairs.

Krylov, Ivan Andreevich (1768-1844). "Ovsianikov, the Freeholder," in *A Hunter's Sketches*. The face of Ovsianikov reminded people of Krylov, who was noted for his obesity and his famous fables.

Ksandryk, Roksolan Mediarovich. *Rudin* (1). The benefactor of Pandalevskii. In the character of Ksandryk, Turgenev was parodying Aleksandr Skarlatovich Strudza (1791-1854), a writer of religious and political books. In a sentimental article about Strudza in a journal Turgenev disliked, the *Moskvitianin*, Strudza was called the "wise old man" (starets). Turgenev used the term "wise old man" for Ksandryk to belittle the journal's article.

Kubenskaia, Princess. *A Gentry Nest*. An old aunt of Ivan Lavretskii who married a young French tutor and left her wealth to him instead of Ivan.

Kubyshkin, Nazar. "Lebedian'," in *A Hunter's Sketches*. The groom of Chernobei.

Kudriashev, Vasilii. "Hamlet of the Shchigrovskii District," in *A Hunter's Sketches*. A former steward of the Russian Hamlet.

Kukol'nik, Nestor Vasil'evich (1809-1868). *Virgin Soil* (8). A second-rate poet whom Kallomeitsev preferred to Pushkin because he had more "protoplasm."

Kukshina, Avdotia Nikitishna. *Fathers and Sons*. An independent divorcée and landowner who lived in a provincial capital.

Kuleshov, Gregorii Efimovich. *Resurrection*. A merchant in the jury at Katiusha Maslova's trial.

Kulibin, Ivan Petrovich (1735-1818). *Smoke* (14). An inventor whom Potugin mentioned. Kulibin created a clock in the shape of an egg which was presented to Ekaterina II.

Kulikov, Fedor. "Petr Petrovich Karataev," in *A Hunter's Sketches*. The father of the Matrena, the mistress of Petr Petrovich.

Kulikova, Matrena Fedorovna. "Petr Petrovich Karataev," in *A Hunter's Sketches*. The serf whom Petr Petrovich abducted but who returned to her mistress in order to save Petr from financial ruin.

Kul'nev, Iakov Petrovich (1763-1812). "Dubrovskii" (2, 9). The Russian general who distinguished himself in the war with Sweden in 1808. He was killed in the War of 1812.

Kupria (Kuprian Afanasevich). "The Office," in *A Hunter's Sketches*. The man appointed to be a stove tender.

Kuragin, Prince Anatol' Vasil'evich. *War and Peace*. The troublesome son of Prince Vasilii who failed to marry Mar'ia Bolkonskaia and tried to abduct Natasha Rostov, a scandal that led to his exile.

Kuragin, Prince Ippolit Vasil'evich. *War and Peace*. The younger son of Prince Vasilii who was ugly and was considered a fool by his father.

Kuragin, Prince Vasilii Sergeevich Kuragin. *War and Peace*. An aristocrat who succeeded in marrying his daughter Elena to the wealthy Pierre Bezukhov but failed to marry his son Anatol' to the heiress Mar'ia Bolksonskaia.

Kuragina, Princess Aline. *War and Peace*. The wife of Prince Vasilii.

Kurbeev. *Rudin*. The man with whom Rudin went into business in an effort to make a river navigable.

Kurbskii, Prince Andrei Mikhailovich (1528-1583). *War and Peace* (E, 2, 4). The writer and warrior who betrayed Russia during the reign of Ivan the Terrible. His correspondence with Ivan while he was in exile is extant.

Kurichkin, Taras. *The Captain's Daughter*. The man who assisted Pugachev in a steam bath.

Kurnatovskii, Egor Andreevich. *On the Eve*. The man Stakhov wanted his daughter Elena to marry, but he married Zoia.

Kutuzov, Mikhail Illarionovich, Prince of Smolensk (1745-1813). "Tat'iana Borisovna and Her Nephew," in *A Hunter's Sketches*. The Russian general who defeated Napoleon in 1812. *War and Peace* (1, 1, 3). The Supreme Russian Commander during the War of 1812. He was rebuked for surrendering Moscow without a fight; but his tactics proved correct, and the French retreated from the country.

Kutuzov, Pavel Ivanovich. See Golenishchev-Kutuzov.

Kuzia. "Lebedian'," in *A Hunter's Sketches*. A jockey for Sitnikov.

Kuz'ma. *Anna Karenina*. A servant at Levin's estate.

Kuzov, Semen. *The Captain's Daughter*. The owner of the house where Grinev was billeted at the Belozorsk Fortress.

Kuzovkin, Stepan Sergeich. "Petr Petrovich Karataev," in *A Hunter's Sketches*. A district inspector.

Kuzovlev, Prince. *Anna Karenina*. A rival racer with Vronskii at the horse race where Anna cried after Vronskii had fallen.

Kvytskii. *Anna Karenina*. The man killed in a duel with Priachnikov.

Ladislas. *Virgin Soil*. A Moscow publicist whom Kallomeitsev lauded as the writer who would put the nihilists to shame. Nezhdanov belittled him.

La Fontaine, Avguste Heinrich Julius (1778-1831). *Evgenii Onegin* (4, 50). The author of numerous novels about family life whom Pushkin mentioned when commenting on marriage.

La Fontaine, Jean de (1621-1695). *Spring Freshets* (6). The French writer noted for his fables. Turgenev quoted his line "Cêt age est sans pitie" after Emilio Roselli had laughed at Pantaleone Cippatola's singing.

Lais. *A Gentry Nest.* Ivan Petrovich Lavretskii ran after beauties who often had classical names such as Lais.

Landau. *Anna Karenina.* A clairvoyant whom Karenin and Lidia Ivanovna gave considerable attention.

Lanfrey, Pierre (1828-1877). *War and Peace* (E, 2, 2). The French publicist and historian who pictured Napoleon as an enemy of liberty and of the people. In his *Histoire de Napoleon* (5 vols., 1867-1875), he minimized Napoleon's military and administrative abilities.

Langeron, Aleksandr Fedorovich (1763-1831). *War and Peace* (1, 3, 11). The French émigré who became a Russian general and fought for Russia against his homeland in 1805 and 1812. He knew Pushkin in Odessa when the poet was in exile.

Lankovskii. *Anna Karenina.* The owner of the horse named Powerful which Vronskii considered buying.

Lannes, Jean, Duke of Montebello (1769-1809). *War and Peace* (1, 2, 12). A marshal of France who participated in the campaigns of 1805 and 1806. In 1809 he commanded a corps and was mortally wounded at Essling, Austria.

Lanskoi, Vasilii Sergeevich (1754-1831). *War and Peace* (4, 2, 1). The senator (1812) who became vice deputy (1815) of the Kingdom of Poland.

Laocoön. *War and Peace* (E, 1, 8). The son of Priam, the priest of Apollo of Troy. The sculpture of his death with his two sons was discovered in 1506 and is now in the Vatican.

Laplace, Peter Simon (1749-1827). *Virgin Soil* (2). The physicist Paklin cited in a conversation with Ostrodumov.

Larin, Dmitrii. *Evgenii Onegin.* The deceased father of Tat'iana and Ol'ga Larina.

Larina, Ol'ga. *Evgenii Onegin.* The youngest daughter in the Larin family who loved Lenskii but married another soon after Lenskii's fatal duel.

Larina, Pashette. *Evgenii Onegin.* Tat'iana's mother, who adjusted to country life after the birth of her daughters.

Larina, Tat'iana. *Evgenii Onegin*. The heroine of Pushkin's famous novel in verse. Her loyalty to her husband was used as an example of fidelity throughout the nineteenth century.

La Rochefoucauld, François de Marsillac de la (1613-1680). *Rudin* (7). The famous French writer noted for his maxims. Rudin quoted his "Believe in yourself and others will believe in you."

Larrey, Baron Dominique Jean (1766-1842). *War and Peace* (1, 3, 19). Napoleon's doctor who served as Head Medical Inspector of all major French military marches.

Laska. *Resurrection*. A peasant boy in Nekhliudov's village.

Lassalle, Ferdinand (1825-1864). *Anna Karenina* (3, 27). One of the organizers of the German labor movement. He was mentioned in a conversation between Levin and some regional landowners. *Smoke* (4). Litvinov mentioned Lassalle in a conversation with Gubarev.

Lasunskaia, Countess. *Spring Freshets*. Polozova was dining with the countess when Sanin arrived.

Lasunskaia, Dar'ia Mikhailovna. *Rudin*. The wealthy landowner who had a reputation for oddity in society and who served as hostess for Rudin. She ordered Rudin from her home when she discovered that her daughter was infatuated with him.

Lasunskaia, Natalia Alekseevna (Natasha). *Rudin*. Dar'ia's daughter.

Lasunskii, Petia. *Rudin*. One of Dar'ia Lasunskaia's young sons.

Lasunskii, Vania. *Rudin*. One of Dar'ia Lasunskaia's young sons.

Laura. *Anna Karenina*. A name mentioned in conversation between Vronskii and the Baroness Shilton.

Lauriston, Marquis de. See Law, Jacques-Alexandre.

Laventer, Johann Kaspar (1741-1801). "Dubrovskii" (2, 9). The Swiss author of *Physionomy*, which advanced the theory that the capabilities of a man are expressed in his figure and mainly in the structure of his head. *War and Peace* (1, 1, 1). Prince Vasilii Kuragin quoted Laventer as the originator of the remark "I lack the bump of paternity."

Lavra, St. *War and Peace* (4, 1, 12). The Russian saint mentioned by Platon Karataev in a prayer.

Lavrentii. *Anna Karenina*. An old butler of Countess Vronskaia.

Lavretskaia, Ada. *A Gentry Nest*. Varvara's small daughter.

Lavretskaia, Anna Pavlovna. *A Gentry Nest*. The grandmother of Fedor Lavretskii.

Lavretskaia, Glafira Petrovna (Glashka). *A Gentry Nest*. The aunt of Fedor Lavretskii who was noted for her irritable nature and who left him her estate.

Lavretskaia, Malania Sergeevna. *A Gentry Nest*. A servant girl whom Ivan Lavretskii married. After the birth of her son Fedor, the father deserted her and she died young.

Lavretskaia, Varvara Pavlovna (Varia). *A Gentry Nest*. The wife of Fedor Lavretskii. She was reported dead, but returned and destroyed the happiness of Liza and Fedor.

Lavretskii, Andrei Afanasevich. *A Gentry Nest*. Fedor Lavretskii's fiery great-grandfather who greatly enhanced the family's wealth.

Lavretskii, Fedor Ivanich. *A Gentry Nest*. The landowner who fell in love with Lizaveta Kalitina and planned to marry her. His wife, who was reported dead, returned and ruined his plan.

Lavretskii, Ivan Petrovich. *A Gentry Nest*. The father of Fedor Lavretskii, reared as a Voltairean liberal.

Lavretskii, Petr Andreevich. *A Gentry Nest*. Fedor Lavretskii's grandfather.

Lavrushka. *War and Peace*. Denisov's orderly at Braunau.

Law, Jacques Alexandre Bernard, Marquis de Lauriston (1768-1828). *War and Peace* (4, 2, 2). The friend of Napoleon from artillery school who was made an adjutant by him in 1800. He was in the campaigns of 1805 and 1809. In 1811, he was made Ambassador to Russia. In 1812, he held a command in the Grande Armée. He was captured in the retreat from Leipzig and held prisoner of war until the fall of the empire.

Lazarchuk. *War and Peace*. A soldier in Denisov's batallion.

Lazarev. *War and Peace*. The soldier of the Preobrazhenskii infantry corps who accepted a medal from Napoleon at Tilsit.

Lazarus. *Fathers and Sons* (20). Bazarov told his father to quit playing the beggar like the Biblical Lazarus (Luke X, vi).

Lebrun, Mme. (1755-1842). "The Queen of Spades." The two portraits that hung in the Countess Anna Fedotovna's bedroom were painted by the noted French portraitist.

Lecouvreur, Adrienne (1692-1730). "The Death of Ivan Il'ich." The noted French actress whom Voltaire named as his mistress when her body was denied the last rites of the church. A play based on her life by Eugène Scribe in 1849 was seen by Fedor Petrovich.

Leda. *Smoke* (5). The mythical daughter of an Aetolian ruler who was praised for her beauty by Zeus. When Litvinov and Potugin were discussing the future of Russia, the expression "from the eggs of Leda" meant "from the earliest times."

Lejeune, Franz Ivanych. "Ovsianikov, the Freeholder," in *A Hunter's Sketches*. The narrator's neighbor who had been a drummer boy in Napoleon's army. He was saved from drowning by the Russians and stayed in Russia. After a career in the government, he became a landowner.

Lel'. *Evgenii Onegin* (5, 10). A pagan god of love and the grove. Lel' hovered over Tat'iana Larina as she slept. Tat'iana had a nightmare.

Lelorgme d'Ideville. *War and Peace*. The interpreter for Napoleon during his entrance into Moscow.

Lemarrois, Jean Leonard François (1776-1836). *War and Peace* (1, 2, 17). The French general who was an adjutant of Napoleon.

Lemm, Christoph Theodor Gottlieb. *A Gentry Nest*. Liza Kalitina's old music teacher of German descent.

Lenochka. A diminutive for Elena. *A Gentry Nest*. See Elena Kalitina.

Lenore, *Evgenii Onegin* (8, 4). The heroine of a famous ballad "Lenore" (1773) by the German poet Gottfried August Burger (1747-1794). The poem was translated into Russian by V. A. Zhukovskii in 1808. *Spring Freshets* (42). Polozova felt like Lenore when riding with Sanin in the mountains.

Lenskii, Vladimir. *Evgenii Onegin*. The handsome young landowner who loved Ol'ga Larina and died in a tragic duel, killed by his friend Onegin. *Spring Freshets* (19). When Sanin said farewell to Gemma, he remembered Lenskii's parting from Ol'ga Larina in Pushkin's work. *Virgin Soil* (37). In a note which Nezhdanov left for Silin before suicide, Nezhdanov mentioned Lenskii.

Lepic. *A Gentry Nest*. A watchmaker whose name was inscribed in a watch which the Princess Kubenskaia gave to I. P. Lavretskii.

Leppich (b. 1775). *War and Peace* (3, 2, 18). The Dutchman who tried unsuccessfully to construct a balloon at Vrontsovo to destory the French army.

Lermontov, Mikhail Iur'evich (1814-1841). *A Gentry Nest* (33). The author of the poem "The Thought" in 1838.

Lerois, Julien (1686-1759). "The Queen of Spades." The Countess Anna Fedotovna's bedroom had many porcelain figures made by Lerois.

Leshchetitskii. "The Death of Ivan Il'ich." The celebrated specialist who treated Ivan Il'ich Golovin during his mortal illness.

Levin, Konstantin Ivanovich. *Anna Karenina*. An idealistic, athletic country gentleman who was greatly concerned with philosophical, social and political problems. He married Kitty Shcherbatskaia and settled down to an active life in the country.

Levin, Nikolai Ivanovich. *Anna Karenina*. Konstantin's brother who died of consumption.

Levshin, Platon (1737-1812). *Evgenii Onegin* (7, 4). The Metropolitan of Moscow who was known as a typical representative of church mentality during the Age of Reason.

Levushka. *Resurrection*. Madame Charskaia's nephew who worked in the senate.

Lezhnev, Mikhailo Mikhailych. *Rudin*. The wealthy landowner and frequent visitor at Dar'ia's who was the first to warn her of Rudin's barren intellectuality.

Lezhnev, Misha (Mishuk). *Rudin*. The son of Lezhnev.

Lichtenfels, Count. *War and Peace*. The man cited by Bilibin as his source for details about the French parade in Vienna.

Lichtenstein, Prince Johann Joseph (1760-1835). *War and Peace* (1, 3, 11). The Austrian field marshal who conducted peace talks in St. Petersburg after the Battle of Austerlitz.

Lidia Ivanovna, Countess. *Anna Karenina*. A matron of a conservative set called the "Conscience of Petersburg Society." She rebuked Anna and befriended Karenin during their marital dispute.

Liebig, Baron Justus von (1803-1873). *Fathers and Sons* (6). The natural scientist to whom Nikolai Kirsanov referred in a conversation with Bazarov.

Ligne, Charles Joseph (1735-1814). *War and Peace* (2, 3, 9). The Belgian political writer who was a friend of Joseph II of Austria and Ekaterina II of Russia. He was known for his cleverness and wit.

Ligovskaia, Princess Mary. "Princess Mary," in *A Hero of Our Time*. The heroine of the story who loved Pechorin but could not win his affection.

Likhachev. *War and Peace*. A cossack in Denisov's guerrilla detachment during the retreat of the French from Russia.

Lili. *Anna Karenina*. The infant daughter of Dolly and Stepan Oblonskii. *War and Peace*. A woman suggested to Nikolai Rostov by the governor's wife in Voronezh.

Lille, Duc de. *Anna Karenina* (33). A French author thought up by Tolstoi as a parody of the Parnassian poet Le comte de Lille (1818-1894). The famous Saturday meetings at the home of the comte helped unite and establish the Parnassian poets.

Linchen. "Hamlet of the Shchigrovskii District," in *A Hunter's Sketches*. The daughter of a German professor. The Russian Hamlet loved her but did not marry her.

Lindamandol, Karlo Karlich. "The Office," in *A Hunter's Sketches*. The agent who did not have the power to make any agreements.

Linon, Mlle., *Anna Karenina*. The French teacher of the Shcherbatskii daughters.

Lipina, Aleksandra Pavlovna. *Rudin*. A widow who lived with her brother Valynzev and who later married Lezhnev.

Lise. French for Liza. See Liza.

List, Fredrich (1789-1846). *Resurrection* (2, 30). The German author of a book on criminology which Nekhliudov read to understand the persecuted in criminal cases and those who judged them.

Liszt, Franz (1811-1886). *A Gentry Nest* (15). The famous Hungarian pianist who twice played for Varvara Lavretskaia. *Spring Freshets* (39). Herr R____ imitated Liszt when he laughed in a constrained way with a sob. *Resurrection* (1, 26). When Nekhliudov first went to Maslova in prison, he heard Liszt's music being played in the inspector's quarters. Later he found out that the inspector's daughter was an aspiring musician.

Litvinov, Gregorii Mikhailovich. *Smoke*. The thirty-year-old, swarthy hero of the novel whose visit to Baden brought him love and despair.

Litvinova, Madame. *Smoke*. Gregorii's mother who died when the youth entered Moscow University.

Liubomirski, General Konstantin Ksaverevich (1782-1843). *War and Peace* (3, 2, 1). An aide-de-camp of Aleksandr I. Liubomirski demanded that Barclay de Tolly take a stand against the French as they advanced on Moscow. Barclay despatched him to St. Petersburg.

Liubov' Petrovna. *Evgenii Onegin*. Tat'iana Larina's relative who had the habit of telling lies.

Liubozvonov, Vasilii Nikolaich. "Ovsianikov, the Freeholder," in *A Hunter's Sketches*. A young landowner who inspired fear and surprise in his serfs.

Liudmila. *Evgenii Onegin* (1, 2). The heroine of Pushkin's "Ruslan and Liudmila" (1820) which the author mentioned while addressing his readers.

Liza. A diminutive of Lizaveta (Elizaveta). *A Gentry Nest*. See Kalitina, Liza. "The Kreutzer Sonata." Pozdnyshev's favorite daughter. "The Queen of Spades." See Lizaveta Ivanovna. *Smoke*. At Irina Ratmirova's party, the Countess Liza (Lise) was a very superstitious lady who talked about mediums. *War and Peace*. See Bolkonskaia, Liza.

Lizan'ka. A diminutive of Lizaveta (Elizaveta). *Resurrection*. Agrafena Petrovna's married niece.

Lizaveta Ivanovna (Lise, Lizan'ka). "The Queen of Spades." The countess's ward and companion who was a domestic martyr. Her love for Hermann led her to disillusionment.

Lizaveta Petrovna. *Anna Karenina*. Kitty's midwife.

Loktev, Sergei Nikolaevich. *Fathers and Sons*. The deceased father of Anna Odintsova and Katerina Lokteva.

Lokteva, Anna. See Odintsova, Anna.

Lokteva, Katerina Sergeevna (Katia). *Fathers and Sons*. The attractive sister of Anna Odintsova. She married Arkadii Kirsanov.

Lombroso, Caesare (1836-1909). *Resurrection* (2, 30). The Italian criminologist whom Nekhliudov studied when he was trying to understand the behavior of judges and prisoners.

Lopukhin, Ivan Vladimirovich (1756-1816). *War and Peace* (2, 5, 3). A dinner guest at Prince Nikolai Bolksonskii's in Moscow. He was a well-known Mason and mystic who lived in Moscow where he was a senator. Tolstoi erred in calling him a prince.

Lorrain. *War and Peace*. A doctor from St. Petersburg who was brought to Count Bezukhov.

Losniakova, Elena Nikolaevna, "The Office," in *A Hunter's Sketches*. The mistress of the Ananevo estate.

Lothario. *Fathers and Sons* (23). The fictional libertine from Nicholas Rowe's tragedy *The Fair Penitent*. Bazarov congratulated himself on joining the ranks of Lotharios after giving Fenichka the kiss observed by Pavel Kirsanov.

Louis, Bourda (1632-1704). *Fathers and Sons* (12). The French prophesizer whose works were translated into Russian at the beginning of the nineteenth century.

Louis XI (1423-1483). *War and Peace* (E, 2, 4). The King of France from 1461 to 1483.

Louis XIV (1638-1715). *Rudin* (5). Of recent historical figures,

Mlle. Bancourt knew only of Louis XIV, the King of France. *War and Peace* (E, 2, 1). The King of France from 1643 to 1715.

Louis XV (Quinze) (1710-1774). *Anna Karenina* (2, 6). Tushkevich was described as having something Louis Quinze in him by a group of gossips at Princess Betsy Tverskoi's. *War and Peace* (1, 1, 3). The King of France from 1715 to 1765.

Louis XVI (1754-1793). *War and Peace* (1, 1, 4). The King of France from 1765; he was beheaded in 1793.

Louis XVIII (1755-1824). *War and Peace* (E, 2, 1). The King of France from 1814 to 1824.

Louis Philippe (1773-1850). *Fathers and Sons* (7). The French king at whose court Pavel Kirsanov was supposed to have dined with the Duke of Wellington.

Lovaiskii III, Mikhail Feklich. *War and Peace*. A confederate of Denisov in a guerrilla detachment.

Lovelace. *Evgenii Onegin* (2, 30). The principal male character in Samuel Richardson's novel *Clarissa Harlowe* (1747). He was a selfish man of fashion whose sole ambition was to seduce women.

Lozinskii. *Resurrection*. A young revolutionary of Polish descent who was condemned to death.

Lucca, Paulina (1841-1908). *Anna Karenina* (7, 6). The noted opera singer whom Levin praised merely because he was trying to make conversation with the Countess Bohl.

Ludmila. *Evgenii Onegin* (1, 2). See Liudmila.

Lucia di Lammermoor. "The Steward," in *A Hunter's Sketches*. The opera by Gaetano Donizetti. Arkadii Penochkin hummed melodies from the work while he was playing cards. See Donizetti.

Luisa. *Spring Freshets*. A servant of Roselli.

Luke. *Resurrection* (1, 1). Tolstoi began the novel with four Biblical quotations, one of which is from St. Luke (6, 40).

Lukeria. "Dubrovskii." The woman who kept the night watch. "Living Holy Relics," in *A Hunter's Sketches*. A paralyzed girl who once worked for the narrator's mother but who was living in a hut in a remote village when he found her. *Virgin Soil*. A name which Nezhdanov used in his discussion with Mariana about teaching.

Lukeria L'vovna. *Evgenii Onegin* (7, 45). Tat'iana's relative who was old but still used makeup.

Lukin. *Smoke*. A deacon who was supposed to have devoured, on a wager, thirty-three herrings.

Lupikhin, Petr Petrovichk. "Hamlet of the Shchigrovskii District," in *A Hunter's Sketches*. A well-known wit who claimed he was actually being malicious and people didn't realize it.

Lupoiarov. *On the Eve*. The man who met Insarov in Moscow and visited him in Venice.

Lushchikin, Khalampy. *On the Eve*. A Moscow drunkard known as the "funnel" who confessed to Shubin that he would never amount to anything.

Lushin. "First Love." One of Zinaida Zavekina's admirers. He was supposed to be very frank in his speech.

Luther, Martin (1483-1546). *War and Peace* (E, 2, 3). The German reformer who was mentioned by Tolstoi in his interpretation of history.

Luzhin, Monsieur. *Smoke*. The young traveler with a stony face. Irina Ratmirova asked him to bring a live crab for the medium, Mr. Fox. She wanted the medium to stop the crab's movements by thought control, but he couldn't.

L'vov, Prince Arsenii. *Anna Karenina*. A diplomat married to Natal'ia Shcherbatskaia L'vova.

L'vova, Princess Natal'ia (Shcherbatskaia). *Anna Karenina*. The eldest of the daughters in the Shcherbatskii family.

M____, Prince. *Smoke*. An acquaintance of Ratmirov. They accompanied each other on a carriage ride.

Macaulay, Thomas Babington (1800-1859). *Fathers and Sons* (13). The English statesman whom Mme. Kukshina cited and Sitnikov denounced in a discussion on women. *Smoke* (3). Voroshilov called Macaulay obsolete, which surprised and perplexed Litvinov.

Mack von Leiberich, Baron Karl (1725-1828). *War and Peace* (1, 2, 1). The Austrian general who surrendered to Napoleon in 1805 when his forces were surrounded at Ulm. After his court-martial, he lost his rank and medals.

Maecenas, Gaius Cilnius (d. 8 B. C.). *On the Eve* (9). The Roman statesman who was a friend to men of letters. Shubin called Prince Chikurovov a "Maecenas of Tartar origin." *Rudin* (6). Lezhnev said that Dar'ia Lazunskaia was a female Maecenas.

Magnitskii, Mikhail Leontevich (1778-1855). *War and Peace* (2, 3, 18). A reactionary statesman who was chairman of the Committee on Army Regulations to which Prince Andrei Bolkonskii was appointed (2, 3, 5). He was also a guest at Speranskii's.

Maidanov, "First Love." A poet and admirer of Zinaida Zasekina.

Maistre, Joseph M. (1754-1821). *War and Peace* (4, 3, 19). The diplomat and writer who was the French Ambassador in St. Petersburg in 1802.

Makar Alekseevich. *War and Peace.* A name mentioned by a doctor at the wretched hospital where Denisov stayed when he was ill with typhus.

Makarin. *War and Peace.* A retired hussar who was to be a witness at the mock marriage between Natasha and Anatol'.

Makarka. *War and Peace.* Anatol' Kuragin's nickname for Makarin.

Makarov, Semen. *Resurrection.* A poor peasant on Nekhliudov's estate.

Makeev. *War and Peace.* The *fel'dsher* in the hospital where Denisov stayed. They were the only two still on their feet in a filthy room filled with dying soldiers (2, 2, 17). Also a Russian soldier in the Russians' Eighth Company doing reconnaisance raids during the French retreat from Moscow (4, 4, 8).

Makhotin. *Anna Karenina.* The owner of the horse named Gladiator in the race with Vronksii.

Maksim. "Death." *A Hunter's Sketches.* The woodsman who was hit by a falling tree. *War and Peace.* A gardener at the Rostov country estate.

Maksim Maksimovich. *A Hero of Our Time.* The officer up from the ranks who befriended Pechorin but who was treated coolly by him. Maksim gave the narrator Pechorin's diary.

Maksimich. *The Captain's Daughter.* The sergeant who was a stalwart young cossack at the Belogorsk Fortress.

Malania. "Death." *A Hunter's Sketches.* Pavel approached each visitor to the hospital with an appeal for permission to marry Malania who had long been dead. "Ermolai and the Miller's Wife," in *A Hunter's Sketches.* Arina wanted Malania to take her job as maid for Zverkova. *Resurrection.* The woman who took Katiusha Maslova's baby to a foundling home where it died.

Malasha. *War and Peace.* The six-year-old granddaughter of Andrei Svastianov.

Malbroug. *War and Peace* (1, 1, 26). The hero of a song based on the life of the Duke of Marlborough, the famed English commander John Churchill (1650-1722).

Malek-Adel'. "First Love" (14). The subject of a picture entitled "Malek-Adel' Carrying Off Matilda," which Vladimir B____ remembered hanging in his home. *Evgenii Onegin* (3, 9). The Moslem general who was a character in the novel *Matilda* (1805) by Sophie Cottin (1773-1807).

Malevskii, Count. "First Love." One of Zinaida Zasekina's admirers.

Malfilâtre, Charles Louie Clinchamp (1733-1767). *Evgenii Onegin*. The epigraph to Chapter Three is from his poem "Narcisse, ou l'île de Vénus" (1768).

Maltishcheva. *Anna Karenina*. The lady who was the subject of gossip one evening at the Princess Betsy Tverskaia's.

Malts, Carl (1792-1848). *Spring Freshets* (6). Emilio Roselli asked his sister Gemma to read Sanin a comedy by Malts, who was known for his humorous lines written in local dialects.

Mal'vina. *Evgenii Onegin* (5, 23). The name of the heroine in a a novel by that name written in 1800 by Sophie Cottin (1773-1807). *War and Peace*. A beautiful woman referred to by Nikolai Rostov when he tried to explain his love for his wife Mar'ia Rostova (née Bolkonskaia).

Malvinskii. *Anna Karenina*. A man mentioned at the Kursk train station by Koznyshev.

Malvintseva, Anna Ignatevna. *War and Peace*. The aunt of Princess Bolkonskaia in Voronezh who tried to find a bride for Nikolai when he went there to buy horses for the army.

Mamonov. See Dmitriev-Mamonov.

Mamonova. *Anna Karenina*. A lady mentioned as a profligate society member.

Mamontova, Princess Katerina Semenovna. *War and Peace*. A cousin of Pierre Bezukhov whom Pierre supported in style after the death of his father. She had expected poor treatment from Pierre but worshiped him for his kindness.

Mamontova, Princess Ol'ga. *War and Peace*. A cousin of Pierre Bezukhov whom Pierre supported after his father's death.

Mamontova, Princess Sophia. *War and Peace*. A cousin of Pierre Bezukhov whom Pierre allowed to stay in the family mansion after his father's death.

Manfred. *Rudin* (6). The hero of Byron's poem of this name (1817) who sold himself to the Prince of Darkness and is wholly without human sympathies. Lezhnev told Lipina that she wrote drama in an imitation of *Manfred*.

Manzoni, Alessandro Francesco Tommaso Antonio (1785-1873). *Evgenii Onegin* (8, 35). The Italian poet and dramatist whom Evgenii read while trying not to think of Tat'iana.

Marat, Jean Paul (1743-1793). *Smoke* (7). The French revolutionary whom Litvinov dared to condemn aloud because of the Frenchman's popularity among young members of the Russian intelligentsia. *War and Peace* (2, 2, 6). Anna Pavlovna mentioned Marat while talking about Pierre Bezukhov.

Marfa. *Resurrection*. A poor peasant at Nekhliudov's estate.

Marfa Dmitrievna. "Ovsianikov, the Freeholder," in *A Hunter's Sketches*. The lady who was insulted by Porfirii Ovchinikov.

Marfa Efimovna. *Anna Karenina*. The nurse at the Karenins' home.

Maria (spelled "Mar'ia" if the accent is on the first syllable). *Anna Karenina*. The Countess Vronskaia's maid when the old lady was informed of Anna's suicide.

Maria Bogdanovna. *War and Peace*. A midwife at Bald Hills.

Maria Borisovna, Countess. *Anna Karenina*. The woman who was jokingly suggested for the position of Minister of War at the birthday reception in the palace.

Maria Borisovna, Princess. *Anna Karenina*. Kitty's godmother.

Maria Fedorovna, Empress (1759-1828). *War and Peace* (1, 1, 1). Born the Princess of Wertemberg, she was the wife of the Emperor Pavel and the mother of Aleksandr I.

Maria Genrikhovna. *War and Peace*. The wife of the regimental doctor at the Battle of Saltonov.

Maria Il'inichna. "Petr Petrovich Karataev," in *A Hunter's Sketches*. The old landowner who opposed Petr Karataev's plans to buy a peasant girl for his mistress. The old woman's obstinacy caused him to take radical measures which led to his ruin.

Maria Ivanovna. "The Kreutzer Sonata." The woman whose eldest daughter's life was saved by the doctor Zakhar Ivanovich.

Maria Karlovna. *Resurrection*. A warden in the penal institution.

Maria Nikolaevna. *Anna Karenina*. The companion of Nikolai Levin who stayed with him until his death. *War and Peace*. The mother whose child was saved by Pierre Bezukhov during the Moscow conflagration.

Mar'ia Petrovna. *On the Eve*. When Shubin chanted "Long life to Mar'ia Petrovna," he was repeating the words of a student song based on words by N. M. Iazykov (1803-1846).

Maria Theresa (1717-1780). *War and Peace* (1, 2, 12). Archduchess of Austria, Queen of Hungary and Bohemia, and the wife of the Holy Roman Emperor Franz I.

Mar'ia Vasil'evna. "Ovsianikov, the Freeholder," in *A Hunter's Sketches*. The narrator's grandmother. *Resurrection*. The married woman with whom Nekhliudov was having an affair until he decided to marry.

Maria Viktorovna. *War and Peace*. The woman whose misfortunes were mentioned at a dinner party at Anna Pavlovna Scherer's.

Mariana. *Virgin Soil*. See Sinetskaia, Mariana Vikentevna.

Marie. *Anna Karenina*. The granddaughter of Countess Vronskaia. *War and Peace*. A name for Princess Mar'ia Bolksonskaia.

Marie Louise, Empress (1791-1847). *War and Peace* (3, 1, 2). The daughter of the Emperor of Austria. She was Napoleon I's second wife.

Mariette. *Anna Karenina*. A housemaid at the Karenins' mansion.

Marin, Sergei Nikiforovich (1775-1813). *War and Peace* (3, 2, 22). The poet and adjutant of Aleksandr I whose poem was quoted by Kutuzov on the eve of the Battle of Borodino.

Markelov, Sergei Mikhailovich (Serge). *Virgin Soil*. Valentina Sipiagina's brother, who had a small estate near the Sipiagin factory. He was a revolutionary.

Markov, Count. See Morkov, Ardakii Ivanovich.

Marks. *Smoke*. The owner of a bookstore in Baden mentioned by Potugin.

Marks, Karl. See Marx, Karl.

Marlinskii. The pseudonym of Aleksandr Aleksandrovich Bestuzhev (1797-1837). "Chertopkhanov and Nedopiushkin," in *A Hunter's Sketches*. The author whose works Pantelei Chertopkhanov knew and loved.

Marmontel, Jean François (1723-1799). *Evgenii Onegin* (5, 23). An obscure French writer whom Tat'iana read.

Mars. See Boutet, Mars.

Martin. "Kassian from Fair Strath," in *A Hunter's Sketches*. The carpenter who died.

Marusia. *Resurrection*. The prison inspector's daughter who played the piano when Nekhliudov went there on business.

Marx, Karl (1818-1883). *Resurrection* (3, 12). When Kondratev was exiled after successfully organizing a strike that led to the destruction of a factory, he kept himself busy with crafts and with reading the works of Marx.

Mary Magdalene. *Resurrection* (1, 39). In a prison church service, a priest spoke of Christ's appearing to Mary Magdalene before He entered the Kingdom of Heaven.

Masha. A dimunitive of Maria or Mar'ia. *Anna Karenina*. See Maria Nikolaevna. *The Captain's Daughter*, See Mar'ia Ivanovna Mironova. "Chertopkhanov and Nedopiuskin," in *A Hunter's*

Sketches. The gypsy who lived with Chertopkhanov. "Dubrovskii." See Troekurova, Masha. "The End of Chertopkhanov,"
in *A Hunter's Sketches*. The gypsy girl who left Chertopkhanov
because she felt weariness. "First Love." The maid in the
Petrovich household. "The Kreutzer Sonata." Pozdnyshev's
daughter. *Rudin*. The maid of Natalia who accompanied her
mistress on an early morning meeting with Rudin. *War and
Peace*. A diminutive for Princess Mar'ia Bolkonskaia.

Mashurina, Fekla. *Virgin Soil*. The thirty-year-old revolutionary
who studied obstetrics. She was in love with Nezhanov.

Maslennikov, (Mikii). *Resurrection*. The vice-governor of the city
where the prison was located. Nekhliudov had no respect
for him; yet he had to visit the official to ask for favors for
the prisoners and Katiusha Maslova.

Maslennikova, Anna Ignatevna. *Resurrection*. The vice-governor's
wife, who played up to Nekliudov during his visits.

Maslova, "Little Miss." *Anna Karenina*. The governor's nickname
in the Corps of Pages.

Maslova, Katerina Mikhailovna (Katiusha) (Liubov'). *Resurrection*.
The orphan who was seduced by Nekhliudov at his aunt's
and whom he later faced in a jury trial when she was being
tried for murder. His guilt caused him to change his life and
work for Maslova's salvation.

Maslova, Maria Ivanovna. *Resurrection*. The older of Nekhliudov's
aunts. She wanted to raise Katiusha as a servant.

Maslova, Sofia Ivanovna. *Resurrection*. Nekhliudov's aunt who wanted
to raise Katiusha as a lady.

Massalskii, K. P. (1802-1861). *Fathers and Sons* (8). The Russian writer
whose book *The Streltsy* (1832) was in Fenichka's room.

Matilda. *On the Eve*. See Malek-Adel'. *Smoke*. A princess who was
mentioned once. *War and Peace*. A name recalled by Nikolai
Rostov while in the military service at Braunau.

Matrena. *Rudin*. The sick woman whom Lipina visited.

Matrena Filimonova. *Anna Karenina*. The nurse and friend of Dolly
Oblonskaia.

Matrena Kharina (Simenikha). *Resurrection*. Katiusha Maslova's aunt
with whom the girl stayed during her pregnancy.

Matrena Kuzmichievna. *Smoke*. The leader of a religious sect of
Old Believers.

Matrena Matrevna. *War and Peace*. A gypsy girl whose sable coat
was taken by Anatol' Kuragin for Natasha Rostova when he
planned to elope with her.

Matrena Pavlovna. *Resurrection*. A maid of Nekhliudov's aunts.

Matrena Timofeevna. *War and Peace*. A maid of the Countess Rostova.

Matreshka. *War and Peace*. A canteen woman typical of the sort the average soldier thought about when he had idle time.

Matthew. *Fathers and Sons*. The name Pavel Kirsanov called Matvei Il'ich Koliazin. *Resurrection* (1, 1). Tolstoi began the novel with four Biblical quotations, two of which are from St. Matthew (18, 21) (7, 3).

Matvei. *Anna Karenina*. A valet of Prince Stepan Oblonskii.

Matvei Ivanovich. *Resurrection*. The police doctor.

Matvei Nikitich. *Resurrection*. The kind and cheerful judge of the civil court who was always late and who had obtained his position through his wife's patronage.

Maudsley, (1835-1918). *Resurrection*. The English psychiatrist whose works Nekhliudov read while trying to figure out why the condemned and those that condemn them in court are the same kind of people.

Mausfield, Amelie de. *War and Peace* (2, 2, 1). The heroine of a book by Madame de Souza which Pierre Bezukhov read while traveling. See Souza-Botelho.

Mavra, *Resurrection*. The wife of a factory worker.

Mavra Kuzminishna. *War and Peace*. The former housekeeper who suggested that the wounded stay in the Rostov mansion while the family was away. Natasha loved the idea and convinced her parents to agree.

Mavrusha. A diminutive of Mavra. *War and Peace*. A maid of the Rostovs' in St. Petersburg and in Moscow.

Max. *On the Eve* (12). The hero of the opera *Der Freischütz*, by Karl Maria von Weber (1786-1826). Max stealthily approaches Agatha in scene three of the second act. Shubin stated that he as stealthily came to Bersenev.

Mazankov. *Anna Karenina*. Recalled by Serpukhovskoi as a man whose amorous affairs ruined his career.

Medintsev. *Resurrection*. A very personable visitor at the prison where Maslova was.

Medvedev. *War and Peace*. A member of Tushin's artillery battery.

Meinen. Lizaveta Karlovna. *War and Peace*. Princess Liza Bolkonskaia's name before her marriage.

Melektrissa. "Death," in *A Hunter's Sketches*. The cook in the hospital.

Melinskii. "The Death of Ivan Il'ich." During an interval in his trial, the court members learned of the death of Ivan Golovin.

Meliukova, Pelageia Danilovna. *War and Peace*. A widow who lived near the Rostov estate.

Meliukova, Sasha. *War and Peace*. A child of the widow who lived near the Rostovs in the country.

Melmoth, Sebastian. *Evgenii Onegin* (3, 12). The hero of *Melmoth the Wanderer*, by Charles Maturin (1820), the author of many Gothic novels.

Melpomene. *Evgenii Onegin* (7, 50). The muse of tragedy in Greek mythology.

Mendelei. *Virgin Soil*. The man who was nicknamed "the Porpoise." He was a worker for the revolutionaries' cause when he was sober, but a coward when drunk.

Mendelssohn, Felix (1809-1847). *Virgin Soil*. The German composer whose "Song without Words" was played by Mariana for the Sipiagins' guests.

Menelaus. *Anna Karenina* (3, 13). The Spartan ruler and husband of Helen of Troy, who deserted him. Karenin remembered him while thinking of various deceived husbands.

Menshov, Dmitrii. *Resurrection*. The man who was framed by a village innkeeper. Nekhliudov procured his release.

Menshova. *Resurrection*. The old woman who was in prison with her son. Katiusha Maslova asked Nekhliudov to help them, and he obtained their release.

Mephistopheles. "The Queen of Spades." According to Tomskii, Hermann had the soul of Mephistopheles. *Rudin* (4). Rudin said that Pigasov feigned to be Mephistopheles.

Meriver. *War and Peace*. A French doctor in Moscow in 1811.

Merkalov, Liza. *Anna Karenina*. A member of a select St. Petersburg circle entitled "les sept merveilles du monde."

Mérope. *Spring Freshets* (7). The heroine of Voltaire's tragedy by the same name (1743). Panteleone wanted Gemma to declaim from Voltaire's work instead of from a German comedy.

Merzhkov. *Anna Karenina*. A Moscow family that gave dull balls, in Kitty's opinion.

Meshcherskii. Prince Petr Sergeevich (1779-1856). *War and Peace* (2, 5, 21). The guest at the Bolkonskiis' mansion in Moscow who was a senator during the reign of Aleksandr I.

Meshkov, Petr Alekseevich (b. 1780). *War and Peace* (3, 3, 25). A political prisoner in Moscow as the French entered. He was a governmental employee from 1793 to 1812, when he was involved in the Vereshchagin scandal. Judged guilty, he was deprived of rank and service, and put in the army. Aleksandr I forgave him in 1816. See Vereshchagin.

Mesmer, Franz Anton (1734-1815). "The Queen of Spades." The Austrian mystic who believed that he had magnetic healing power in his hands. His "mesmerism" was in the Countess's bedroom, according to Pushkin's description.

Metrov. *Anna Karenina*. A well-known St. Petersburg scholar.

Metternich, Prince Klemens Wenzel Lothar von (1773-1859). *A Gentry Nest* (40). The Austrian Chancellor and Foreign Minister of great fame. Turgenev wrote that Panshin's career undertakings almost led him to Metternich. *War and Peace* (3, 1, 1). The Foreign Minister of Austria for thirty-eight years. He was an ardent champion of the Holy Alliance.

Meyerbeer, Giocomo (1791-1864). *Smoke* (14). The composer Potugin recalled while talking with Litvinov.

Miakhaia, Princess. *Anna Karenina*. An aristocrat famed for her harsh manners.

Miakhii, Prince Bibish. *Anna Karenina*. An aristocrat who sent 12,000 rifles and two nurses to the Turkish front.

Miakhov. *Anna Karenina*. A governmental official who promised Nikolai Levin a position.

Miaskin. *Anna Karenina*. A gambler whom Levin knew.

Michael. See Mikhail.

Michaud-de-Boretur, Count Aleksandr Frantsovich (1771-1841). *War and Peace* (3, 1, 10). A military engineer who accompanied the tsar on a tour of the Drissa fortifications. Later he was sent by Kutuzov to inform the tsar about the Russian evacuation of Moscow.

Michelangelo Buonarroti (1475-1564). *Resurrection* (2, 9). When Nekhliudov decided to give up his land to his peasants, he had his bailiff call the peasants in Kuzminskoe together. One of them looked like Michelangelo's statue of Moses.

Michelet, Jules (1798-1874). *Fathers and Sons* (13). The French author of *L'Amour*, which Mme. Kukshina called a "miracle."

Micheli. *Anna Karenina*. A name thought up by Tolstoi to designate one of the writers Levin thought about when he studied how to improve his lands and the lot of his peasants (3, 29).

Midian. *War and Peace* (3, 1, 18). A Biblical figure mentioned in a prayer by Natasha. He was the son of Abraham (Gen. 25, 2).

Mignon. "Taman,'" in *A Hero of Our Time*. The heroine of Goethe's *Wilhelm Meister* (1795-1796). She went insane from unreciprocated love for Wilhelm. Pechorin thought that he had found a Mignon in the Undine who so captivated him.

Mignonette. *On the Eve.* The name Insarov whispered to Bersenev as the Bulgarian lay desperately ill.

Mikhail. *Resurrection.* A poor peasant on the Nekhliudov estate. *War and Peace.* An old servant of the Rostov family. Also Prince Mikhail was the name the valet Tikhon mentioned to Count Nikolai Bolkonskii when his master asked about whom the guests had discussed at dinner.

Nikhail Danilovich. "The Death of Ivan Il'ich." The family doctor.

Mikhail Ivanovich. *War and Peace.* The architect of lower-class background who was seated with Prince Nikolai Bolkonskii at the table, at the prince's insistence.

Mikhail Kirilich. *War and Peace.* An acquaintance of Count Il'ia Rostov at the opera.

Mikhail Mikhailovich. "The Death of Ivan Il'ich." Ivan Il'ich's partner in bridge who was upset when Ivan missed a grand slam by three tricks in the card game.

Mikhail Mitrich. *War and Peace.* A battalion commander whom Kutuzov addressed at his headquarters at Braunau.

Mikhail Nikanorych (Diadiushka). *War and Peace.* The flamboyant, distant relative of the Rostovs who lived on a small estate near the Rostovs' country place. Diadiushka accompanied the Rostovs on a hunt, and then entertained Natasha, Petia and Nikolai at his home. Natasha danced, and Diadiushka's peasant mistress served refreshments.

Mikhail Pavlovich, Grand Duke. *Spring Freshets.* Polozov remembered that a Grand Duke had ordered him to ride his horse at a trot when he was the Duke's orderly officer.

Mikhail Petrovich. *Resurrection.* A gloomy, serious member of the civil court who was always arguing with his wife.

Mikhail Sidorich. *War and Peace.* A name mentioned by Semen Chakmar while hunting with the Rostovs.

Mikhailevich. *A Gentry Nest.* A schoolmate of Fedor Lavretskii who visited Fedor at his country estate and discussed current political issues with him.

Mikhailo. *War and Peace.* The younger brother of Platon Karataev.

Mikhailo Ivanovich. "Two Landowners," in *A Hunter's Sketches.* The name Khvalynskii pronounced "Mikhal Vanych."

Mikhailo Savel'ich (Fog). "Raspberry Spring," in *A Hunter's Sketches.* A former butler who fished with Stepushka.

Mikhailov. *Anna Karenina*. A Russian artist living abroad, and an acquaintance of Anna and Vronskii.

Mikheevskii, Fedor. "Bezhin Meadow," in *A Hunter's Sketches*. The man with whom Il'iusha spent the night in a paper mill.

Mikhei. "Tat'iana Borisovna and Her Nephew," in *A Hunter's Sketches*. Tat'iana's coachman.

Mikheich. *Virgin Soil*. The bartender in the shop where Nezhdanov became drunk, thus losing the respect of his fellow revolutionaries.

Mikhelson, General Ivan Ivanovich (1740-1807). *The Captain's Daughter*. The leader of the Russian forces pursuing Pugachev. *War and Peace* (1, 1, 23). Count Nikolai Bolkonskii mentioned the general whose army helped vanquish Pugachev and who was head of Russian troops on the Western border in 1805.

Mikhnev. *Smoke*. A name mentioned in a conversation between Bambaev and Madame Sukhanchikova.

Mikholai Mikholaich. "The Steward," in *A Hunter's Sketches*. The middleman in the boundary settlement with Sofron Iakovlich.

Mikishin. *Resurrection*. A well-known lawyer.

Mikita. "Dubrovskii." Troekurov's blacksmith.

Mikolka. *War and Peace* (2, 2, 15). A folk hero who was the subject of tales told by soldiers around a campfire.

Milanovskii. *Smoke*. A society member who was supposed to have snored when he had been put to sleep by a medium.

Mileev. *Anna Karenina*. The person a certain Laura was living with.

Mill, John Stuart (1806-1873). *Anna Karenina*. The English philosopher of the utilitarian school who was mentioned in a newspaper article Oblonskii read.

Miller. "The Death of Ivan Il'ich." The man who lost his position to Zakhar Ivanovich.

Miloradovich, Mikhail Andreevich (1771-1825). *War and Peace* (1, 3, 11). The Russian general who participated in the Wars of 1805 and 1812. He later became Governor-General of St. Petersburg and was mortally wounded in the Decembrists' uprising of 1825.

Mimi, Mlle. "Dubrovskii." Mar'ia Troekurova's teacher who was the mother of a son by Troekurov.

Minchen. "Hamlet of the Shchigrovskii District," in *A Hunter's Sketches*. Linchen's sister.

Miniaich. "Khor' and Kalinych," in *A Hunter's Sketches*. The guard of the abandoned countinghouse.

Minikh, Count. *The Captain's Daughter*. The aristocrat under whom Andrei Petrovich Grinev served.

Mironov. *War and Peace*. A cadet who ducked every time a cannonball flew over him during the fighting near Enns.

Mironov, Ivan Kuzmich. *The Captain's Daughter*. The commandant of the Belozorsk Fortress and the father of Masha. He was killed during the raid by Pugachev.

Mironova, Maria Ivanovna (Masha). *The Captain's Daughter*. The daughter of the captain who fell in love with Grinev and saved his life when he had been unjustly accused of treason.

Mironova, Vasilisa Egorovna. *The Captain's Daughter*. The commandant's wife who was killed in the Pugachev uprising.

Misha. *War and Peace*. A serving boy at the Rostov estate.

Mishka. *Anna Karenina*. A laborer on Levin's estate. "Two Landowners," in *A Hunter's Sketches*. Stegunov's servant. *War and Peace*. A page left at the Rostov mansion during the French occupation.

Missy. *Resurrection*. See Maria Korchagina.

Mitenka. *War and Peace*. Count Rostov's name for Dmitrii Vasil'evich, his overseer.

Mitia (a diminutive for Dmitrii [Dimitry]). *Anna Karenina*. Kitty's infant son. "The Death of Ivan Il'ich." Ivan's brother. "Dubrovskii." The boy who was caught taking the ring from the hollow of the oak tree. *Fathers and Sons*. The infant son of Nikolai and Fenichka, born out of wedlock. "Ovsiannikov, the Freeholder," in *A Hunter's Sketches*. Ovsiannikov's nephew who was always causing trouble in his efforts to do good deeds.

Mitin. *Resurrection*. The revolutionary who was arrested. Shustova thought his arrest was her fault, but it was not.

Mitinka. *Resurrection*. Nekhliudov's father's illegitimate peasant son.

Mitiukha. *Anna Karenina*. The peasant Fedor's name for the innkeeper Kirilov. *Fathers and Sons*. The coachman for Nikolai Kursanov.

Mitka. "Bela," in *A Hero of Our Time*. Pechorin's orderly. *War and Peace*. A groom of Count Il'ia Rostov. Also a coachman and balalaika player for Uncle Mikhail Nikanorych.

Mitrich, Ivan. *War and Peace*. A name mentioned as a typical soldier in any battle.

Mitrodora. "Chertopkhanov and Nedopiuskin," in *A Hunter's Sketches*. The sister of Tikhon.

Mitrofan. "Raspberry Spring," in *A Hunter's Sketches*. A gardener.

Mochalov, P. S. (1800-1848). *A Gentry Nest* (12). A Russian actor who was famous for playing Hamlet. "Petr Petrovich Karataev," in *A Hunter's Sketches*. Petr asked the narrator if he had seen Mochalov as Hamlet.

Möena. *Evgenii Onegin* (1, 17). The heroine of V. A. Ozerov's tragedy *Fingal* (1805).

Molière (1622-1673). *War and Peace* (2, 1, 6). The name taken by the French actor and dramatist Jean Baptiste Poquelin.

Moller, Fedor Antonovich (1812-1874). *Virgin Soil* (17). The Russian artist whose painting "The Kiss" hung in Golushkin's house.

Moloch. *Virgin Soil* (32). The God of the Ammonites (2nd Kings, 23, 10) who symbolizes any influence which demands from anyone the sacrifice of what he holds most dear.

Molodenkov, Fedka. *Resurrection*. The sweetheart of the red-haired cell mate of Maslova.

Monaco, Principessa di. *Spring Freshets* (38). When Sanin appeared in Polozova's drawing room, Polozova sent away the secretary of the principessa.

Montgolfier. "The Queen of Spades." The name of the French brothers who flew their fifty-seven-foot balloon in Paris in 1783.

Montmorency. *War and Peace* (1, 1, 1). The French family dating from the tenth century to which the Vicomte de Mortemart was related.

Montesquieu, Baron de La Brède et de. Charles de Secondat (1689-1755). *War and Peace* (2, 3, 5). The French philosopher and man of letters who was noted for his *Lettres Persanes* (1721) which criticized the society of the time.

Morand, Louis Charles (1771-1835). *War and Peace* (3, 2, 27). The French general who participated in many Napoleonic wars and was wounded at Borodino. In that engagement, he commanded a division with the specific instructions from Napoleon to support the troops under the command of the Emperor's stepson, Beauharnais.

Mordvinskii. *Anna Karenina*. A member of the board of directors where Stepan Oblonskii wanted a position.

Moreau, Mlle. *A Gentry Nest*. The French governess of Liza Kalitina in her childhood.

Moreau, Jean Victor Marie (1763-1813). *War and Peace* (1, 1, 24). In 1800, Moreau opposed Napoleon and was exiled from France. He went to America. In 1813, he was called to Europe to fight Napoleon and was mortally wounded in a battle near Dresden.

Morel. *War and Peace*. An orderly for Captain Ramballe in Moscow.

Morio, Abbé. *War and Peace* (1, 1, 2). A guest at Anna Pavlovna Scherer's soiree. When Tolstoi mentioned Morio's plan for eternal peace, he referred to a plan created by the Abbot Piatolii, who was the prototype of Abbot Morio. Piatolii's plan caused great interest in St. Petersburg because Russia was to play a major role in creating world peace.

Morkov, Arkadii Ivanovich (1747-1827). *War and Peace* (1, 3, 9). The Russian diplomat who served in Paris (1801-1803) but was recalled because of his sharp behavior toward Napoleon.

Morpheus. *Evgenii Onegin* (8, 28). The god of sleep in Greek mythology. Onegin thought only of Tat'iana before sleep came.

Mortemort, Vicomte de. *War and Peace* (1, 1, 1). An aristocrat whom Anna Pavlovna called a "good" émigré. See Montmorency.

Mortier, Édouard Adolphe Casimir Joseph, Duke of Trevino (1768-1835). *War and Peace* (1, 2, 9). The French Marshal who participated in the campaigns during the French Revolution and during Napoleon's reign. In 1812, he commanded a squadron.

Moses. *Anna Karenina* (5, 6). The legendary founder of the Jewish religion. He was mentioned in the prayer in Kitty and Levin's wedding ceremony in the Russian Orthodox Church. *Resurrection* (3, 12). The peasant prisoner Nabatov never cared about the creation of the universe whether it was from Darwin or from Moses. He was content without explanation. *War and Peace* (3, 1, 18). Natasha mentioned the Biblical figure in a prayer.

Moshel, Leiba. "End of Chertopkhanov," in *A Hunter's Sketches*. The Jew who sold Pantelei a magnificent horse for saving him from a mob.

Mouton-Duvernet, Baron Regis Bartelemy (1779-1816). *War and Peace* (4, 2, 18). The French general who urged Napoleon to return to France by the nearest familiar road after the French retreat from Moscow. During the reign of Louis XVIII, Mouton was executed.

Mozart, Wolfgang Amadeus (1756-1791). *Fathers and Sons* (16). Katia played Mozart's "Sonata Fantasia in C Minor" for

Arkadii when they first met. *A Gentry Nest* (40). "La ci darem" duet is from his *Don Giovanni* (1787). *Smoke* (14). Potugin recalled the Austrian composer while talking with Litvinov. *Virgin Soil* (2). Paklin referred to Mozart in conversation with Ostrodumov.

Mucius, Scaevola. See Scaevola Mucius.

Mudrov, Matvei Iakovlevich (1772-1831), *War and Peace* (3, 1, 16). A well-known doctor in Moscow who was a professor of medicine in the university. Tolstoi made him one of the doctors for Natasha after her scandalous affair with Anatol' Kuragin.

Muffel, Baron. *Rudin*. An aristocrat from St. Petersburg.

Müller, Johannes (1752-1809). *Smoke* (4). The German historian and political writer mentioned by Voroshilov when he finally managed to interrupt Madame Sukhanchikova.

Muller, Zoia Nikitishna (Zoe). *On the Eve*. The Russian-German girl who had been engaged by Anna Vasil'evna as a companion for her daughter, but Anna Vasil'evna kept the girl busy as her own personal servant. See Stakhova, Anna Vasil'evna.

Murat, Carolina (1782-1839). *War and Peace* (3, 1, 4). The younger sister of Napoleon and wife of Murat, the King of Naples.

Murat, Joachim, King of Naples (1767-1815). *War and Peace* (1, 2, 10). The French marshal who was one of Napoleon's closest generals. In 1805 he commanded a French cavalry unit. In 1812 he was in charge of all French cavalry. He was King of Naples from 1810 to 1815.

Mylov, Pavel Lukich. "The Country Doctor," in *A Hunter's Sketches*. The judge at whose house the doctor received the note that requested that he come to see a widow's dying daughter.

N____. *Evgenii Onegin*. Prince N____ was Tat'iana's husband and an old friend of Onegin. *A Gentry Nest*. Mikhalevich tutored a Count N____. "Lebedian'," in *A Hunter's Sketches*. Prince N____ was a local potentate and gambler. "Maksim Maksimich," in *A Hero of Our Time*. Pechorin spent the night in Vladikavkaz with a colonel N____.

N____ N____. *Rudin*. The Minister N____ N____ had a most remarkable dog, according to Lazunskaia. *War and Peace*. N____ N____ was the lover of Elena Bezukhova whom she decided to marry while Pierre was away at Borodin.

Nabatov. *Resurrection.* A peasant and political prisoner who grew up believing in the fundamentals of revolution. He spent his life trying to enlighten people, always believing in man's essential goodness.

Nadenka. *Anna Karenina.* The niece of Lidia Ivanovna who was a friend of Serezha Karenin.

Nakhimov, Akim N. (1783-1815). "Khor' and Kalinych," in *A Hunter's Sketches.* A Russian poet and writer of satirical epigrams.

Napoleon I (1769-1821). *Evgenii Onegin* (2, 14). Pushkin wrote that we all aspire to be Napoleons. *Fathers and Sons* (21). When Vasilii Bazarov noted that players took great risks in a game of whist, his son mentioned that "It was the Napoleonic rule!" "Princess Mary," in *A Hero of Our Time.* After trying to see Vera, Pechorin slept the sleep of Napoleon after Waterloo. "The Queen of Spades." Tomskii said that Hermann had a profile of Napoleon. *Rudin* (5). Napoleon was one of the historical names which Mlle. Bancourt knew. "Tat'iana Borisovna and Her Nephew," in *A Hunter's Sketches.* Policarp taught his grandson to hate Napoleon. *War and Peace.* The Emperor of France from 1799 to 1815, who invaded Russia and occupied Moscow before being forced to retreat. He died in exile on the island of St. Helena.

Napoleon II, Francis Charles Joseph, The King of Rome (1811-1832). *War and Peace* (3, 2, 26). The son of Napoleon I and Marie Louise of Austria. In 1814, Napoleon abdicated his throne in his son's favor.

Napoleon III, Louis (1808-1873). *Fathers and Sons* (20). Vasilli Bazarov discussed the French ruler as he walked around the table where his son and Arkadii were eating. *Smoke* (4). He was mentioned by Madame Sukhanchikova in a conversation with Voroshilov. *Virgin Soil* (7). Kallomeitsev considered him to be an outstanding fellow. *War and Peace* (E, 2, 4). Tolstoi referred to the French ruler (1852-1870) in his interpretation of history.

Narkizov, Kosenkin. "The Office," in *A Hunter's Sketches.* A clerk.

Narrator. *A Hero of Our Time.* Maksim Maksimich told the narrator, an educated officer, the story of Pechorin and gave the narrator Pechorin's diary. The narrator published it. *A Hunter's Sketches.* It is assumed that the narrator was Turgenev himself.

Narumov. "The Queen of Spades." The Officer of the Guards in whose home Tomskii told the story of the three cards that so aroused the imagination of Hermann.

Naryshkin, Aleksandr L'vovich (1760-1826). *War and Peace* (2, 1, 3). The aristocrat who was the director of the imperial theaters from 1799 to 1819.

Naryshkina, Maria Antonovna (1779-1854). *War and Peace* (2, 3, 16). A member of a famous noble family who was the wife of D. L. Naryshkin and the mistress of Aleksandr I.

Naryshkina, Natal'ia Kirilovna (1651-1694). *Spring Freshets* (38). The second wife of Tsar Aleksei Mikhailovich and the mother of Petr I. Polozova compared herself with the former tsarina.

Nash, Thomas (1567-1601). *Smoke* (4). The English pamphletist and dramatist who was recalled by Voroshilov when he was finally able to interrupt Madame Sukhanchikov.

Nastas'ia Ivanovna. *War and Peace.* A woman who acted like a buffoon in the Rostov household.

Nast'ia. The diminutive of Anastas'ia. *Anna Karenina.* The sister-in-law of Sviazhskii who Levin knew was an eligible mate. *A Gentry Nest.* Liza's maid. "The Fatalist," in *A Hero of Our Time.* The daughter of the sergeant where Pechorin lived.

Natal'ia Nikitishna. *Smoke.* An upper-class matron who conversed with the Princess Osinina at a ball.

Natalie. A diminutive for Natal'ia.

Natal'ka. "Two Landowners," in *A Hunter's Sketches.* The daughter of the woman whose hens went into the forbidden garden.

Natasha. A diminutive for Natal'ia. *Resurrection.* See Rogozhinskaia, Natal'ia Ivanovna. *War and Peace.* See Rostova, Natal'ia Il'-inicha.

Nazar Tarasych. "The Office," in *A Hunter's Sketches.* The person to whom the narrator was advised to go for tea when he walked into the remote office in the country. When the narrator offered money, tea was provided in the office itself.

Nazarov. "Bezhin Meadow," in *A Hunter's Sketches.* The overseer who advised the boys to sleep in the paper mill so they could start work early in the morning.

Nebuchadnezzar (6th Cent. B. C.). *Virgin Soil.* The ancient Babylonian ruler of whom Mariana was reminded when she heard about the Subochevs' penchant for living in the past.

Necker. See Staël, de.

Nedopiuskin. "Chertopkhanov and Nedopiuskin," in *A Hunter's Sketches*. Tikhon's father, who was poor and persecuted by fate.

Nedopiuskin, Tikhon Ivanych. "Chertopkhanov and Nedopiuskin," in *A Hunter's Sketches*. The weakling who was saved from embarrassment by Chertophkanov, and who became the latter's listener and living companion. "The End of Chertophkanov," in *A Hunter's Sketches*. Nedopiuskin died, thus leaving Chertophkanov with a void in his life.

Negulina Ustinia, *The Captain's Daughter*. The woman who quarreled with the corporal over a tub of hot water.

Nekhliudov, Dmitrii Ivanich (Mitinka). *Resurrection*. The Prince whose life was changed when he confronted a woman he had wronged. He spent the rest of his life trying to correct his wrongdoing.

Nekhliudova, Elena. *Resurrection*. Nekhliudov's deceased mother.

Nekhliudova, Natasha. *Resurrection*. The name of Nekhliudov's sister before she married Rogozhinskii. See Rogozhinskaia, Natal'ia.

Neledinskaia, Iulia. *Anna Karenina*. A woman supposedly cured by Landau.

Nelly. *Fathers and Sons*. The Princess R___ was referred to as Nelly by Pavel after his duel with Bazarov.

Nepomniashchii. *Resurrection*. The prisoner who was a tramp and who was flogged with Vasil'ev for agreeing with him.

Neptune. *Virgin Soil* (14). The Roman god of the sea whom Sipiagin brought to mind when he thought of himself.

Neptunova, Liza. *Anna Karenina*. A profligate society member.

Nereid. *Evgenii Onegin* (8, 4). Any sea nymph in Greek mythology. Onegin heard one in the waves of the sea.

Nero, C. Caludius (54-68). "Princess Mary," in *A Hero of Our Time*. Pechorin stated that poets who called women angels also dubbed Nero a demi-god.

Nesvitskii. *War and Peace*. A staff-officer comrade of Prince Andrei Bolkonskii at Braunau.

Nevedovskii. *Anna Karenina*. A former university professor who was elected the Marshal of Nobility in Kashin province.

Neverov. *Resurrection*. A revolutionist who was a poet at heart and who committed suicide while imprisoned in an insane asylum with Petlin.

Neverovskii, Dmitrii Petrovich (1771-1813). *War and Peace* (3, 2, 1).

The Russian divisional commander wounded near Leipzig. Tolstoi mentioned him as the officer who turned down Barclay's battle plan for Smolensk because he detested the man.

Newton, Sir Isaac (1642-1727), *Rudin* (3). The English scientist whom Rudin admired. *War and Peace* (E, 2, 11). Tolstoi cited Newton in a discussion on free will. If one freely moving body existed, then Newton's laws would cease to exist. If there is a single action due to free will, then not a single historical law is valid.

Ney, Michel (1769-1815). *War and Peace* (3, 2, 27). The French marshal who participated in many Napoleonic wars and was granted the title of the King of Moscow in 1812.

Nezhdanov, Aleksei Dmitrievich (Alesha). *Virgin Soil*. The handsome illegitimate son of an aristocrat who became disillusioned with revolutionary activity and committed suicide.

Niedermeyer, Louis (1802-1861). *On the Eve* (15). The French composer of "Le Lac," which Zoia sang during the outing at Tsaritsino.

Nikifor Il'ich. "Freeholder Ovsianikov," in *A Hunter's Sketches*. The arbitrator who gathered the peasants for the land division.

Nikiforov. *Resurrection*. The councillor who was on Maslova's jury.

Nikita. *War and Peace*. An old footman at the Rostov estate.

Nikita Ivanich. *War and Peace*. The husband of the woman with whom Nikolai Rostov flirted in Voronezh when he went there to buy horses for the army.

Nikiteno. *Resurrection*. A name mentioned by Charskaia as a typical name for the fools who work in the senate.

Nikitin. *Resurrection*. The severe and formal jurist who voted down Maslova's appeal.

Nikitin, Filipp. *Anna Karenia*. An old civil servant and office colleague of Stepan Oblonskii.

Nikitinko. *War and Peace*. The soldier ahead of Nikolai Rostov when his horse was shot from under him in battle near Schöngraben.

Nilolaeva. *Anna Karenina*. A guest at Kitty's wedding.

Nikolaevich. "The Death of Ivan Il'ich." The doctor who treated Ivan Il'ich Golovin.

Nikolai. *War and Peace*. See Rostov, Count Nikolai Il'ich.

Nikolai I (1796-1855). *Resurrection* (3, 24). Nekhliudov dined at the

magnificent table of a former lady-in-waiting from the court
of Nikolai, the tsar from 1825 to 1855.

Nikolai, Saint. *Fathers and Sons* (8). The Russian saint known as the
"miracle worker" whose image was in the icon in Fenichka's
room. "First Love." Vladimir Petrovich remembered Saint
Nikolai's day as the date he left town for the villa near
Kaluga. *War and Peace* (4, 1, 12). The Russian saint mentioned
in a prayer by Platon Karataev.

Nikolai Ivanich. "The Singers," in *A Hunter's Sketches*. The shrewd
saloon owner.

Nikolai Ivanovich. *War and Peace*. The general who danced the *trepak*
at Echkino when General Kikin gave a party.

Nikolenka. A diminutive for Nikolai. *Anna Karenina*. Dolly and Stepan
Oblonskii's small boy. *War and Peace*. See N. Bolkonskii.

Nikolev, Nikolai Petrovich (1758-1815). *War and Peace* (2, 1, 3). The
poet who wrote the verses quoted in honor of Bagration at
the party given for the general by Count Il'ia Rostov.

Nikolushka. A diminutive for Nikolai. *War and Peace*. See N. Bolkonskii.

Nikulin. *War and Peace*. A family whose yard Pierre Bezukhov crossed
on his way to save a child from a fire.

Nillson, Christina (b. 1843). *Anna Karenina* (2, 4). The Swedish
soprano who sang in the Paris Opera and toured Russia.

Nina. *Evgenii Onegin*. Triquet substituted the name Nina for Tat'iana
in his stanza for her.

Nirmatskii. "First Love." A retired captain and admirer of Zinaida.

Noah. *Anna Karenina* (1, 24). Levin remembered that when his brother
Nikolai went on a fast he was teased and called Noah, after
the Biblical figure.

Nogent, Saint Laurens (1814-1871). *Virgin Soil* (19). A French
lawyer during the reign of Napoleon III. Fomushka Subochev called him a bandit and an example of the malicious
nature of the present-day French people.

Nordston, Countess Mary. *Anna Karenina*. A friend of Kitty's who
was very nervous and enjoyed teasing Levin.

Nordston, Count Vasilii. *Anna Karenina*. The obedient husband of
Countess Nordston.

Nostit, Gregorii Ivanovich (d. 1838). *War and Peace* (1, 2, 3). The
Austrian general who entered Russian service in 1807 and
became an adjutant general.

Novalis, Fredrich Leopold von Hardenberg (1772-1801). *Rudin.*
The pseudonym of von Hardenberg, who was a German
Romantic poet and novelist known for his mystical poems.
Novodvorov. *Resurrection.* A political prisoner who saw good in no
man and who believed that the masses worship power only.
Novosiltsev, Nikolai Nikolaevich (1761-1836). *War and Peace* (1, 1, 1).
Aleksandr I's minister who sent dispatches about Napoleon
to St. Petersburg from France.

O____. *Smoke.* General O____ was a brilliant but rude officer. *War
and Peace.* Brother O____ was a fellow Mason of Pierre
Bezukhov when he was studying to be a Mason.
Oberon. *A Gentry Nest* (4). Gedeonovskii was not able to find the
overture to the opera *Oberon*, by Karl Maria von Weber
(1786-1826). *On the Eve* (1). The legendary magician whom
Bersenev recalled when speaking of love in springtime. He
was somewhat embarrassed by his own words.
Oblonskaia, Dar'ia Aleksandrovna (Dolly). *Anna Karenina.* Stepan
Oblonskii's deceived wife, whom Anna Karenina consoled
and reunited with her husband. She was the sister of Kitty
and Natal'ia Shcherbatskaia.
Oblonskii, Prince Petr. *Anna Karenina.* A sixty-year-old relative of
Stepan Oblonskii. He saved his "soul" by going regularly to
Paris.
Oblonskii, Prince Stepan Arkad'evich (Stiva). *Anna Karenina.* The
brother of Anna Karenina. He was noted for his extravagance
and joie de vivre. His marriage problems brought his sister
to Moscow, where she met Vronskii.
Obolenskii, Fedia. *War and Peace.* A friend of Petia Rostov. When he
joined the hussars, Petia also wanted to enter the military
service.
Obrenovich, Prince Mikhail III (1823-1868). *Virgin Soil* (5). A
Serbian prince whom Kallomeitsev claimed as a friend. He
was killed in 1856 by a member of a rival princely family,
the Karageorgeviches.
Obrenovich, Prince Milan (1854-1901). *Anna Karenina* (8, 5). After
ruling under the liberal regent Ristich from 1872 to 1882,
Milan proclaimed himself King of Serbia in 1882. When
Koznyshev met Vronskii on the train heading for the Southern front, he offered to write to either Milan or Ristich on
behalf of his acquaintance. Vronskii, saddened by the death
of Anna, refused the offer.

Odintsova, Anna Sergeevna. *Fathers and Sons.* The attractive, aloof twenty-nine-year old widow who refused Bazarov's love but visited his deathbed.

Odrý, Jacques Charles (1781-1853). *A Gentry Nest* (15). The French actor who caused Varvara Lavretskaia to laugh when he did slapstick comedy.

Odyntsova, Kitty. *War and Peace.* The acquaintance of the Bolkonskiis who married an old man.

Offenbach, Jacques (1819-1880). *Anna Karenina* (3, 21). The French operetta composer whose music was played during a party for Vronskii's regiment at Colonel Denin's country estate.

Ogarkova, Nastas'ia Karpovna. *A Gentry Nest.* A widowed companion of Marfa Pestel'.

Okhotin. *Resurrection.* A thief who was a humorous prisoner.

Oldenburg, Duke Peter Freidrich Ludwig (1755-1825). *War and Peace* (2, 5, 3). The father-in-law of Aleksandr I's sister the Grand Duchess Ekaterina Pavlovna.

Old Woman. "Taman,'" in *A Hero of Our Time.* The old woman who pretended to be deaf but heard enough to defend the blind boy from Pechorin.

Ol'ga (Ol'ia). *Evgenii Onegin.* See Larina, Ol'ga. "My Neighbor Radilov," in *A Hunter's Sketches.* The sister of Radilov's deceased wife. Law forbade them to marry; so they ran off together, abandoning his old mother.

Omir. *Evgenii Onegin* (5, 36). Homer is Omir in old poetic Russian.

Onatas (5th Cent. B. C.) *Smoke* (3). An ancient Greek sculptor recalled by Voroshilov in a conversation with Litvinov.

Onegin, Evgenii. *Evgenii Onegin.* The hero of Pushkin's novel in verse form who has Byronic characteristics but escapes the true Byronic mold. To avoid accusations of self-description, Pushkin included himself as one of Onegin's friends in the work. Onegin represented a typical young dandy of the time. He scorned a maiden's love, only to find out later that he wanted her affection desperately.

Onisim. "Death," in *A Hunter's Sketches.* A friend of Maksim.

Onufrich, Dmitrii. *War and Peace.* The Bezukhov family lawyer.

Orłassanov, "Hamlet of the Shchigrovskii District," in *A Hunter's Sketches.* The man who had run for the position of Marshal of Nobility.

Orleans, Duc Louie Phillippe Joseph d' (1747-1793). "The Queen of Spades." The man to whom the Countess Anna Fedotovna lost a great sum of money playing faro.

Orlov, Count Aleksei Grigorevich (1737-1807). *War and Peace* (1, 1, 1). The man noted for his participation in the placing of Ekaterina II on the throne. He was also one of her lovers.

Orlov-Chesmenskii, Count Aleksei Gregor'evich (1737-1807). "Ovsianikov, the Freeholder," in *A Hunter's Sketches*. A grandee in the time of Ekaterina II. He loved hunting and had a brilliant military career.

Orlov-Denisov, Count Vasilii Vasil'evich (1775-1843). *War and Peace* (4, 2, 6). During Napoleon's retreat, Count Orlov-Denisov ordered General Grekov to return from an expedition which would have captured Murat if it had continued.

Orpheus. *Rudin* (2). The son of Apollo and Callipe. His music moved not only hearts but rocks as well. Dar'ia Lasunskaia mentioned that Orpheus calmed wild animals with music when she asked Konstantin Pandalevskii to play an étude.

Osinin, Prince Pavel Vasil'evich. *Smoke*. The descendant of an ancient family who lived beneath the standard he was used to.

Osinina, Princess Cleopatrinka. *Smoke*. A daughter of Prince Osinin who was not so vivacious as her sister Viktorinka.

Osinina, Princess Praskovia Danilovna. *Smoke*. Pavel's wife, who was a former maid-of-honor at court.

Osinina, Princess Irina Pavlovna. *Smoke*. See Ratmirova, Irina.

Osinina, Princess Victorinka. *Smoke*. The daughter of Prince Osinin. She was attractive but spoke with a lisp.

Osten. *Resurrection*. A diplomat and a friend of the Korshagins.

Ostermann-Tolstoi, Aleksandr Ivanovich (1770-1857). *War and Peace* (2, 2, 9). A Russian general who participated in the Wars of 1805 and 1812. He commanded the Fourth Army Corps of the First Western Army. He was mentioned by Bilibin in a letter to Prince Andrei Bolkonskii.

Ostrodumov, Pimen. *Virgin Soil*. The young man who distributed letters among the members of the revolutionary group to which Nezhdanov belonged.

Ostrovskii, Aleksandr Nikolaevich (1823-1886). *Virgin Soil* (3). The Russian playwright whose *Stick to Your Station* (1853) was given in St. Petersburg. Sipiagin and Nezhdanov met at a performance of the play.

Othello. "First Love" (17). The hero of the tragedy by Shakespeare (1604). Othello, the Moor, killed Desdemona, because of unfounded jealousy. Realizing his error, he then killed himself. Vladimir B____ felt that he was as jealous of Zinaida Zasekina as Othello was of his beloved.

Otrep'ev, Gregorii Bogdanovich (Grishka). *The Captain's Daughter.* Known as the "False Dmitrii" in history, he pretended to be the son of Tsar Ivan IV. When captured, he was beheaded and burned, and his ashes were shot from a cannon.

Oudinot, Charles Nicolas, Duke of Reggio (1767-1847). *War and Peace* (2, 2, 15). The Marshal of France who commanded a corps of grenadiers in 1805.

Ovchinikov, Porfirii. "Ovsianikov, the Freeholder," in *A Hunter's Sketches.* A land manager.

Ovid (Publius Ovidius Naso) (43 B. C.-17 A. D.). *Evgenii Onegin* (1, 8). The Roman poet and author of *Metamorphoses.* Onegin occupied himself with art of soft passion which Ovid sang about.

Ovsianikov, Luka Petrovich. "Ovsianikov, the Freeholder," in *A Hunter's Sketches.* A man of tradition and cordial manners who was a successful farmer. "My Neighbor Radilov," in *A Hunter's Sketches.* A neighbor of Radilov's who was the hero of the narrator's next tale.

Ovsianikov, Petr. "Ovsianikov, the Freeholder," in *A Hunter's Sketches.* Luka's father, who had petitioned the courts because his land had been taken by a neighboring gentleman. The neighbor flogged him and kept the land.

Ovsianikova, Tat'iana Il'inichna. "Ovsianikov, the Freeholder," in *A Hunter's Sketches.* Ovsianikov's wife.

Ozerov, Vladislav Aleksandrovich (1769-1816). *Evgenii Onegin* (1. 18). The Russian author who, Pushkin wrote, shared tears and plaudits with the young actress Katerina Semenov. Ozerov wrote the classical tragedies in which Semenova acted.

P____. *Spring Freshets.* Herr P____ was the Wiesbaden critic who stuck his head in the door of Polozova's opera box and was shooed away.

Pachette, Princess. *Smoke.* The wife of a provincial governor.

Pahlen, Count Fedor Petrovich von (1780-1863). *War and Peace* (1, 1, 27) The Russian diplomat who did service in America, Brazil and Germany. He was sent by Alexandr I to America to persuade Moreau to come to Russia and enter Russian service.

Pakhomovna. "Dubrovskii." The postmaster's wife.

Paklin, Sila Samsonich. *Virgin Soil*. A small, hunched man noted for his cynical vivacity and revolutionary activities.

Palashka. A diminutive for Pelageia. *A Gentry Nest*. Mar'ia Dmitrievna Kalitina's hairdresser. *The Captain's Daughter*. The laundry maid seduced by Beaupré.

Palmerston, Henry George Temple (1784-1865). *On the Eve* (34). The English Minister of the Interior whom Lupoiarov cited when he visited Insarov in Venice.

Pandalevskii, Konstantin Diomidych. *Rudin*. A bright, young Russian who lived as Dar'ia Lasunskaia's adopted son. He informed the woman of her daughter Natal'ia's infatuation with Rudin.

Panin. *War and Peace* (2, 3, 20). An aristocratic family mentioned in a description of Berg's dinner party.

Panshin, Vladimir Nikolaich. *A Gentry Nest*. A handsome, petty official on duty from St. Petersburg who captivated the Larin household as well as Varvara Lavretskaia after her return from abroad.

Pantelei. See Chertopkhanov, Pantelei.

Panteleone. See Cippatola, Panteleone.

Paramanov, Stepan. *The Captain's Daughter*. The barber who treated Grinev after his duel with Shvabrin over Mar'ia Mironova.

Parasha. "Two Landowners," in *A Hunter's Sketches*. Ermil's wife.

Parcae. *A Gentry Nest* (11). The Latin name of the Fates who carried out the will of the gods. When Fedor Lavretskii was a small boy, he was under the supervision of three women who carried out their duties like the Parcae.

Parfan. *Anna Karenina*. A serf who died at Levin's estate.

Paris. *Evgenii Onegin* (5, 37). Pushkin ironically compared Petushkov with Paris, the legendary Greek hero. *War and Peace* (1, 2, 4). Paris was the son of Priam, King of Troy, and Hecuba; his abduction of Helen caused the siege of Troy.

Parmenov, Ivan. *Anna Karenina*. A laborer at Levin's estate.

Parny, Evariste Désiré Desforges, Chevalier de (1753-1814). *Evgenii Onegin* (3, 29). The French poet who is known for his love poems. Pushkin wrote that Parny was out of fashion in Onegin's time.

Paromoshka. "Dubrovskii." Troekurov's kennel attendant who defended his master's treatment of his serfs.

Paskudin, Count. *Anna Karenina*. The person mentioned by Karenin as a man whose wife was unfaithful.

Patti, Adelina Juana Maria (1843-1919). *Smoke* (15). The famous singer who was mentioned by a pretentious guest at Irina Ratmirova's party. *Spring Freshets* (43). Sanin had a ticket to hear Patti sing in St. Petersburg but left the city in search of Gemma Roselli.

Patti, Carlotta (1840-1889). *Anna Karenina* (5, 32). The singer who performed the night Anna Karenina dared to face society by attending the opera. Anna was snubbed so badly by former acquaintances that she left the performance mortified.

Paul. See Pavel. *Rudin* (7). *Paul and Virginia* was the book by Bernardin de St. Pierre which Lezhnev mentioned. *Anna Karenina.* A figure mentioned by an English governess at Anna's.

Paul, Saint. *War and Peace* (2, 2, 10). The Biblical apostle whose image was in the icon that greeted Pierre Bezukhov when he visited one of the villages he owned.

Pauliicci, Marquis Phillipe Osipovich (1779-1849). *War and Peace* (3, 1, 9). The French adjutant-general who served in the French army. In 1807-1829, he was in Russian service and in 1812 was head of the First Army Headquarters.

Paulina, Princess. See: Polina Princess.

Pavel. "Death" *A Hunter's Sketches.* A woodcarver who was subject to fits of madness. *Fathers and Sons*, See Kirsanov, Pavel.

Pavel I (1754-1801). *Resurrection.* The Baron Vorobev was proud of his title, but his grandfather was the footman at the court of Pavel I. The Emperor suddenly made his grandfather a baron for some service the menial did that pleased him. *War and Peace* (3, 2, 9). Aleksandr I's father, who was assassinated so that Aleksandr could take the throne.

Pavel Andreich. "The Office," in *A Hunter's Sketches.* A doctor's assistant.

Pavel Egorich. *Virgin Soil.* Solomin's trustworthy attendant in the factory.

Pavel Petrovich. *War and Peace.* See Pavel I.

Pavel Timofeich. *War and Peace.* An acquaintance of Pierre Bezukhov's in Moscow.

Pavel Vasil'evich. "Two Landowners," in *A Hunter's Sketches.* The man who was called Pael Asilich by Khvalynskii.

Pavlusha. A diminutive for Pavel. "Bezhin Meadow," in *A Hunter's Sketches.* A homely but sensible boy whom the narrator met at a campfire in the woods when he lost his way.

Pechorin, Gregorii Aleksandrovich. *A Hero of Our Time.* The hero of the book, seen as an arrogant egotist through the eyes of other characters in the first part. After a belittling episode ("Taman'"), the hero's personal diary is presented and a more sympathetic figure emerges. *Rudin* (5). Lezhnev compared Rudin to Pechorin, the proud fictional hero.

Peel, George (1558-1597). *Smoke* (4). The English dramatist and contemporary of Shakespeare mentioned by Voroshilov when he managed to interrupt Madame Sukhanchikova.

Peel, Sir Robert (1788-1850). *A Gentry Nest* (18). The English statesman whom Lavretskii remembered for no reason at all while traveling. *Fathers and Sons* (24). Pavel Kirsanov told his brother Nikolai that Anglomaniacs and Peel were the cause of the duel he had with Bazarov. *Virgin Soil* (8). Sipiagin tried to copy Peel's manner of speech.

Pekhterkhov, Sergei Sergeich. "L'gov," in *A Hunter's Sketches.* A former owner of Suchok.

Pelageia Nikolaevna. *Evgenii Onegin.* Tat'iana Larina's relative who had long had the same dog, same friend, and same husband.

Pelageiushka. *War and Peace.* One of Maria Bolkonskaia's "God's folk" at Bald Hills.

Pelikanov. *Smoke.* The man Madame Sukhantchikova maintained was a spy.

Pelin. *Resurrection.* A noted revolutionist who was sentenced to hard labor.

Pelouze, T. J. (1807-1867). *Fathers and Sons* (17). The French chemist whose book *Notions générales de Chimie* was recommended to Madame Odintsova by Bazarov when he decided to leave, rather than stay and give her chemistry lessons.

Penochkin, Arkadii Pavlych. "The Steward," in *A Hunter's Sketches.* A landed proprietor who regarded himself as stern but just, and who lived near the narrator.

Perekhodov, Bor'ka. "Freeholder Ovsianikov," in *A Hunter's Sketches.* The man whom Mitia defended in court for stealing governmental money.

Perepentev, Arkhip. *Virgin Soil* (38). The man whom Paklin mentioned when he stated that Russians are always seeking something.

Perepreevskii. *On the Eve.* A nonexistent noble family that was supposed to have a particular type of neck.

Perevlessov (The Wild Squire). "The Singers," in *A Hunter's Sketches.* The large man who rarely showed emotion but was moved by the singing in the competition. He drank little and kept away from women.

Perfishka. "The End of Chertopkhanov," in *A Hunter's Sketches*. Pantelei's servant. *Virgin Soil*. The Subochevs' aged coachman who was so slow it took him five minutes to take a pinch of snuff.

Pernetti, General. *War and Peace*. The commander of the French First Artillery Corps at Borodino.

Peronskaia, Maria Ignatevna. *War and Peace*. A lady-in-waiting at court who was a guest of the Rostovs in St. Petersburg and who took them to a grand ball.

Pestov, Dmitrii. *A Gentry Nest*. A cousin of Ivan Lavretskii and a brother of Marfa. Ivan took his bride to Dmitrii's after his secret marriage.

Pestova, Marfa Timofeevna. *A Gentry Nest*. An aunt of Maria D. Kalitin who was noted for her outspokenness.

Peter, See Petr.

Peter of Amiens (1050-1115). *War and Peace* (E, 2, 4). The ascetic French monk who organized the First Crusade and who was mentioned by Tolstoi in his interpretation of history.

Petia. A diminutive of Petr. "Lebedian'," in *A Hunter's Sketches*. A groom of Sitnikov. *War and Peace*. See Rostov, Petr Il'ich.

Petin'ka. *War and Peace*. A name referred to by Prince Nikolai Bolkonskii in a letter to his son Prince Andrei.

Petito, Jean (1607-1691). *A Gentry Nest* (8). Enamel snuff boxes made by Petito were popular at the French court before the revolution of 1789. Many of the boxes came with French émigrés to Russia.

Petr. "The Death of Ivan Il'ich." The footman of Ivan Il'ich. *Fathers and Sons*. A servant of Nikolai Kirsanov. "The Office," in *A Hunter's Sketches*. A clerk.

Petr, Saint. *Resurrection* (1, 1). The Biblical figure mentioned in the quotation from St. Matthew which Tolstoi used as an epigraph to Chapter I. *War and Peace* (2, 2, 10). The Biblical apostle whose image was in the icon that greeted Pierre Bezukhov when he visited one of the villages he owned.

Petr I, Velikii (the Great) (1672-1725). *Anna Karenina* (3, 27). The Russian tsar mentioned by a landowner in conversation with Levin to show his erudition. "Bela," in *A Hero of Our Time*. There was a legend in the Caucasus that Petr I put a cross on a mountain top where the narrator traveled; however, the tsar was never in that area. "Khor' and Kalinych," in *A Hunter's Sketches*. The tsar who was praised for liking the good and accepting the sensible. *Smoke* (5). Potugin blamed Petr I for bringing in foreign words into the Russian language. *War and Peace* (2, 5, 3). The Emperor of Russia from 1682 to 1725; he was famous for Westernizing his country.

Petr III (1728-1762). *War and Peace* (3, 2, 9). The Russian Emperor from 1761 to 1762; he was killed by followers of his wife Ekaterina II. She then ascended the throne.

Petr Gerasimovich. *Resurrection*. The juryman who was a former tutor of the children of Natal'ia Rogozhinskaia (née Nekhliudova). He assumed a familiarity with Nekhliudov at the trial.

Petr Il'ich, Count. "Raspberry Spring," in *A Hunter's Sketches*. A deceased rich grandee.

Petr Ivanovich. "The Death of Ivan Il'ich." The close acquaintance of Ivan Il'ich Golovin who announced Ivan's demise to his colleagues in the court.

Petr Petrovich. "The Death of Ivan Il'ich." The new person in the chain of command in the ministry where Ivan obtained a position. "Living Holy Relics," in *A Hunter's Sketches*. The hunter and narrator of the story.

Petr Vasil'evich (Petrushka). "Ermolai and the Miller's Wife," in *A Hunter's Sketches*. The footman whom Arina loved but was not allowed to marry because her master, Zverkov, would not give her permission.

Petrarch, Francesco (1304-1374). *Evgenii Onegin*. The Epigraph to Chapter Six is from *In vita de Laura* (Canzone XXVIII). Also (1, 49). The famed Italian poet whose love poems, Pushkin said, would come to his lips while in a gondola with an Italian miss.

Petrishchev. "The Death of Ivan Il'ich." The young examining magistrate who courted Liza Golovin ardently.

Petrishchev, Dmitrii Ivanovich. "The Death of Ivan Il'ich." The father of the young man who courted Liza Golovina so fervently that Ivan Golovin spoke to his wife about their daughter's conduct.

Petritskii. *Anna Karenina*. A fellow officer and poor friend of Vronskii.

Petrov. *Anna Karenina*. A hall porter at the Karenins. Also a poor, sick painter at a German spa who painted Kitty Shcherbatskaia's picture and seemed enamoured of her. *Resurrection*.

A jailer disliked by the prisoners. Also a noted revolutionary who ended his life by cutting his throat with a piece of glass in prison. Also the policeman who questioned Shustova. *War and Peace*. A soldier in Tushin's famous battery which set fire to Schöngraben in 1805.

Petrova. *Anna Karenina*. The painter's wife at the German spa who let Kitty Shchbatskaia know of her disapproval of Kitty's kindness toward her husband.

Petrovskii. *Anna Karenina*. An aristocrat who was five million roubles in debt, but who lived in a grand style and had a position in the treasury department.

Petrushka. A diminutive for Petr. *War and Peace*. A cook in a crowd in Moscow when news of the fall of Smolensk had the city in near panic. Also a coachman at the Bolkonskii estate.

Petushkov. *Evgenii Onegin*. A neighborhood dandy who loved to dance and who performed at the Larins' ball.

Pfühl, Karl Ludwig Avgust (1757-1826). *War and Peace* (3, 1, 6). A Prussian military theoretician in Russian service in 1806.

Phaedra. *Evgenii Onegin* (1, 17). In classical mythology, the daughter of Minos, King of Crete, and the wife of Theseus, who fell in love with her stepson. When he refused her, she told her husband that his son had made advances toward her. The young man was put to death, and Phaedra strangled herself in remorse. Onegin saw a theatrical performance based on Phaedra.

Phidias (5th Cent. B.C.). *Smoke* (3). The Greek sculptor of the Periclean age who was recalled by Voroshilov in a conversation with Litvinov.

Philaret (V. M. Drozdov) (1783-1867). *Virgin Soil* (33). The Metropolitan of Moscow whose portrait Golushkin contributed to a gymnasium after his arrest.

Phillip. See Filipp.

Phillis. *Evgenii Onegin* (3, 2). Onegin named Phillis as a common name in sentimental poems.

Phoebus. *Evgenii Onegin* (3, 13). An epithet of Apollo, the sun god and the god of poetry, whose storms of inspiration were disliked at one time by Pushkin.

Photius (1792-1838). *War and Peace* (E, 1, 1). The archimandrite who was known as the persecutor of the Masons.

Phryne. *A Gentry Nest* (8). The Greek courtesan of the fourth century B.C. whose name was popular for young girls in the later eighteenth century. Ivan Petrovich Lavretskii might have courted a girl with such a name. "The Kreutzer Sonata" (14). Pozhnyshev mentioned Phryne when he stated that women are only for the amusement of men.

Pichukov. "Khor' and Kalinych," in *A Hunter's Sketches*. Polutykin's neighbor.

Pierre. French for Petr. *Anna Karenina*. The Baroness Shilton called Petritskii by the French spelling. *War and Peace*. See Bezukhov, Pierre.

Pifagor (650 B.C.). *On the Eve* (29). Shubin said that Nikolai Stakhov was as eloquent as the ancient philosopher.

Pigasov, Afrikan Semenich. *Rudin*. The eccentric, splenetic woman-hating landowner who had failed in the civil service, marriage and nearly everything else.

Pilate, Pontius. *Anna Karenina* (5, 11). The Biblical figure whom Mihailov painted with Christ. When he showed the picture to Anna and Vronskii, he was delighted with their comments but Vronskii's remarks about technique grated the artist's ear.

Pinna. "Khor' and Kalinych," in *A Hunter's Sketches*. A novel written by M. A. Markov (1810-1876) in 1845.

Pinselchen. *On the Eve* (3). Avgustina Kristianovna called Nikolai Strakhov "my Pinselchen" (simpleton) in letters to her cousin.

Pirogov. *Smoke* (20). A character from Gogol''s story "Nevskii Prospect" (1834). Litvinov insulted Pishchalkin, but the latter soothed himself with food as did Gogol''s Pirogov.

Pishchalkin. *Smoke*. An arbitrator of peace between serfs and landowners on the distribution of land.

Pitt, William (1759-1806). *War and Peace* (1, 1, 13). The son of William Pitt, Earl of Chatham; he was an English statesman during the Napoleonic period.

Pius VII (1740-1823). *War and Peace* (2, 5, 3). The Pope who crowned Napoleon in 1804 and then excommunicated the Emperor in 1809. For the latter, he was arrested.

Platoche. *War and Peace*. A Frenchman's name for Platon Karataev.

Plato (427?-347 B.C.). *Anna Karenina*. The Greek philosopher whom Levin read and reread in his search for meaning in life. He concluded that philosophers created an artificial train of reasoning.

Platon. *Anna Karenina*. A well-to-do peasant known for his kindness. *War and Peace*. See Karataev, Platon.

Platon, Levshin Petr Gregorievich (1737-1812). *War and Peace* (4, 1, 1). The Moscow Metropolitan (1787-1812) who sent a letter to Aleksandr I with the Holy Icon of St. Sergei to St. Petersburg as the French approached Moscow.

Platosha. *War and Peace*. A diminutive for Platon Karataev.

Platov, Matvei Ivanovich (1751-1818). *War and Peace* (3, 2, 4). A cossack who achieved great success and popularity during the War of 1812. His exploits were discussed at an inn in Smolensk before the city's fall.

Plenkovich, Churilo. *Smoke* (14). The hero of an ancient *bylinni* which Potugin recalled in his description of an old-time dandy.

Pleskachev. *Smoke*. Madame Sukhanchikova told a tale about a merchant by that name who had starved twelve girls to death.

Plutarch (46-120 A.D.). *War and Peace* (3, 2, 6). The Greek writer who wrote biographies of many ancient Greeks and Romans.

Podsalaskinskii. *On the Eve*. A nonexistent noble family which was said to have a particularly long nose.

Pokorskii. *Rudin*. The intellectual friend of Rudin and Lezhnev during their student days who managed to mix love and humanity in his actions.

'Poleon. *War and Peace*. Soldiers' name for Napoleon.

Polezhaev, Aleksandr Ivanovich (1805-1838). The Russian writer who was exiled to Siberia for his part in the Decembrist Revolution of 1825. "Petr Petrovich Karataev," in *A Hunter's Sketches*. Petr asked the narrator if he read Polezhaev. "Tat'iana Borisovna and Her Nephew," in *A Hunter's Sketches*. The narrator remarks that secondhand Polezhaevs are unbearable.

Polezhaev, Ivan. *The Captain's Daughter*. Vasilisa Mironova's friend whose house was so crowded that Vasilisa did not want Petr Grinev to live there when he came to the fortress.

Polia. *War and Peace*. A maid at the Rostov country estate.

Poliakov, Vasilii. "Living Holy Relics," in *A Hunter's Sketches*. The betrothed of Lukeria who married another after Lukeria's accident and loss of health.

Policarp. "Tat'iana Borisovna and Her Nephew," in *A Hunter's Sketches*. The valet who was a reader, fiddler and former soldier.

Polina. *Evgenii Onegin.* The name which Mme. Larina called her servant Praskov'ia. "The Queen of Spades." The princess whom Tomskii courted and finally married.

Pollux. *Fathers and Sons* (21). The mythological hero and son of Zeus whom Vasilii Bazarov was reminded of when he saw his son Evgenii Bazarov with Arkadii Kirsanov.

Polly. *Virgin Soil.* An Irish girl whom Solomin saw in London.

Polonius. "First Love" (11). The sententious old courtier in Shakespeare's *Hamlet* who was the father of Ophelia and also was the Lord Chamberlain to the King of Denmark. Lushin mentioned Polonius's description of clouds as sails.

Polozov, Ippolit Sidorovich (Puffy). *Spring Freshets.* The boarding-school comrade of Sanin and the servile husband of Maria. She nicknamed him Puffy.

Polozova, Maria Nikolaevna (née Kolyshkina). *Spring Freshets.* The rich wife of an old friend of Sanin.

Poltavskii. *Anna Karenina.* Mentioned by Karenin as a man whose wife was unfaithful.

Polutykin. "Khor' and Kalinych," in *A Hunter's Sketches.* A petty landowner in Kaluga.

Polutykin, Nikolai Kuzmich. "Khor' and Kalinych," in *A Hunter's Sketches.* Polutykin's father, who gave Khor' permission to live by the marsh and pay quitrent.

Poniatowski, Prince Joseph (1763-1813). *War and Peace* (3, 2, 27). The nephew of Polish King Stanislas-Augustus. In 1807 he was the Minister of War of the Principality of Warsaw. He went with Napoleon's forces into Russia in 1812 as the commander of a Polish corps.

Porfirii Platonich. *Fathers and Sons.* An old neighbor of Madame Odintsova who played cards with her and Bazarov. The latter lost a considerable sum.

Porpoise. *Virgin Soil.* The nickname for Eremei Golopletskii.

Potap. "Khor' and Kalinych," in *A Hunter's Sketches.* Khor' 's son.

Potemkin, Prince Grigorii Aleksandrovich (1739-1791), *War and Peace* (1, 1, 24). The Russian statesman and favorite of Ekaterina II who was remembered by Count Nikolai Bolkonskii.

Potier, Robert Joseph (1699-1772). *War and Peace* (3, 3, 29). A French judge and professor in Orleans mentioned in a conversation about France when Pierre was imprisoned in Moscow.

Potocka, Countess. *War and Peace* (3, 1, 3). An ancient Polish family name. Boris Drubetskoi wanted to ask the Countess to dance but ran into the Tsar Aleksandr I while looking for her.

Potugin, Irinarkh. *Smoke*. An uncle of Sozont Potugin who was a state councillor and for whom Sozont had worked for twenty-two years.

Potugin, Sozont Ivanovich. *Smoke*. The retired court councillor who advised Litvinov in his love affair with Irina Osinina.

Pozdnyshev, Vasilii (Vasia). "The Kreutzer Sonata." The landowner and Marshal of the Nobility who stabbed and killed his wife in a fit of jealousy and was acquitted for defending his honor. He had never known peace of mind since his trial.

Pozdnysheva. "The Kreutzer Sonata." The murder victim who asked that her husband not be allowed to have their children after her death.

Pozen. *Resurrection*. The man who killed Kamenskaia's son in a duel.

Pozniakov. *War and Peace* (4, 2, 10). The family whose house on Great Nikitin Street was made into a theater during Napoleon's stay in Moscow.

Pradt, Abbé Dominique de (1759-1817). *Evgenii Onegin* (4, 43). The French political writer whom Pushkin stated one might read in the winter when one could not go riding.

Praskov'ia. *Evgenii Onegin* (2, 33). The servant whom Mrs. Larina called Polina in a French fashion.

Praskov'ia Iakovlevna. *Smoke*. The person whom Madame Sukhanchikova mentioned as the source for some gossip she was telling. Turgenev first wrote her name as Avdot'ia Iakovlevna because he had in mind a lady by that name who was the common-law wife of N. A. Nekrassov. See Nekrassov.

Praskov'ia Savishna. *War and Peace*. Mar'ia Bolkonskaia's old nurse.

Pravdin. *Anna Karenina*. A pan-Slav agitator abroad who wrote to Countess Lidia Ivanovna.

Prepalovenskii. *Fathers and Sons*. The former landlord of Nikolai Kirsanov whose daughter became Nikolai's wife.

Priachnikov. *Anna Karenina*. The man who killed Kvytskii in a duel over his wife. He was mentioned in front of Karenin at a dinner at the Oblonskiis.

Priam. *Evgenii Onegin* (7-4). The Trojan King who was the father of many children. Pushkin referred to girls living in the country as Priam's children.

Prianichnikov. *War and Peace*. An old man cited in conversation at Count Kochubei's.

Priazhentsov. *Rudin*. Rudin's friend who took a job to support a family of peasants.

Pripasov. *Anna Karenina.* A name thought up by Tolstoi to designate an author who wrote on the subject of perception. Koznyshev discussed the subject with Levin (1, 7).

Prokhorov. *The Captain's Daughter.* The corporal who quarreled with Negulina.

Prokofii. *War and Peace.* A strong footman of the Rostovs.

Prokovich. *Fathers and Sons.* An old servant at the Kirsanov estate.

Prolasov. *Evgenii Onegin.* A neighbor of the Larins who was noted for his baseness.

Proudhon, Pierre Joseph (1809-1865). *Fathers and Sons* (13). The French philosophic anarchist was cited by Madame Kukshina in a conversation with Bazarov about women. *On the Eve* (34). Lupoiarov had the French socialist's latest book when Insarov visited in Venice. *Virgin Soil* (9). Kallomeitsev referred to the French philosopher in a conversation with Valentina Sipiagina. (16) Nezhdanov recalled the author of *What Is Property?* (1840) in a conversation with Markelov.

Prozorovskii, Prince Aleksandr Aleksandrovich (1732-1809). *A Gentry Nest* (21). The author of a tract that Lavretskii found among his aunt's things after her death. *War and Peace* (2, 2, 4). The commander of Russian troops fighting the Turks in 1808. Because of ill health, he relied on his confederate Kutuzov.

Prussia, King of. *War and Peace* (1, 1, 1). When Prince Vasilii Kuragin suggested that Anna Pavlovna Scherer should have been sent as a diplomat to the King of Prussia, he referred to Frederick Wilhelm III (1770-1840).

Pryshchova, Khavronia. *Virgin Soil.* A lady whom Paklin once knew and who maintained that at her death the name Henri V would be found on her heart. Turgenev was ironically referring to the Countess E. B. Salias de Turnemir (née Kobilina), who became a follower of the pretender to the French throne.

Przazdzieska, Panna. *War and Peace.* The person for whom the hussars were planning a ball which Nikolai Rostov regretted he would miss when he retired from the military service in 1809.

Przhibyshevskii, General Ignatii Iakovlevich (1755-?). *War and Peace* (1, 3, 12). An officer who participated in the War of 1805.

Ptolemy (Claudius Ptolemaeus) (2nd Cent. A.D.). *War and Peace.* (E, 2, 12). The ancient Greek astronomer and mathematician who stated that the sun and stars revolve around the earth.

Pufka. *Virgin Soil.* The Subochevs' maid who was a dwarf.

Pugachev, Emel'ian Ivanovich (1744-1775). *Anna Karenina* (8, 15). The famous leader of a peasant rebellion whom Levin recalled in a discussion with Koznyshev about Russian social problems. *The Captain's Daughter.* The pretender to the Russian throne who claimed to be Peter III. Pushkin gave Pugachev human qualities during a period of strict censorship in Russia. *Resurrection* (2, 40). Nekhliudov thought of Pugachev when thinking of the deplorable mentality of governmental officials. *Virgin Soil* (34). Sipiagin remembered Pugachev when Paklin stated that the Russian lower classes needed a legend to arouse them to action. *War and Peace* (E, 1, 15). Tolstoi mentioned the cossack rebel in his interpretation of history.

Pupyr, Andrei. "L'gov," in *A Hunter's Sketches.* The serf who was ordered to the paper mill as a water carrier.

Pushkin, Aleksandr Sergeevich (1799-1837). *Evgenii Onegin.* Pushkin included himself in his famous novel in verse so that critics could not say that he wrote a biography of himself in the character Onegin. *A Gentry Nest* (16). Varvara Lavretskaia read Pushkin's poetry. *Fathers and Sons* (3). Nikolai Petrovich quoted Pushkin while riding with Arkadii around their estate. "First Love" (9). Maidanov read Pushkin at Zinaida's request. Also Vladimir Petrovich B____ read Pushkin's poetry. "Petr Petrovich Karataev" in *A Hunter's Sketches.* Gornostaev read Pushkin to Matrena. *Rudin.* Natal'ia read books which Mlle. Bancourt had never heard of. Among them were works by Pushkin. *Spring Freshets* (5). Sanin translated Pushkin's poem "I Remember a Wondrous Moment" for the Roselli family. "Two Landowners," in *A Hunter's Sketches.* Pushkin's comment on Saadi was quoted. *Virgin Soil* (8). The famous Russian poet whom Kallomeitsev considered second-rate compared to the poet Kukul'nik.

Pushkin, Vasilii L'vovich (1767-1830). *War and Peace* (3, 2, 17). The poet whose *bouts-rimes* were read in Moscow before the siege by the French. He was the uncle of A. S. Pushkin.

Pustiakov. *Evgenii Onegin.* A fat neighbor of the Larins who came for Tat'iana Larina's name-day party.

Putiatov. *Anna Karenina.* The man who received the Order of Aleksandr at the same time Karenin did.

Pykhtin. *Evgenii Onegin.* One of the suitors whom Tat'iana Larina rejected.

Queen of Petersburg. *War and Peace*. Society's name for Countess Elena Bezukhova.

Queen of Spain. *War and Peace*. The royal personage mentioned as a former patient of the doctor who treated Elena Bezukhova.

Queen of the Wasps. *Smoke*. See Countess Sh____.

R____, Princess. *Fathers and Sons*. The woman for whom Pavel Kirsanov forsook his military career. At her death, he settled on the family estate with his brother Nikolai Kirsanov.

R____, Andrei Karlovich. *The Captain's Daughter*. The old friend of Petr Grinev's father; Petr was sent to him for army service.

R____R____ *Smoke*. The person who, it was said, preserved the social ideas of the 1840s.

Rabelais, François (1495-1553). *Resurrection* (1, 23). When Nekhliudov was frustrated with court proceedings, Tolstoi mentioned a story which Rabelais told about a judge who finally asked two contending parties to throw dice to decide the winner in a court case.

Rachel, Élisa Félix (1820-1858). *A Gentry Nest* (15). The French tragic actress who had retired from the stage before Varvara Lavretskaia became well-known in Paris. *Virgin Soil* (26), Valentina Sipiagina quoted the famous actress, but Mariana Sinetskaia told her that she did not say the actress's lines very well. Turgenev himself saw the actress in several theatrical productions.

Racine, Jean (1639-1699). *Evgenii Onegin* (5, 22). The French dramatist whose works were not on Tat'iana Larina's bed after her nightmare.

Radcliffe, Ann (1764-1823). *Fathers and Sons* (24). The English writer of Gothic novels who, Bazarov said, considered the Russian peasant the "mysterious unknown." "Dubrovskii" (2, 9). Pushkin wrote that Mar'ia Troekurova was impregnated with Radcliffe's horrors.

Radilov, Mikhailo Mikhailovich. "Freeholder Ovsianikov," in *A Hunter's Sketches*. The narrator met Ovsianikov in Radilov's house. "My Neighbor Radilov," in *A Hunter's Sketches*. The retired landowner who eloped with his sister-in-law.

Radilova. "My Neighbor Radilov," in *A Hunter's Sketches*. The old mother of Radilov, who abandoned her.

Raevich. "Princess Mary," in *A Hero of Our Time*. A Moscow dandy who had a beard and haircut *à la muzhik*.

Raevskii, Aleksandr Nikolaevich (1795-1868). *War and Peace* (3, 1, 7). The son of the famous general of the War of 1812. He fought alongside his father and brother.

Raevskii, General Nikolai Nikolaevich (1771-1829). *War and Peace* (3, 1, 7). The famed general of many Russian wars. He was commander of the Seventh Infantry Corps in 1812. His redoubt in the middle of the Borodino battlefield became known by the name Raevskii.

Raevskii, General Nikolai Nikolaevich (1801-1843). *War and Peace* (3. 1. 7). The son of the famous general of the War of 1812. His participation with his father in battle won him fame. He was a friend of the poet A. S. Pushkin, who dedicated his work *The Caucasian Prisoner* to him.

Ragozov, Ivan Ivanich. *Anna Karenina*. The person who Levin said had declared war on the Turks.

Ramballe. *War and Peace*. The French officer whose life Pierre Bezukhov saved in Moscow.

Rambouillet, Marquise Catherine de (1588-1665). *Anna Karenina* (2, 7). The brilliant French hostess whom Karenin recalled to Princess Betsy at the latter's party in order to compliment her.

Rameau. *War and Peace*. The French official who issued propaganda proclamations to Russian peasants after Napoleon's invasion of Russia.

Rantseva, Emily. *Resurrection*. The political prisoner who had become a revolutionary because of her faith in her husband's viewpoints.

Raphael (Raffaello Sanzio) (1483-1520). *Anna Karenina* (1, 33). The Italian Renaissance painter whom Karenin liked to discuss to impress others with his knowledge. *Fathers and Sons* (10). Bazarov said that Raphael was not worth a farthing. *Spring Freshets* (10). Sanin was impressed by the elegant beauty of Gemma's hands and compared them with those of Raphael's "Fornarina." "Tat'iana Borisovna and Her Nephew," in *A Hunter's Sketches*. Turgenev wrote that the ignorant never call Raphael simply Raphael but something like the "divine Sanzio." *Virgin Soil* (2). The Italian artist to whom Paklin referred in conversation with Ostrodumov.

Rapp, Count Jean (1772-1821). *War and Peace* (3, 2, 29). The general on duty in Napoleon's tent at Borodino. In 1809 he prevented an attempt on the life of the Emperor. He was wounded at Borodino in 1812.

Rappeau. *Smoke* (14). Potugin stated the name Rappeau while commenting on art and style. The name signifies strength. Rappeau was a strong man who performed feats of strength in Russia.

Rarey. "First Love" (8). The tamer of wild horses.

Rastopchin, Fedor Vasil'evich (1763-1828). *War and Peace* (2, 1, 2). The Governor of Moscow during the War of 1812; he was a friend of the Emperor Pavel.

Rastrelli, Franchesco Bartholomeo (1770-1771). *Rudin*. The Italian architect whose drawings influenced the construction of Dar'ia Lazunskaia's house on a hill.

Ratmirov, Valerian Vladimirovich. *Smoke*. The rich general who was the husband of Irina.

Ratmirova, Irina (née Osinina). *Smoke*. The daughter of the Prince and Princess Osinin who caused Litvinov to forsake Tat'iana for an affair of passion. See Shestova, Tat'iana.

Raumer, Friedrich Ludwig Georg von (1781-1873). *On the Eve* (5). The German historian who wrote *Geschichte der Hohenstaufen und ihrer Zeit* (1825). Bersenev read from Volume 11 after talking with Shubin about his love for Elena Stakhova.

Raynal, Guillaume (1713-1797). *A Gentry Nest* (8). The philosophical writer whom Fedor Lavretskii's father studied in his youth.

Rayner. *Resurrection*. The governess of Maria Korchagina's little sister.

Razin, Stepan Timofeevich (d. 1671). *Resurrection* (2, 40). The leader of a peasant rebellion whom Nekhliudov remembered while thinking of the deplorable mentality of governmental officials.

Razumovskii, Prince Andrei Kirillovich (1752-1836). *War and Peace*. The Russian envoy in Vienna (1790-1799, 1801-1807) whom Bilibin mentioned to Prince Andrei Bolkonskii when the latter was on duty there (1, 2, 10). The family was also mentioned at a Rostov party (1, 1, 7).

Rebecca. *Anna Karenina* (1, 34). Petritskii had in mind the beautiful Rebecca from *Ivanhoe* (1820), by Sir Walter Scott.

Rebekah. *Anna Karenina* (3, 4). In the Old Testament, the wife of Isaac. She was mentioned in a prayer at Kitty and Levin's marriage.

Récamier, Julie (1777-1849). *Rudin* (4). The hostess of a literary salon who created a new fashion which acquired her name.

Regulus, Marcus Atilius (d. 250 B. C.). *Evgenii Onegin* (6, 5). The Roman commander noted for his heroic behavior in captivity. Pushkin ironically contrasted him with Zaretskii.

Reisenbach, Count. *Smoke*. Prince Osinin's first cousin, who presented Irina Osinina to high society and who was a chamberlain of the court.

Renan, Joseph Ernest (1823-1892). *Anna Karenina* (5, 9). The French philosopher whom Golonishchev criticized in a conversation with Anna and Vronskii. Renan was famous for his book *The Life of Christ*. *Smoke* (4). He was mentioned by Voroshilov when he was finally able to interrupt Mme. Sukhanchikova.

Rendich. *On the Eve*. The Dalmatian fisherman whom Insarov sought in Venice to arrange for passage for himself and his wife Elena (née Stakhova) to Bulgaria.

Repin, Il'ia Efimovich (1844-1930). *Resurrection* (1, 27). The princess Sophia Vassil'evna said that the famous Russian painter Repin had told her that Nekhliudov had art talent. Nekhliudov knew that she was lying.

Repnin, Prince Nikolai Grigorievich (1778-1833). *War and Peace* (1, 3, 19). The general who commanded a regiment of Emperor Aleksandr I's Horse Guards. He was captured with Prince Andrei and interviewed by Napoleon.

Retz, Jean François Paul de Gondi (1614-1679). *Spring Freshets* (36). One of the main members of the Fronde, a political party organized to oppose Cardinal Mazarin. Polozova was mentioned in Retz's memoirs as having a great gift of "familiarité."

Reumont, Alfred (1808-1887). *Smoke* (4). The German historian and diplomat recalled by Voroshilov when he managed to interrupt Madame Sukhanchikova.

Rezunov, Fedor. *Anna Karenina*. The head of a cooperative peasant group.

Rhipheus. *War and Peace* (2, 1, 3). See Riphaei.

Riabinin. *Anna Karenina*. A wood merchant who came to Levin's estate.

Richardson, Samuel (1689-1761). *Evgenii Onegin* (2, 30). The English writer whom Tat'iana loved. He was known for his contributions to the study of character and social manners in the development of the form of the novel.

Richelieu, Duc de. Cardinal de. Armand Emmanuel du Plessis (1766-1822). "The Queen of Spades." The famous French statesman in the reign of Louis XIII who paid court to Countess Anna Fedotovna when she was a fashionable beauty in Paris.

Richelieu, Duc de. Louis François Armand du Plessis (1696-1788). *A Gentry Nest*. The grandnephew of Cardinal Richelieu who was noted for his daring duels and deeds. The Princess Kubenskaia was perfumed with a scent *à la Richelieu*.

Riehl, William Hentry (1823-1797). *Smoke* (3). The German publicist and writer cited by Voroshilov in a conversation with Litvinov.

Rigolboche. "The Kreutzer Sonata" (5). The nickname which the noted French dancer Marguerite Bodelle gave herself from the word "rigolo" and "bouche." The name developed a negative connotation for a particular type of dancer.

Rikher, Herr von. *Spring Freshets*. Donkhov's comrade.

Rinaldini, Rinaldo. "Dubrovskii." The bandit hero in a book by C. A. Vulpius (1767-1827). *Spring Freshets* (4). The portrait of Gemma's deceased father reminded people of Rinaldo. *Virgin Soil* (14). The peasant Fitiuev had a face resembling a description of the fictional character.

Riphaei. *War and Peace* (2, 1, 3). Tolstoi referred to the ancient name for the Ural mountains. In Latin: *Riphaei montes*. Bagration would be of mountainous stature at home, according to the way the term is used in the poem dedicated to the famous general.

Ristich-Kudzhitskii, Ivan (1831-1899). *Anna Karenina*. The Serbian statesman who was admired by the Countess Lidia Ivanovna because of his views on Slavic matters.

Riurik (830?-879?). *Smoke* (7). The legendary Varengian prince who is supposed to have accepted an invitation to rule Russia. Old Russian families dating from the early period are called Riurikivichi and many have the title Prince. They looked down on aristocrats with the title "Count" because Petr the Great created that title in the eighteenth century in Russia as an award for service to the crown. *War and Peace* (1, 1, 24). The Bolkonskiis were supposed to be Riurikivichi.

Robert le Diable. *Fathers and Sons* (21). Vasilii Bazarov sang an air from Jacob Meyerbeer's opera *Robert le Diable* when he went to breakfast with his son and Arkadii. *Spring Freshets* (36).

Sanin heard an orchestra play a potpourri from *Robert le Diable* in the garden in Wiesbaden.

Robespierre, Maximilien François (1758-1794). *Smoke* (7). The French revolutionary whom Litvinov worshipped for a time. Russian intellectuals of the period considered such men as freedom fighters. *War and Peace* (2, 1, 6). Robespierre helped institute the Reign of Terror during the French Revolution. He was overthrown by the Ninth Thermidor in 1794 and sent to the guillotine.

Robinson Crusoe. "The Office," in *A Hunter's Sketches*. Seeking refuge from a rain, the narrator walked into a shed where he found an old man who reminded him of the famous literary character by Daniel Defoe (1719).

Rodemacher, Johan Gottfried (1772-1849). *Fathers and Sons* (20). The German scholar to whom Vasilii Bazarov referred when talking about medical affairs in his province.

Rodia. "Dubrovskii." A shepherd at the Dubrovskii estate.

Rogozhinskaia, Natal'ia Ivanovna (Natasha). *Resurrection*. Dmitrii's sister who was torn between her love for her brother and her love for her husband. They were virtually enemies.

Rogozhinskii, Ignatii Nikiforovich. *Resurrection*. Natasha's husband who was a jurist and who artfully maneuvered between liberalism and conservatism, whichever benefited him more at the time.

Rohans. *War and Peace* (1, 1, 1). The distinguished French family dating from the twelth century. Anna Pavlovna Scherer called it one of the best families in France.

Rolandaki. *Anna Karenina*. A family that invited Anna to a fete at Tsarskoe Selo.

Romulus. *Evgenii Onegin* (1, 6). The legendary founder of Rome. Onegin remembered anecdotes from the time of Romulus to his own time.

Roselli, Emilio. *Spring Freshets*. The brother of Gemma. He was saved from death by Sanin but later died a glorious death fighting with the famous Giuseppe Garibaldi (1807-1882).

Roselli, Gemma. *Spring Freshets*. The daughter of an Italian confectioner who became the object of Sanin's love. When he deserted her, she married another and moved to New York.

Roselli, Giovanni Battista. *Spring Freshets*. Gemma's deceased father, who, Turgenev suggested, belonged to the democratic society founded in 1808 for the freedom of Italy.

Roselli, Lenore. *Spring Freshets.* The mother of Gemma and widow of Giovanni Battista Roselli.

Rosen, K. M. *Rudin.* See Aibulat.

Rossini, Gioacchino Antonio (1792-1868). *A Gentry Nest* (40). Varvara Lavretskaia and Panchin sang "Mira la bianca luna" from Rossini's *Soirée Musicale* (1835).

Rostov, Andriusha. *War and Peace.* The eldest child of Mar'ia and Nikolai Rostov.

Rostov, Count Il'ia Andreevich Rostov. *War and Peace.* An extravagant, kind and well-meaning aristocrat who lived beyond his means and was forced to sell properties in order to meet his debtors. The father of Nikolai, Natasha, Vera and Petia.

Rostov, Mitia. *War and Peace.* The son of Nikolai and Maria Rostov.

Rostov, Count Nikolai Il'ich. *War and Peace.* The eldest son of the Rostov family, who fought in the 1805 and 1812 campaigns. His love for Sonia, a relative, was scorned by his mother, who wanted him to make a brilliant marriage and save the family from financial ruin. Circumstances brought him into the life of Mar'ia Bolkonskaia, whom he came to love and finally marry.

Rostov, Count Petr Il'ich (Petia). *War and Peace.* Count Il'ia's youngest son, who was killed in a raid during the War of 1812.

Rostova, Countess Natal'ia. *War and Peace.* Count Il'ia's forty-five-year-old wife, who looked tired from many pregnancies. A kind mother whose concern was only for the welfare of her children: Nikolai, Natasha, Petia and Vera.

Rostova, Countess Natal'ia Il'inichna (Natasha). *War and Peace.* The younger daughter of Count Il'ia who fell in love with Prince Andrei Bolkonskii but who carried out a flirtation with Prince Anatol Kuragin which caused a scandal. After the death of Prince Andrei, whom she nursed, she married Pierre Bezukhov and had a family.

Rostova, Natasha. *War and Peace.* The small daughter of Mar'ia and Nikolai Rostov in the Epilogue of the novel.

Rostova, Countess Vera Il'inichna Rostova (Berg). *War and Peace.* The eldest daughter of Count Il'ia whose marriage to Berg was not considered desirable. They proved to be a pretentious couple and a financial drain on the Rostov family.

Rousseau, Jean Jacques (1712-1778). *A Gentry Nest* (8). The French philosopher whom Courtin de Vaucelles greatly admired.

Evgenii Onegin (1, 24). Pushkin mentioned in passing that
Rousseau could not understand how the dignified writer
M. Grimm dared to clean his nails in front of him. *Fathers and
Sons* (21). Vasilii Bazarov believed that Rousseau was correct
when he stated that one must labor to be happy. *War and
Peace* (E, 1, 10). Pierre Bezukhov related Rousseau's theory
on breast feeding to Natasha, whereupon she nursed her own
child, a practice frowned upon in society at that time.

Rovigo, Henri Jean Marie René Savary de (1774-1833). *War and Peace*
(1, 3, 11). The French general who was close to Napoleon after
1800. In 1805 and 1807 he participated in Napoleon's military
campaigns.

Rozovskii, Iosif Isaakovich (1860?-1880). *Resurrection* (3, 6). The
young Jewish boy condemned to death for revolutionary
activities. He was hanged in Kiev, and his execution was
painfully described by Tolstoi.

Rtishchev, Maria Evgenievna. *Anna Karenina*. A Moscow society
woman at the German spa where the Shcherbatskiis visited.

Rubens, Peter Paul (1577-1640). *Anna Karenina* (5, 4). When
Mikhailov showed Rubens' painting of Christ and Pilate to
Anna and Vronskii, he thought of Rubens' interpretation
of the Christ figure and decided that his own composition
was weak in comparison.

Rudin, Dmitrii Nikolaevich. *Rudin*. The protagonist of the novel.
He had a supreme intellectual gift, which he wasted while
moving from one patron to another. Discharged from Daria's
home because of his affair with Natal'ia, he continued
moving around until he was killed in the Paris uprising of
June, 1848.

Rumiantsev, Nikolai Petrovich (1754-1826). *War and Peace* (1, 1, 5).
During the reign of Pavel I, this statesman was a senator.
Under Aleksandr I, he was Minister of Commerce (1802-1811).

Rumiantsev, Petr Aleksandrovich (1725-1796). *The Captain's
Daughter*. An outstanding Russian general of the eighteenth
century whose memorial monument was in the park at Tsarskoe Selo when Mar'ia met Empress Ekaterina II.

Ruslan. *Evgenii Onegin* (1, 2). The hero of a famous poem by
A. S. Pushkin, *Ruslan and Liudmila* (1820).

Rustan. *War and Peace* (3, 1, 5). Napoleon's bodyguard who was
an Egyptian Mameluke captured by Napoleon on a campaign near the pyramids close to Cairo in 1798.

S____. "The Fatalist," in *A Hero of Our Time*. It was at Major S____'s that the group of officers discussed fatalism.

S____ S____. *War and Peace*. The person to whom Prince Boris Drubetskoi alluded during the Rostovs visit in St. Petersburg.

Saadi (Muslish-ud-Din) (1184-1291). *Evgenii Onegin* (8, 51). The Persian poet whom Pushkin quoted in the last stanza of his novel in verse. "Two Landowners," in *A Hunter's Sketches*. A reference was made to Pushkin's quotation from Saadi.

Sadovskii, Prov Mikhailovich (1818-1872). *Virgin Soil* (3). An artist of the Moscow theater who played yearly in St. Petersburg. Nezhdanov found little entertainment in his acting.

Saint-Germain, Comte de (c. 1710-c. 1780). "The Queen of Spades." A celebrated adventurer who was called der Wundermann. He knew nearly all European languages and was a capable violinst. He pretended to have a secret for removing flaws from diamonds and to possess a liquid which could prolong life. He himself claimed to be 2000 years old. He appeared at the French court about 1748 and was employed on secret missions by Louis XV. Forced to leave France in 1760 on account of the hostility of the Duke of Choiseul, he went to London. In St. Petersburg in 1762, he was supposed to have aided the forces that dethroned Peter III and placed Ekaterina II on the throne. According to Cagliostro, Saint-Germain was the founder of Freemasonry in Germany.

Saint Priest. *Evgenii Onegin*. See Sen-Pri.

Saint-Simon, Claude Henri de Rouvroy, Comte de (1760-1825). *Smoke* (14), The French philosopher and social reformer who believed that all property should belong to the state and that a worker could then share in it according to the amount and quality of his work. He is considered the father of French socialism. Potugin mentioned Saint-Simonism in a conversation with Litvinov.

Saint-Thomas. *War and Peace*. A corporal in the shed where Pierre Bezukhov was a prisoner in Moscow during the French occupation.

Sakhar Medovich (Sugar Honey). "Hamlet of the Shchigrovskii District," in *A Hunter's Sketches*. One of the guests at the party where the narrator met the Russian Hamlet was referred to as Mr. Sugar Honey.

Salamatov. *Resurrection*. The friends of the Korchagins with whom they played tennis.

Salomoni. *War and Peace* (1, 1, 9). An operatic singer who appeared in a German troup in Moscow during the winter of 1805-1806.

Saltykov, Prince Nikolai Ivanovich (1736-1816). *War and Peace* (3, 1, 3). A field marshal in 1812 and a representative on the governmental Committee of Ministers.

Saltykova, Praskov'ia Fedorovna. *A Gentry Nest*. The person who received a decoction for the relief of chest ailments.

Samanov. *Resurrection*. A very rich old man whose affairs were managed by Shenbok.

Samovar. *Anna Karenina*. A nickname for the Countess Lidia Ivanovna.

Samson. *Anna Karenina* (4, 9). In the Old Testament (Judges, 13, 16) the hero whose strength depended on the fact that his hair had never been cut. Observing Levin's biceps under his coat, Oblonskii called him the Biblical man of strength. *War and Peace* (1, 1, 6). Anatol' Kuragin called Pierre Bezukhov by that name.

Samuel. *Virgin Soil*. The Old Testament judge (Samuel, Books I and II), whom the Subochevs cited when they thought of the strength of their horses.

Sancho. *Rudin* (11). Don Quixote's servant in Cervantes's masterpiece, *Don Quixote de la Mancha* (1605). Rudin said that he felt like Don Quixote when the fictional character told his servant that one should be happy if he has a piece of bread and is not obligated to anyone for it.

Sand, George (Amantine Lucile Aurore Dupin) (1804-1876). The famous French writer known for her numerous love affairs and novels with socialistic and humanitarian themes. *Fathers and Sons* (13). Madame Kukshina called the French writer "out of date." *A Gentry Nest* (40). George Sand's novels made Varvara Lavretskaia indignant.

Sanin, Dmitrii Pavlovich. *Spring Freshets*. The Russian who fell in love with an Italian girl. Although his intentions were admirable, circumstances separated him from her and their love was lost forever.

Sannazaro, Jacopo (1456-1530). "Tat'iana Borisovna and Her Nephew," in *A Hunter's Sketches*. The Italian writer noted for his work *Arcadia*, which started the genre in Italian literature known as pastoral. A play by N. V. Kukol'nik based on the life of Sannazaro was mentioned by the narrator as a dramatic piece for people who know nothing about art.

Santo-Fiume, Contessa Rocca di. *Virgin Soil*. The name Miss Mashurina was using when Paklin met her in 1870 in St. Petersburg. He tried to find out if she was still working in revolutionary activities, but she would not answer directly.

Sapozhnikov, Pierre. *Fathers and Sons*. An acquaintance of Eudoxie Kukshina in a provincial town.

Sardou, Victorien (1831-1908). *Smoke* (15). At Irina Ratmirova's party, the pretentious guests spoke of the notorieties of the Parisian demimonde, mentioning the French playwright Sardou who wrote *Tosca* (1887), *Fedora* (1882) and *Madame Sans Gene* (1893) for Sarah Bernhardt.

Sarkisov. *Smoke*. The person whom Madame Sukhanchikova called a liar.

Sarmatskii. *Anna Karenina*. The family at whose home the children of Kitty Levina (née Shcherbatskaia) went for a party.

Sasha. A diminutive for Aleksandr. "Dubrovskii." The illegitimate son of Troekurov and Mimi, a French turoress. Mlle. Mimi was sent away to another estate after her child was born. Troekurov reared the boy as his own, even though there were on the estate several peasant boys with the master's features.

Sauerbrengel. *Smoke*. The doctor who wrote a book on prisons in Pennsylvania.

Savary. See Rovigo.

Savel'ich. *The Captain's Daughter*. Grinev's faithful tutor who went with the young officer to the remote fortress. "Dubrovskii." The sexton at Troekurov's estate. *War and Peace*. The servant who advised Pierre Bezukov to rebuild at the end of the War of 1812.

Savelii Alekseevich. "Ermolai and the Miller's Wife," in *A Hunter's Sketches*. The miller who bought Arina's freedom.

Savishna, Anna (Arina). *Fathers and Sons*. Fenichka's mother, who had been an innkeeper before becoming the housekeeper at the Kirsanov estate.

Savostianov, Andrei. *War and Peace*. A peasant in whose hut the Russian generals met after the Battle of Borodino.

Say, Jean Baptiste (1767-1832). *Evgenii Onegin* (1, 42). Pushkin wrote that society dames might interpret the French economist but that their conversation was mostly twaddle.

Sbogar, Jean (1822). *Evgenii Onegin* (3, 12). A novel by Charles Nodier (1780-1844), who was known for his Gothic stylistic effects.

Scaevola, Mucius. *War and Peace* (E, 1, 16). A legendary Roman who showed his fearlessness in captivity by placing his hand in fire, winning his freedom. The boy Nikolenka mentioned Mucius Scaevola when he wanted to prove his own worth to his uncle.

Scharmer. "The Death of Ivan Il'ich." The fashionable tailor who made Ivan's clothes.

Scheller. *Rudin*. A student friend of Rudin and Lezhnev.

Schelling. *War and Peace*. The tutor mentioned by Nikolai Rostov in his letter to his family while he was in the War of 1805.

Schelling, Friedrich Wilhelm Joseph von (1775-1854). *Anna Karenina* (8, 9). One of the German philosophers whom Levin read in his search for meaning in life. He decided that philosphers set a verbal trap which is remote from life. *On the Eve* (4). Bersenev said his father was a follower of the German philosopher. *War and Peace* (E, 1, 1). Tolstoi mentioned Schelling in his interpretation of history.

Scherer, Anna Pavlovna. *War and Peace*. The Empress's lady-in-waiting who was known for her evening parties.

Schiff, Seymour. *Fathers and Sons* (13). The composer of the song "Granada Lies Slumbering," which Madame Kukshina played on an out-of-tune piano and sang in a hoarse voice.

Schiller, Johann Christoph Friedrich von (1759-1805). *Evgenii Onegin* (2, 9). Lenskii appreciated the works of the German philosopher. *Fathers and Sons* (6). Pavel Kirsanov denounced Schiller when speaking with Bazarov. "First Love" (1). Vladimir Petrovich read Schiller's *The Brigands* when he was sixteen. *A Gentry Nest* (21). Lemm had set to music Schiller's ballad "Fridalin." "Hamlet of the Shchigrovskii District," in *A Hunter's Sketches*. The Russian Hamlet recited a poem by Schiller. *On the Eve* (5). Shubin said that Bersenev's interest in Schiller had attracted Elena to him. "Tat'iana Borisovna and Her Nephew," in *A Hunter's Sketches*. A guest at Tat'iana's mentioned the German philosopher.

Schlegel, Avgust Wilhelm von (1767-1845). *A Gentry Nest* (5). The translator of Shakespeare into German whose works Lemm read in his solitude.

Schlosser, Friedrich Christoph (1776-1861). *War and Peace* (E, 2, 2). The German bourgeois historian who, Tolstoi said, proved that Napoleon was a product of the French Revolution and who at another time plainly stated that the campaign of 1812 was simply the product of Napoleon's misdirected will.

Schmidt, Friedrich (1743-1809). *War and Peace* (1, 2, 9). The general of the Austrian Army who was closely connected with Kutuzov in the War of 1805. He was killed in the battle at Krems.

Schneider. *War and Peace*. An adjutant of Kutuzov's before and during the retreat from Moscow by the Russian forces.

Schopenhauer, Arthur (1788-1860). *Anna Karenina* (8, 9). The pessimistic German philosopher whom Levin read in his search for meaning in life. He received comfort by substituting the word "love" for the word "will" in Schopenhauer's writings, but he decided that the philosopher was alien to real life. "The Kreutzer Sonata" (11). Poznyshev said that Schopenhauer would be correct if there was no aim to life. *Resurrection* (2, 23). Nekhliudov did not feel that Schopenhauer's philosophy could satisfy him.

Schopenhauer, Johanna. "Death," in *A Hunter's Sketches*. The narrator thought that Von der Koch was reading a novel by this writer.

Schoss, Louisa Ivanovna. *War and Peace*. The member of the Rostov household mentioned by Nikolai Rostov in a letter to his family while he was in the War of 1805.

Schubert, Franz Peter (1797-1828). *A Gentry Nest* (33). When Panshin became irritated with Lavretskii, he tried to change the conversation to Schubert's music, but to no avail. *Fathers and Sons* (9). Nikolai Kirsanov played Schubert's "Expectation" on the cello, and Bazarov was greatly amused, to the chagrin of Arkadii. *Rudin* (2). Pandalevskii played Schubert's "Erlkönig" at Rudin's request.

Schubert, Karl Bogdanovich. *War and Peace*. The regimental commander of the Pavlograd Hussars. He dined at the Rostovs.

Schulze-Delitsch, Hermann (1808-1883). *Anna Karenina* (3, 27). The German economist who was mentioned in a conversation between Levin and regional landowners. *Smoke* (4). Gubarev, who led a campaign among some workers for cooperative brotherhoods of laborers, mentioned the German economist.

Schuzburgs. *Anna Karenina*. A banking family recalled by Princess Betsy Tverskaia.

Schwartz. "The Death of Ivan Il'ich." A colleague of Petr Ivanovich.

Schwartzenberg, Prince Karl Philipp Fürst zo (1771-1820). *War and Peace* (2, 2, 7). The field marshal who was a minister in St.

Petersburg in 1808 and commanded an Austrian army in 1813. He was named at one of Anna Pavlovna's soirées.

Scott, Sir Walter (1771-1832). *Evgenii Onegin* (4, 43). The Scotch poet and novelist whom Pushkin suggested one could read in the wintertime. *A Gentry Nest* (32). Panshin loaned a novel by Scott to Liza Kalitina.

Scribe, Augustin Eugène (1791-1861). *A Gentry Nest* (40). The French writer whom Varvara Lavretskaia saw as a great connoisseur of the human heart.

Sebastiani, Count Horace (1775-1851). *War and Peace* (4, 2, 9). The French marshal whom Napoleon ordered to watch the movements of Russians on the roads outside Moscow after the French occupied the city.

Sedmoretskii. *War and Peace.* The divisional commander cited by Bilibin in a letter to Prince Andrei Bolkonskii.

Selenin. *Resurrection.* The public prosecutor on Maslova's appeal who, after successfully defeating the appeal, worked to help her receive the Emperor's clemency.

Selivanov. *War and Peace.* A merchant in Smolensk during the War of 1812.

Seliverstych. "Death," in *A Hunter's Sketches.* The local medic who did not arrive in time to save Maksim's life after the tree had fallen on him.

Semen. *Anna Karenina.* A contractor who lived near Levin's estate. *Resurrection.* A cross old man on the Nekhliudov estate. *War and Peace.* The first violinist in Count Rostov's orchestra.

Semen Ivanovich. *Resurrection.* A friend of the author Fanarin. He was the advocate Nezhdanov went to on behalf of Katiusha Maslova's appeal.

Semen Petrovich. *Evgenii Onegin.* A relative of the Larins who was very tight with his money.

Semen Stolpnik. "Living Holy Relics," in *A Hunter's Sketches.* The saint who stood on a pillar for thirty years.

Semenenko. *Resurrection.* Charskaia mentioned this name as one typical of the fools who worked in the senate.

Semenov. *Anna Karenina.* Recalled by Karenin as a man whose wife had been unfaithful.

Semenova, Nymphodora (1787-1876). *Evgenii Onegin* (1, 18). Pushkin wrote that the noted actress shared tribute with V. A. Ozerov, who wrote some of the plays she acted in. *War and Peace* (2, 5, 8). The Russian operatic actress who was more famous for her acting than her voice. Pushkin, Griboedov and other famous writers knew her well.

Sénancour, Étienne Pivert de (1770-1846). *A Gentry Nest* (28). The French author of the pessimistic novel *Obermann* (1804).

Seneca, Lucius Annaeus (4 B.C.-65 A.D.). *Evgenii Onegin* (5-22). Tat'iana was not reading the Roman writer in bed.

Sen-Pri, Count (1806-1828). *Evgenii Onegin* (8, 26). A young French émigré who drew caricatures of noblemen in young girls' albums.

Serezha. A diminutive of Sergei. *Anna Karenina*. Anna's eight-year-old son.

Sergei, Prince. *War and Peace*. The aristocrat whom Pierre Bezukhov called a splendid man when he returned to Natasha at Bald Hills after being in St. Petersburg on business.

Sergei Nikolaevich. "First Love." The corpulent guest who stated that his first love began with his second love.

Serpukhovskoi. *Anna Karenina*. A classmate of Vronskii's at the Corps des Pages who became a general in three years.

Sestrin. *Anna Karenina*. The starter at the horse race.

Sh___, Countess. *Smoke*. The well-known dictator of fashion who attended Irina's party.

Shabashkin. "Dubrovskii." The magistrate whom Troekurov asked to deprive Dubrovskii of his estate.

Shakespeare, William (1564-1616). *Anna Karenina* (1, 33). The English poet and dramatist whom Karenin liked to discuss to show off his reading interests. *A Gentry Nest* (5). Lemm liked to read the English writer in solitude. *Smoke* (4). The English playwright recalled by Voroshilov rather cuttingly to Bambaev, who had interrupted him.

Shakhovskaia. *Anna Karenina*. A girl Dolly predicted would marry a Mr. Breteln, and she did.

Shakhovskoi, Aleksandr Aleksandrovich (1777-1846). *Evgenii Onegin* (1, 18). The playwright known for his caustic comedies.

Shapovalov. *War and Peace*. The cossack on a reconnoitering patrol who stumbled on the left flank of Murat's army encamped deep in a forest without any guard.

Shchapov, Afanasii Prokof'evich (1830-1876). *Smoke* (4). The Russian historian and publicist mentioned by Voroshilov when he was finally able to interrupt Madame Sukhanchikova.

Shcheglov. *Resurrection*. A prisoner who was continually escaping.

Shchentinnina, Maria Pavlovna. *Resurrection*. The political

prisoner who was imprisoned voluntarily and who thought
that physical love for a man was wrong. She had a positive
influence on her fellow prisoners, and they respected her.

Shchepetenko. "The Singers," in *A Hunter's Sketches*. The man to
whom a high-ranking landowner bowed when he passed him.

Shcherbatii, Tikhon (Tishka). *War and Peace*. A member of Denisov's guerrilla detachment.

Shcherbatov, Prince Dmitrii Mikhailovich (1760-1839). *War and Peace*
(4, 1, 10). The son of the famous historian M. M. Shcherbatov
whose Moscow house was occupied by the Duke of Eckmühl
during the French occupation.

Shcherbatskaia, Princess. *Anna Karenina*. The mother of Natal'ia,
Dolly and Kitty. She regretted that marriages were no longer
arranged by parents, as in her time.

Shcherbatskaia, Princess Dar'ia. *Anna Karenina*. See Oblonskaia,
Dolly.

Shcherbatskaia, Princess Kitty. *Anna Karenina*. The heroine who
married Levin after her infatuation with Vronskii. She
settled for the life of a country gentlewoman.

Shcherbatskaia, Princess Natal'ia. *Anna Karenina*. See L'vova,
Natal'ia.

Shcherbatskii, Prince Aleksandr. *Anna Karenina*. The father of
Kitty, Dolly and Natal'ia. He disliked Vronskii and was glad
that Kitty married Levin.

Shcherbatskii, Prince Nikolai Aleksandrovich. *Anna Karenina*. A
cousin of the family who appeared at the skating rink when
Levin skated with Kitty.

Shcherbinin. *War and Peace*. The orderly on duty at the General
Staff when Bolkhovitinov brought the news of the French
retreat from Moscow.

Shchitov. *Rudin*. A student friend of Rudin and Lezhnev.

Shebek, Ivan Egorovich. "The Death of Ivan Il'ich." The members
of the court met in his room when they heard of Ivan's death.

Shelgunov, Nikolai Vasil'evich (1824-1891). *Smoke* (4). The publicist
and literary critic of the democratic camp who was mentioned by Voroshilov when he was finally able to interrupt
Madame Sukhanchikova.

Shenbok. *Resurrection*. Nekhliudov's friend in the guards who
owed 200,000 roubles in debts. He was finally able to have a
rich man turn over the management of his estates to him.

Shestova, Kapitolina Markovna. *Smoke*. An elderly spinster and the aunt of Tania. The old woman loved to flaunt her anti-social behavior.

Shestova, Tat'iana Petrovna (Tania). *Smoke.* The deserted girl friend of Gregorii Mikhailovich Litvinov. She was very kind and good-natured. After his ruinous affair with Irina Ratmirova, Litvinov returned to Tat'iana and they renewed their love.

Shilton, Baroness. *Anna Karenina.* The girl friend of Lieutenant Petritskii.

Shinshin. *War and Peace.* An old bachelor cousin of the Countess Rostova.

Shinshina, Natal'ia. *War and Peace.* Countess Natal'ia Rostova's name before her marriage.

Shirkov. *Anna Karenina.* A financier in the Kashin province.

Shishkov, Aleksandr Semenovich (1754-1841). *Evgenii Onegin* (8, 14). The conservative writer who was against foreign words in Russian literary works. Pushkin asked his forgiveness when he could not translate a French phrase he used. *War and Peace.* (3, 1, 3). The secretary to Tsar Aleksandr I who was the author of the declaration of war in 1812 and who was Minister of Education from 1824 to 1828.

Shittov. *War and Peace.* A guest at one of Anna Pavlovna Scherer's soirées.

Shönlein, Johann Lucas (1793-1864). *Fathers and Sons* (20). The German doctor whom Vasilii Bazarov referred to when trying to show he was knowledgeable in the medical field.

Shopman from Zhizdra. "Singers," in *A Hunter's Sketches.* The city slicker who was Iashka the Turk's rival in the singing contest.

Shtabel. "The Death of Ivan Il'ich." A candidate for Alekseev's post.

Shtaps, Friedrich (1792-1809). *War and Peace* (3, 3, 27). The German student who tried to assassinate Napoleon in Vienna in 1812 and was shot for his attempt. Pierre Bezukhov recalled the student when he himself plotted Napoleon's demise.

Shubin, Pavel Iakovlich. *On the Eve.* The son of Anna Vasil'evna's second cousin who was a sculptor and made fun of everything. He was in love with Elena Stakhova.

Shuraev. *Anna Karenina.* A renter of some of Levin's land.

Shurochka. *A Gentry Nest.* A nine-year-old orphan companion of Marfa Pestel'.

Shustova, Lidia (Lidochka). *Resurrection.* A political prisoner whom Nekhliudov helped to release from prison.

Shvabrin, Aleksei Ivanovich. *The Captain's Daughter.* The fellow officer who fought Grinev in a duel over Masha. Later he turned traitor and joined Pugachev's rebellion.

Sidor. *Fathers and Sons.* A peasant to whom Bazarov referred when talking with Arkadii about class rights. "Khor' and Kalinych," in *A Hunter's Sketches.* Khor''s son. "The Office," in *A Hunter's Sketches.* The peasant who dealt with the fat clerk.

Sidorich. "Dubrovskii." The postmaster.

Sidorov. *Resurrection.* A prison attendant. *War and Peace.* A soldier overheard talking with a French grenadier as Prince Andrei Bolkonskii rode to the front lines near Grunt in the War of 1805.

Sigonin. *Anna Karenina.* In a good mood, Karenin decided to have his furniture upholstered like Sigonin's. Karenin also mentioned him as a man whose wife was unfaithful.

Silin, Vladimir. *Virgin Soil.* A friend of Nekhliudov to whom the latter wrote many letters.

Silushka. *Virgin Soil.* A diminutive of Sila.

Simon. See Semen.

Simonson, Vladimir. *Resurrection.* A political prisoner who fell in love with Katiusha Maslova; she agreed to marry him. He was a vegetarian and was very outspoken.

Sinetskaia, Mariana Vikentevna. *Virgin Soil.* Mme. Sipiagin's niece. The woman considered her an atheist and a nihilist. The girl was not a beauty, but emanated impetuousness and passion.

Siniavin, Count. *Anna Karenina.* A guest at Kitty's wedding.

Sipiagin, Boris Andreich. *Virgin Soil.* The landowner and pillar of society who hired Nezhdanov as a tutor for his son.

Sipiagin, Kolia. *Virgin Soil.* Valentina and Boris's son.

Sipiagina, Valentina Mikhailovna. *Virgin Soil.* Boris's beautiful and bewitching wife, who could not tolerate revolutionaries.

Sismondi, Jean Charles Leonard (1773-1842). *War and Peace* (E, 1, 16). The French economist and historian recalled by Pierre Bezukhov when he and Natasha were visiting at Bald Hills.

Sistine Madonna. *War and Peace* (3, 2, 26). The eyes of the Infant Child in this picture by Raphael (1518) were similar to the eyes of Napoleon's child in the painting by Gérard.

Sisyphus. "The Kreutzer Sonata" (10). A legendary King of Corinth whose task in the world of shades was to roll a huge stone up the hill till it reached the top. As the stone rolled back constantly, his work was incessant; hence, a "labor of Sisyphus."

Sitnikov. "Lebedian'," in *A Hunter's Sketches*. A well-known horse dealer.

Sitnikov, Victor. *Fathers and Sons*. A friend and disciple of Bazarov.

Skorodumov, Prince. *Anna Karenina*. The name which Anna mentioned to the door servants at her home when she went to see her son.

Skoropikhin. *Virgin Soil*. The art critic referred to by Paklin while conversing with Miss Mashurina.

Skotinin. *Evgenii Onegin* (5, 26). A family that came to Tat'iana Larina's name-day party. The name Skotinin was derived from the word "cattle" (skot) and was first used by D. I. Fonvizin in his comedy *The Ignorant Minor* (1782).

Skovorodnikov. *Resurrection*. The jurist who voted down Maslova's appeal because Nekhliudov's desire to marry the prisoner was repugnant to him.

Skurekhin. *A Gentry Nest*. The one-eyed brigadier guest of Petr Lavretskii.

Slocum, Jeremiah. *Spring Freshets*. The man who married Gemma Roselli and took her to New York where they raised a family in luxury.

Slyndin, Mikhail. *Anna Karenina*. Karenin's private secretary.

Smelkov, Ferapont. *Resurrection*. The guild merchant whom Maslova and two others were accused of murdering.

Smith, Adam (1723-1790). *Evgenii Onegin* (1, 7). The Scotch economist whom Onegin read. *Smoke* (3). Voroshilov recalled the economist in a conversation with Litvinov.

Smolianinov. *War and Peace*. A rhetor of the Masons in St. Petersburg.

Snandulia. *Virgin Soil*. Paklin's hunchbacked sister, who played well on the piano.

Snapochka. *Virgin Soil*. Paklin's name for his sister Snadulia.

Snetkov. *Anna Karenina*. A marshal of the nobility noted for his conservatism.

Socrates (469-399 B.C.). *Anna Karenina* (5, 9). In a conversation with Anna and Vronskii, Golenishchev suggested that artists quit trying to depict Christ and turn to figures from

history such as Socrates, the Greek philosopher. "Khor'
and Kalinych," in *A Hunter's Sketches*. Khor''s face reminded one of Socrates.

Sofia. "Hamlet of the Shchigrovskii District," in *A Hunter's
Sketches*. The daughter of the Russian Hamlet's neighbor
whom "Hamlet" married but who died in childbirth.

Sofia Aleksandrovna. *War and Peace*. A cousin of the Rostovs who
loved Nikolai Rostov but relinquished her feelings when
he married Mar'ia Bolkonskaia. Sofia lived with them as a
governess for their children.

Sofron. "Ermolai and the Miller's Wife," in *A Hunter's Sketches*.
A muzhik whom Ermolai knew.

Sofron Iakovlich. "The Steward," in *A Hunter's Sketches*. The
steward who returned from Perov to see Arkadii Pavlich
Penochkin. He pretended to be kind, but the narrator
learned that he was famous for abusing the serfs.

Sokolov. "The Death of Ivan Il'ich." Ivan's butler. *Resurrection*.
The chief warden who escorted Maslova to her ward. *War and
Peace*. A soldier in the shed where Pierre Bezukhov was a
prisoner in Moscow during the French occupation.

Sokolov, Afanasii (Khlopushka). *The Captain's Daughter*. An ugly
old peasant whom Pugachev made a general.

Sokolov, Il'ia Osipovich (Iliusha). *War and Peace*. A gypsy choir
leader in Moscow.

Solomin, Vasilii Feodotich. *Virgin Soil*. The factory manager and
revolutionary who married Mariana after Nezhdanov's death.

Solomon. *Smoke* (14). The wisest of the kings of Israel, whom
Potugin mentioned while talking with Litvinov. *War and
Peace* (2, 2, 3). The Biblical character mentioned during
Pierre Bezukhov's Masonic initiation.

Solon (c. 560 B.C.). *Smoke* (28). The Athenian lawgiver whom
Litvinov remembered when he accidentally ran into Pishchalkin.

Sonia. "First Love." A chambermaid in the Zasekin household.
War and Peace. A diminutive for Sofia.

Soniakova. "Lebedian'," in *A Hunter's Sketches*. The actress whom
Prince N——— preferred to Verzhembitskaia.

Soniushka. A diminutive for Sofia or Sonia.

Sonnenberg. *A Gentry Nest*. A provincial governor and a relative
of Panchin. He was a general but was not on active duty.

Sophie. A diminutive for Sofia.

Sorbier, General Jean Bartelemy (1762-1827). *War and Peace* (3, 2, 27). A French commander at Borodino.

Sorokina, Princess. *Anna Karenina*. The girl whom Vronskii's mother wanted him to marry.

Sorokoumov, Avenir. "Death," in *A Hunter's Sketches*. A hired tutor who died. He was a fellow student of the narrator.

Sotinin. *Evgenii Onegin*. An old couple who were neighbors of the Larins in the country.

Souza-Botelho, Adelaide Fillend, Marquise de (1761-1817). *War and Peace* (2, 2, 1). A French writer mentioned by Julie Drubetskaia.

Spencer, Herbert (1826-1903). *Anna Karenina* (3, 28). The English sociologist whose philosophy of education was similar to Levin's. *Resurrection* (2, 23). When Nekhliudov was investigating the veracity of the Russian Orthodox Church, he avoided the works of Spencer and turned to Hegel.

Speranskaia, Elizaveta Mikhailovna (b. 1799). *War and Peace* (2, 3, 28). The daughter of M. M. Speranskii who was married to Frolov-Bagreev.

Speranskii, Mikhail Mikhailovich (1772-1839). *Fathers and Sons* (16). The Russian statesman during the reign of Aleksandr I who was the grandson of a deacon. Bazarov was also the grandson of a deacon and was proud of it. *War and Peace* (2, 3, 4). The leader of judicial reforms from 1808 to 1812. In 1812, he fell into disfavor in the government of Aleksandr I.

Spielhagen, F. (1829-1911). *Virgin Soil* (29). The German writer whose works Mariana read aloud to Nezhdanov after the two ran away from the Sipiagin household.

Spinoza, Baruch (1632-1677). *Anna Karenina* (8, 9). The Dutch philosopher whom Levin read in his search for meaning in life. He decided that philosophers are entrapped in words and reason, and fail to see all aspects of life.

Spitin. "Dubrovskii." Troekurov's family bought an estate from him and later sold it to the Dubrovskiis.

Stadnitskii, Boleslav. *Smoke*. A man who, according to Madame Sukhanchikova, had a wonderful nature but was frivolous.

Staël, Mme. de (née Germaine Necker) (1766-1817). *Evgenii Onegin*. The epigraph to Chapter Four is from de Stael's *Considérations sur les principaux événemens de la Révolution française* (1818). Also

(8, 35). The French writer whom Onegin read while trying not to think of Tat'iana. *War and Peace* (4, 1, 7). The celebrated writer and hostess who was exiled from France for her political opposition to Napoleon.

Stahl. *Anna Karenina*. An invalid high-society woman who came to the German spa which the Shcherbatskiis visited.

Stahr, Adolph (1805-1876). *Smoke* (4). The German writer of a series of works on the history of art. He was mentioned by Voroshilov when he managed to interrupt Madame Sukhanchikova.

Stakhov, Nikolai Artemevich. *On the Eve*. Elena's father, who spent most of his time in Moscow with his German mistress.

Stakhov, Uvar Ivanovich. *One the Eve*. Nikolai Artemevich's uncle twice removed who was a retired cornetist and rarely spoke.

Stakhova, Anna Vasil'evna (née Shubina). *On the Eve*. Elena's mother and Shubin's patroness.

Stakhova, Elena Nikolaevna (Lenochka). *On the Eve*. The Stakhov's daughter who secretly married Insarov and left for Bulgaria with him. After his death in Venice, she went on to Bulgaria to serve as a nurse.

Starikov. *Resurrection*. The clerk of a merchant with whom Smelkov had done some business.

Stavasser, Petr Andreevich (1816-1850). *On the Eve* (2). The Russian sculptor who was successful in Italy, according to Shubin.

Stegunov, Mardarii Apollonych. "Two Landowners," in *A Hunter's Sketches*. A landed proprietor and a neighbor of the narrator.

Stein, Freiherr Heinrich Friedrich Karl von und zum (1757-1831). *War and Peace* (3, 1, 6). The Prussian minister whom Napoleon sent into exile from Germany. From 1809 to 1812, he was in Russia. (E, 2, 2). He helped restore the Bourbons to power in France.

Stepan. *Resurrection*. The Korchagin's butler. *Rudin*. Lasunskaia's cook.

Stepan Stepanich. *War and Peace*. The person whom Pierre Bezukhov mentioned to Natasha after the war as his mentor in expressing his experiences.

Stephenson, George (1781-1848). *Virgin Soil* (26). Sipiagin called Solomin a "home-grown Stephenson," referring to the English inventor.

Stepka. "Dubrovskii." A sentry in Dubrovskii's camp.

Stepushka. "Raspberry Spring," in *A Hunter's Sketches*. The old man who lived in the garden of the Shumikhino estate. No one knew him or gave him any attention.

Steshka. "Lebedian'," in *A Hunter's Sketches*. A gypsy singer. *War and Peace*. A name mentioned by Anatol Kuragin to a gypsy girl when he was preparing to elope with Natasha Rostova.

Stevens. *War and Peace*. An English naval officer who attended the wild party at Prince Anatol' Kuragin's.

Stiva. *Anna Karenina*. Society's name for Stepan Oblonskii.

Stolypin, Arkadii Alekseevich (1778-1825). *War and Peace* (2, 3, 18). A senator and writer who was a dinner guest at Speranskii's.

Stolz, Baroness Sappho. *Anna Karenina*. A member of a select Petersburg circle entitled "les sept merveilles du monde."

Stowe, Harriet Beecher (1811-1896). *Smoke* (4). The author of *Uncle Tom's Cabin*. She was supposed to have slapped Tenteleev's face once in Paris.

Stratelates, Theodore (d. 319). *A Gentry Nest* (8). The general in the army of Licinius, by whose order he was tortured and crucified at Heraclea in Thrace.

Strauch, General (d. 1836). *War and Peace* (1, 2, 3). The Austrian general who was attached to Kutuzov's staff in 1806.

Strauss, David Friedrich (1808-1879). *Anna Karenina* (5, 9). The German philosopher whom Golenishchev criticized in a conversation with Anna and Vronskii for his interpretation of Christ. *Smoke* (2). Kapitolina Shestova, an old maid, read the German philosopher in secret because he doubted the holiness of Christ.

Strauss, Johann (1825-1899). *A Gentry Nest* (39). Varvara Lavretskaia played a Strauss waltz on the piano. *Smoke* (1). Strauss waltzes were played on the pavilion at the German resort in Baden where Litvinov stayed.

Stremov. *Anna Karenina*. One of the most influential people in St. Petersburg and an admirer of Lisa Merkalov.

Stroganov, General Pavel Aleksandrovich (1774-1817). *War and Peace* (1, 3, 15). The general who was in Tsar Aleksandr I's review suite at Olmutz in 1805.

Strongman Andreich. *War and Peace*. Count Kochubei's name for Count Arakcheev.

Stur, Ludwig (1815-1856). *Smoke* (4). The author of *The Slavs and the World of the Future* who was recalled by Voroshilov when he finally interrupted Madame Sukhanchikova.

Subbotin. *Rudin*. A poet and student friend of Rudin and Lezhnev.

Subochev, Foma Lavrentievich. *Virgin Soil*. An old relative of Paklin's who was very eccentric and lived in the past.

Subocheva, Evfenia Pavlovna. *Virgin Soil*. Foma's wife, who was a relic from the eighteenth century.

Suchok (The Twig). "L'gov," in *A Hunter's Sketches*. The peasant who was a retired coachman and was made a fisherman.

Sue, Eugène (1804-1857). *A Gentry Nest* (40). The French novelist whom Varvara Lavretskaia read.

Sukhanchikova, Matrena Semenovna. *Smoke*. The childless widow who joined Bambaev, Voroshilov and Litvinov in conversation.

Sukhorukii, Ivanushka. "Bezhin Meadow," in *A Hunter's Sketches*. The peasant who spent the night in a paper mill.

Sukhtelen, Count Pavel Petrovich (1788-1833). *War and Peace* (1,3, 19). The cornet of the Cavalierguard Regiment who, in 1805, was taken prisoner by the French at the Battle of Austerlitz. He returned to Russia in 1806 and became a general.

Sumarokov, Aleksandr Petrovich (1718-1777). *The Captain's Daughter* (4). The Russian writer who was supposed to have praised Grinev's writing at one time.

Super-Sham. *War and Peace*. The name Maria Dmitrievna Akhrosimova used for the dressmaker Madame Chalmé.

Surin. "The Queen of Spades." One of the officers who lost heavily at cards at Narumov's.

Suvorov, Aleksandr Vasil'evich (1730-1800). *Fathers and Sons* (21). Vasilii Bazarov once served under the famous general. *War and Peace* (1, 1, 6). The distinguished military figure during the war with Prussia (1756-1763); the First Turkish War (1768-1774); and the Second Turkish War (1787-1791). In 1799, he commanded the Austro-Russian armies in the war against France.

Svechina, S. P. (1782-1859). *Fathers and Sons* (12). The mystic who knew many statesmen during the reign of Aleksandr I.

Sverlitskii. *Virgin Soil*. A journalist whose writings Kisliakov used as a guide while spreading propaganda among workers.

Svetlana. *Evgenii Onegin* (3, 5). The heroine of Zhukovskii's ballad by that name (1812).

Sviazhskii, Nikolai Ivanovich. *Anna Karenina*. The friend whom Levin went to see in order to avoid calling on the Oblonskiis.

Svintich. *Anna Karenina*. His jubilee was held at the Society of Lovers of Art and Science.

Swedenborg, Emmanuel (1688-1772). *On the Eve* (10). The Swedish scholar who influenced Bersenev's father in his youth.

Taine, Hippolyte (1828-1893). *Anna Karenina* (6, 32). When Anna and Vronskii were living in the country, she read a book by the French critic while Vronskii was away at the elections. *Smoke* (4). Voroshilov mentioned the French philosopher and historian when he was finally able to interrupt Madame Sukhanchikova.

Talleyrand-Perigord, Charles Maurice de (1754-1838). *Anna Karenina* (2, 5). When Vronskii was bragging about his ability to manipulate people, he likened himself to the brilliant French statesman. *Virgin Soil* (35). The governor quoted the French diplomat while talking with Sipiagin. *War and Peace* (3, 1, 1). The French diplomat was Minister of Foreign Affairs during the Napoleonic period.

Talma, Francis Joseph (1763-1826). *War and Peace* (3, 3, 29). A noted French actor mentioned in a description of France while Pierre Bezukhov was imprisoned in Moscow.

Tania. A diminutive for Tat'iania. *Anna Karenina*. Stepan and Dolly's eldest daughter was Tania. Also Kitty and Levin's daughter was Tania. *Smoke*. See Shestova, Tat'iana.

Taniushka. A diminutive for Tat'iana. *Fathers and Sons*. A servant girl of the Bazarovs.

Taporov. *Resurrection*. The head of the Holy Synod who gave Nekhliudov a release for some prisoners because he did not want the case to come to the attention of the tsar.

Taras. *War and Peace*. A cook at the Rostovs. Also a gardener at the Bolkonskiis' Bald Hills estate.

Taras Alekseevich. "Dubrovskii." An official who came to claim the Dubrovskii estate but perished in the fire.

Tarbuskii, Prince. *Spring Freshets*. The man who presented a laurel wreath to Panteleone for his singing.

Tarde, Gabrielle (1843-1904). *Resurrection* (2, 30). The French socialist whom Nekhliudov read when he was studying as to why the persecuted in criminal courts are the same type of people as those who judge them.

Tartar. *Anna Karenina*. A waiter in the restaurant where Levin and Oblonskii had lunch. *War and Peace*. A cossack at Borodino.

Tartuffe. *Rudin* (6). Lezhnev compared Rudin with Tartuffe, the Molière character known as a hypocrite and imposter.

Tasso, Torquato (1544-1595). *Evgenii Onegin* (1, 48). The Italian poet whose octaves inspired many European writers. "Princess Mary," in *A Hero of Our Time*. Dr. Werner compared women with the enchanted forest which Tasso described in his *Jerusalem Liberated* (1581).

Tatarinova, Ekaterina Filipovna (1783-1856). *War and Peace* (E, 1, 13). The spiritualist, recalled by Denisov in conversation, who in 1817 founded a spiritualistic circle in St. Petersburg which lasted until 1837. She was arrested and banned from the city.

Tat'iana. *Evgenii Onegin*. See Tat'iana Larina. "The Office," in *A Hunter's Sketches*. The girl who suffered at the hands of Khvostov, according to Pavel Andreich. *On the Eve*. A maid in the Stakhovs' home who ran away but was caught. Elena remembered her because she herself was going to be a runaway. *Smoke*. See Shestova, Tat'iana.

Tat'iana Osipovna. *Virgin Soil*. Pavel Egorich's wife.

Tat'iana Vasil'evna. "L'gov," in *A Hunter's Sketches*. The woman who sold the estate to Afanasii Nefedych.

Teacher. *Virgin Soil*. The title Sipiagin called Nezhdanov when he arrived in the country to teach Kolia Sipiagin.

Telegin, Mikhail Sergeevich (Misha). *Resurrection*. Korchagin's cousin.

Telianin. *War and Peace*. A member of Denisov's squadron who stole Denisov's money at Braunau.

Telushkin, Petr Stepanovich. *Smoke* (14). The man who climbed the spire of the Admiralty Building in St. Petersburg in 1831 without the help of a ladder.

Tenteleev. *Smoke*. The man who, according to Mme. Sukhantchikova, was slapped by Mrs. Harriet Beecher Stowe in Paris.

Terentii. *War and Peace*. Pierre Bezukhov's servant from Moscow who nursed him at Orel after his liberation from the French.

Tereshchinko. *Anna Karenina*. A servant of Captain Iashvin.

Terlakhov. *Rudin*. The foreign companion of Rudin who told of the hero's unsuccessful love affair.

Terpsichore. *Evgenii Onegin* (1, 19). The Greek muse of dancing and lyric poetry, whom Pushkin recalled when Onegin went to the theater.

Terteresheneva, Princess. "Tat'iana Borisovna and Her Nephew," in *A Hunter's Sketches*. The aristocrat who commissioned Tat'iana's nephew to paint her picture.

Thalberg, Zigizmund (1812-1871). *Rudin* (1). The Austrian pianist whose étude was played by Pandalevskii.

Thalia. *Evgenii Onegin* (7, 50). The Greek Muse of comedy, whom Pushkin described as asleep when Tat'iana had to face society.

Themistocles (527?-460 B.C.). *On the Eve* (13). The Greek warrior who ate dinner on the eve of the Battle of Salamis (480 B.C.). Bersenev mentioned the fact when Elena Stakhova pointed out two Bulgarians who gulped their food.

Theocritus (3rd Cent. A.D.). The Greek bucolic poet who is regarded as the founder of pastoral poetry. *Evgenii Onegin* (1, 7). Evgenii only had scorn for the poet.

Theodore. *A Gentry Nest*. Varvara Lavretskaia's name for Fedor Lavretskii after her return from Paris.

Thérèse. *Anna Karenina* (3, 4). Vronskii's mistress before his involvement with Anna.

Thiers, Louis Adolphe (1797-1877). *Virgin Soil* (35). The French historian who was President of France from 1871 to 1873. Sipiagin liked to imitate him while traveling by pretending to be at work on research. *War and Peace* (3, 2, 7). Tolstoi belittled Thiers's comments about a captured Russian soldier who confronted Napoleon. (4, 2, 10). Tolstoi discredited Thiers's statements concerning Napoleon's campaign plans.

Thomas a Kempis (c. 1380-1471). *War and Peace* (2, 2, 3). The name of the Augustinian writer Thomas Hammerhem (Hammershen, Malleskus), who wrote *An Imitation of Christ* (1427).

Thoreau, Henry David (1817-1862). *Resurrection*. While in Moscow, Nekhliudov remembered the American writer who said, "Under a government which imprisons anyone unjustly, the true place for a just man is in prison."

Tikhon. *War and Peace*. An old servant at the Bolkonskii estate.

Timofei. "The Office," in *A Hunter's Sketches*. The person to whom the narrator was advised to go for tea.

Timofei Nikolaevich. *On the Eve*. See Granovskii, T. N.

Timofeich. *The Captain's Daughter*. Pugachev called this fifty-year-old peasant sometimes by his name and sometimes by the title of Count. *Fathers and Sons*. A steward of the Bazarovs.

Timokhin. *Resurrection*. Smelkov's friend who first brought to the authorities attention that Smelkov might have been poisoned and did not die from too much alcohol. *War and Peace*. A red-nosed captain whom Kutuzov addressed at Braunau during the War of 1805. Also the batallion commander in Prince Andrei's regiment during the Russian retreat from Smolensk.

Timoshka. "Dubrovskii." An infirmary for sick dogs was supervised by this staff surgeon.

Tintoretto (Jacopo Robusti) (1512-1594). *Anna Karenina* (5, 7). Golenishchev advised Anna and Vronskii to see the Tintoretto in the small Italian town where the old school comrades accidentally met. *On the Eve* (33). Elena laughed at Tintoretto's "Saint Mark" leaping from heaven when she and Insarov were in Venice.

Tishka. *War and Peace*. A diminutive of Tikhon.

Tissot (1728-1797). *Evgenii Onegin* (8, 35). A French doctor who was the author of scientific books.

Tit. *War and Peace*. Kutuzov's old cook.

Titian, Vecelli (1477-1576). *Anna Karenina* (5, 11). When Mikhailov showed his paintings of Christ and Pilate to Anna and Vronskii, he thought of Titian's interpretation of the Christ figure and compared it to his own. *On the Eve* (33). Insarov was delighted with Titian's "The Ascension" when he and Elena were in Venice.

Titus. *Anna Karenina*. Levin's instructor in the art of mowing. *A Gentry Nest* (8). *À la Titus* was a short-hair style worn by the French actor Talma for the role of Titus in the play *Brutus* (1783) by Alfieri. When long-haired wigs without powder were forbidden in France in 1790, the hairdresser Duplan thought up the hair style for the French actor, and it became fashionable in Paris.

Titus, Flavius Vespasian (41-81). *War and Peace* (2, 1, 3). The Roman emperor, known for his justice, who was mentioned in the poem read at the reception which Count Il'ia Rostov gave for General Bagration.

Tiutiurev. "The Office," in *A Hunter's Sketches*. The man in whose house Iagushin wanted to meet Vasilii Nikolaevich to discuss a deal.

Tocqueville, Count Alexis Charles Henri Maurice Clérel de (1805-1859). *Rudin* (3). The French historian and author of *De-*

mocracy in America. He was mentioned in conversation between Lasunskaia and Rudin.

Toggenburg. *Fathers and Sons* (17). A hero of a ballad by Schiller. Bazarov felt that the character should have been locked up for his romantic feelings.

Toll, Count Karl Fedorovich (1777-1842). *War and Peace* (3, 1, 11). The Russian general who participated in the War of 1805 and who in 1812 was the Quartermaster General of the Russian Army. He was in almost all the major battles of the Napoleonic wars.

Tolstoi, Count Fedor Petrovich (1783-1873). *Evgenii Onegin* (4, 30). A well-known illustrator.

Tolstoi, Count Nikolai Aleksandrovich (1765-1816). *War and Peace* (1, 3, 11). During the reign of Aleksandr I, Count Tolstoi served as Grand Marshal of the Court in St. Petersburg.

Tolstoi, Count Petr Aleksandrovich (1761-1844). *War and Peace.* (1, 1, 26). The general who headed a detachment of Russian troops sent by ship to Pomerania for action against the French in northern Germany. After the Battle of Austerlitz, the detachment returned by land to Russia.

Tomskii, Pavel Aleksandrovich. "The Queen of Spades." Anna Fedotovna's grandson who related the story about the three secret cards.

Tonkosheev, A. "First Love" (11). The person mentioned by Maidanov as the author of *El Trovador.*

Topcheenko. *War and Peace.* The quartermaster of Denisov's battalion.

Topor. *Anna Karenina.* The person named as the fiancé of Miss Vlaseva at the Princess Betsy Tverskaia's.

Tormasov, Count Aleksandr Petrovich (1752-1819). *War and Peace* (3, 1, 9). The Russian general who commanded the Third Russian Army which defended southern Russia in the War of 1812.

Trediakovskii, Vasilii Kirillich (1703-1769). *The Captain's Daughter.* The Russian writer who was Shvabrin's teacher.

Trifon Ivanovich. "The Country Doctor," in *A Hunter's Sketches.* The doctor who fell in love with his patient Aleksandra Andreevna.

Triquet. *Evgenii Onegin* (5, 27). The Frenchman who came to the Larins' party with the Khalikov family and who presented a poem to Tat'iana, much to her embarrassment.

Trishka. "Bezhin Meadow," in *A Hunter's Sketches*. An amazingly crafty creature, similar to the Antichrist, according to the boys in the meadow.

Troekurov, Kirila Petrovich. "Dubrovskii." The wealthy landowner who considered himself a friend of the older Dubrovskii, but Troekurov took his friend's estate from him. He also forced his daughter to marry a man she did not love.

Troekurova, Maria Kirilovna. "Dubrovskii." The daughter of Kiril Petrovich. She loved Dubrovskii but was forced to marry an older man because of his wealth.

Trofimich. "Bezhin Meadow," in *A Hunter's Sketches*. Il'iusha's grandfather, who saw his deceased master and spoke with him. "Raspberry Spring," in *A Hunter's Sketches*. An old man who knew the genealogy of serfs' families.

Trufonova, Princess. "The Death of Ivan Il'ich." A sister of the distinguished founder of the society called "Bear My Burden." Ivan danced with her at the party which he and his wife gave.

Trukhachevskii. "The Kreutzer Sonata." The friend of Pozdnyshev whom the latter began to suspect of having an affair with his wife. When Pozdnyshev was not able to kill Trukhachevskii, he turned on his wife and murdered her.

Tshibadola. *Spring Freshets*. Richter called Cippatola by this name.

Tuchkov, Nikolai Alekseevich (1761-1812). *War and Peace* (3, 2, 23). The Russian general who participated in the wars of 1799, 1807 and 1808. In 1812 he commanded the Third Infantry Corps. He was mortally wounded at the battle of Borodino.

Turenne, Vicomte de. *War and Peace* (3, 1, 5). A gentleman-in-waiting to Napoleon after the crossing of the Niemen and the invasion of Russia.

Turgenev, Ivan Sergeevich (1818-1883). *Resurrection* (1, 7). One of the Russian writers whose works Nekhliudov gave Katiusha Maslova to read when he first met her at his aunts. She especially liked Turgenev's "A Quiet Place."

Turovtsyn. *Anna Karenina*. A dinner guest at Oblonskii's who was considered silly but good-natured.

Tushin. *War and Peace*. The artillery officer whose battery distinguished itself in the War of 1812 near Shöengraben. Tolstoi heightened Tushin's personality through several humorous incidents; for instance, he was caught off his post without his boots.

212   TUSHKEVICH

Tushkevich. *Anna Karenina*. A handsome young companion of Princess Betsy Tverskaia.

Tutolmin, Ivan Vasil'evich (1751-1815). *War and Peace* (4, 2, 9). The director of a Moscow foundling hospital who stayed in the city during the French occupation to preserve the hospital from destruction. Napoleon sent him to Aleksandr I with a proposal to negotiate peace.

Tvardovskii, Pan. "Lebedian'," in *A Hunter's Sketches*. The opera (1828) by A. N. Versovskii (1799-1862) with a libretto by the Russian writer M. N. Versovskii (1789-1852). The narrator was informed that the opera would be performed in Lebedian'.

Tveritinov, Aleksei Ivanich. *Virgin Soil*. An upper-class man who warned that the peasants would burn the countryside if freed.

Tverskaia, Princess Betsy. *Anna Karenina*. Vronskii's wealthy cousin who was married to a cousin of Anna's. The princess arranged for Anna and Vronskii to meet at her home.

Tyndall, John (1820-1893). *Anna Karenina* (1, 27). In the country, Levin often passed time in reading books such as the English physicist Tyndall's *Treatise on Heat*.

Ul'iana. "Bezhin Meadow," in *A Hunter's Sketches*. The peasant woman who prophesied her own death.

Ul'iashevich. *Virgin Soil*. The official in the governor's chancellery whom Paklin mentioned to Sipiagin.

Ulita. "Biriuk, the Morose One," in *A Hunter's Sketches*. The forester's little girl.

Uncle (Diadiushka). *War and Peace*. See Mikhail Nikanorych. Also the number-one gunner of the second gun crew of Tushin's artillery battery in the War of 1805.

Undine. "Taman,'" in *A Hero of Our Time*. The sweetheart of the bandit Ianko. She tried to drown Pechorin and helped steal his personal possessions.

Uriah. "The Kreutzer Sonata" (22). The Biblical King David sent the soldier Uriah into battle where he would be killed because the king coveted his wife, Bathsheba.

Urusov, Aleksandr Mikhailovich (1766-1853). *War and Peace* (2, 3, 10). A member of the state council referred to in Pierre Bezukhov's diary.

Ustinov. *Resurrection*. The doctor's assistant who pestered Maslova and on whose account she was dismissed from the hospital.

Uvarko. *War and Peace.* A whipper-in during the hunts on the country estate of the Rostovs.

Uvarov, Fedor Petrovich (1773-1824). *War and Peace* (2, 1, 3). A Russian general who commanded a regiment in the Battle of Austerlitz and the Battle of Borodino. From 1813 to 1814, he was in Aleksandr I's general staff.

V——, Brother. *War and Peace.* A member of a Masonic lodge who advised Pierre Bezukhov to stand by Brother A.

Vakhrushkin, Prince. *Smoke.* A cousin of Gubarev.

Vakulov. *Resurrection.* The man in charge of political prisoners in Siberia.

Valerian Petrovich, Count. "Raspberry Spring," in *A Hunter's Sketches.* The son of Count Petr Il'ich, the master of Vlas.

Valia. A diminutive for Valentina. *Virgin Soil.* Sipiagin called his wife Valentina Mikhailovna by this form.

Valuev, Petr Stepanovich (1743-1814). *War and Peace* (2, 1, 2). A Moscow archeologist who held various high governmental positions.

Vampire. "Princess Mary," in *A Hero of Our Time.* An English tale by the name of that fictional monster was written, according to Byron, by a Dr. Polidori. It was translated into Russian and was very popular. Lermontov wrote in the original preface to his novel, "If you believed in the existence of Melmont, the Vampire and others, than why can't you believe in Pechorin?" Pechorin himself said that there were times when he understood the vampire.

Vandyck, Sir Anthony (1599-1641). *Evgenii Onegin* (3, 5). The Flemish painter who studied under Rubens. Onegin said that Ol'ga looked like Vandyck's famous "Madonna": round-faced as the moon.

Vania. A diminutive for Ivan. *Anna Karenina.* A clerk in Levin's office. Levin called him "your Vania" while speaking with his brother Nikolai. "Bezhin Meadow," in *A Hunter's Sketches.* The youngest of the children in the woods around the campfire when the narrator lost his way in the forest. *The Captain's Daughter* (omitted Chapter). Grinev's peasant who was hanged for joining Pugachev. *Evgenii Onegin.* The deceased husband of Tat'iana's nurse. *Resurrection.* A young lad who was being tried for petty burglary.

Van'ka. A diminutive for Ivan. *On the Eve*. A cook in the Stakhovs' home.

Van'ka the Steward. "The Kreutzer Sonata." The subject of an
old folk tale. Van'ka seduced his master's wife, boasted
about the affair and was hanged.

Varenka. A diminutive of Varvara. *Anna Karenina*. The young
helper of Madame Stahl at the German spa who became a
friend of Kitty Shcherbatskaia.

Varia. A diminutive of Varvara. *Anna Karenina*. Vronskii's sister-
in-law, whom Vronskii greatly admired.

Varlamov, Aleksandr Egorovich (1801-1848). *Smoke* (4). The composer of a song which Bambaev started singing in a conversation until someone said he was singing from Verdi's *Il Trova-
tore*.

Varvara, Princess. *Anna Karenina*. A poor aristocrat who lived with
whomever she could. Anna was accompanied by her after returning to St. Petersburg. *A Gentry Nest*. See Lavretskaia.

Vaseek. *Resurrection*. The grandson of the Governor of Siberia.

Vasia. The diminutive of Vasilii. "Bezhin Meadow," in *A Hunter's
Sketches*. Aniutka's lover. "The End of Chertopkhanov,"
in *A Hunter's Sketches*. A peasant boy. "The Kreutzer Sonata."
Pozdnyshev's oldest son. "Khor' and Kalinych," in *A Hunter's
Sketches*. Khor's son. "Petr Petrovich Karataev," in *A Hunter's Sketches*. A servant in the coffeehouse where the narrator
met Karataev. "Tat'iana Borisovna and Her Newphew," in
A Hunter's Sketches. Policarp's grandson. "Two Landowners," in *A Hunter's Sketches*. The butler who was flogged
and said he deserved it. *Virgin Soil*. Golushkin's manager.

Vasil'chikov, General Illarion Vasil'evich (1777-1847). *War and
Peace* (3, 3, 10). The Russian officer who was wounded at the
Battle of Borodino and then commanded the Fourth Cavalry
Corps. He warned Count Rostopchin that there was no pos-
sibility of defending Moscow.

Vasil'chikov. *Anna Karenina*. A successful landowner mentioned by
Levin.

Vasil'chikova. *Anna Karenina*. The woman whom the artist Mikhailov painted.

Vasil'ev. *Anna Karenina*. A person mentioned as a profligate society
member. *Resurrection*. The prisoner who was a clerk and was
liked by his fellow prisoners because he knew the prison
regulations and insisted they be carried out.

Vasil'ev, Feodocii. *Virgin Soil* (17). The founder of a group of Old Believers in the beginning of the eighteenth century which refused to pray for the tsar and refused to pay the tax imposed on Old Believers by Petr I.

Vasil'ev, Vladimir Fedorovich. *War and Peace* (2, 2, 9). According to the memoirs of Denis Davydov, Vasil'ev was the courier whom Bilibin mentioned in his letter to Prince Andrei as having very coarse conduct.

Vasil'evna. *Virgin Soil*. The Subochevs' old nurse.

Vasil'ich. *War and Peace*. A servant of the Rostovs in Moscow.

Vasilii. *Anna Karenina*. A laborer on Levin's estate. Also a hotel clerk whom Stepan Oblonskii knew. "Lebedian'," in *A Hunter's Sketches*." Chernobei's groom. *On the Eve*. The Stakhovs' butler who dragged a legless old man out of a burning hut. *War and Peace*, See Kuragin, Prince Vasilii.

Vasilii Dmitrich. "Death," in *A Hunter's Sketches*. The miller who insisted on dying at home.

Vasilii Ignatich. *War and Peace*. An elderly acquaintance of Count Il'ia Rostov in Moscow.

Vasilii Karlich. *Resurrection*. The German steward who was running Nekhliudov's estate.

Vasilii Lukich. *Anna Karenina*. Serzha's tutor after Anna's departure with Vronskii.

Vasilii Nikolaich. *Virgin Soil*. The head of the Socialist Revolutionary Movement. He was the one who issued orders by letters to the revolutionaries.

Vasilii Nikolaevich. "The Office," in *A Hunter's Sketches*. The head cashier in the hierarchy of clerks in the office.

Vasilii Petrovich. "The Fatalist," in *A Hero of Our Time*. The major at whose house Vulich tested fate by shooting at his head with a loaded revolver.

Vasilii Semenovich. "L'gov," in *A Hunter's Sketches*. The father of Tat'iana Vasil'evna.

Vasilii Vasil'evich. "A Hamlet of the Shchigrovskii District," in *A Hunter's Sketches*. The Russian Hamlet told the narrator to call him by this name since he did not wish to reveal his true identity.

Vasilisa. "Dubrovskii." The woman who kept watch at night. *War and Peace*. An old peasant woman in the Smolensk region who killed many French soldiers in the Partisan War of 1812.

Vasilisa Vasil'evna. "Chertopkhanov and Nedopiuskin," in *A Hunter's Sketches*. The mother of Pantelei.

Vaska. A diminutive for Vasilii. *Anna Karenina*. The young man who accompanied the Baroness Stolz at the Princess Tverskaia's. *Father and Sons*. A serf boy on the Kirsanov estate. *Resurrection*. The sickly child of the peasant Marfa on Nekhliudov's estate. *War and Peace*. Pierrre Bezukhov's servant from Moscow who missed Pierre at Orel.

Vatkovskaia, Princess. *Anna Karenina*. The woman who was jokingly suggested for the military service at a birthday reception at the palace.

Vaucelles, Courtin de. *A Gentry Nest*. The French tutor of Ivan Lavretskii and later the husband of the Princess Kubenskaia.

Vavila. "Bezhin Meadow," in *A Hunter's Sketches*. A copper worker.

Veimar. *War and Peace* (3, 1, 7). The noted German family named by Napoleon at dinner with Balashev.

Venelin, Iuri Ivanovich (Gutsa) (1802-1839). *On the Eve* (11). The Bulgarian folklorist to whom Shubin gave a toast while drinking with Insarov and Bersenev.

Venevskii. *Anna Karenina*. A fellow officer of Vronskii who lost 2,500 roubles playing cards. Vronskii guaranteed the debt.

Venus. *Evgenii Onegin* (1, 25). When Evgenii was dressing, he was described as being similar to a giddy Venus, the goddess of love.

Venus of Milo. "The Kreutzer Sonata" (14). A famous statue of the goddess of love (c. 400 B. C.) Pozdnyshev mentioned the statue when commenting on women as a means of enjoyment.

Venus of Moscow (*la Vénus Moscovite*). "The Queen of Spades." The name given to the Countess Anna Fedotovna when she was a noted beauty in Paris.

Vera. "Hamlet of the Shchigrovskii District," in *A Hunter's Sketches*. The daughter of a neighbor of the Russian Hamlet. "Princess Mary," in *A Hero of Our Times*, See G——va, Vera. *War and Peace*. See Rostova (Berg), Princess Vera Il'inichna.

Verdi, Giuseppe (1813-1901). *On the Eve* (33). Elena and Insarov heard Verdi's *La Traviata* while they were in Venice.

Verdier. *Smoke*. The man who came to Irina's party dressed as a Tyrolian and riding on an ass.

Vereiskii. "Dubrovskii." The rich middle-aged landowner who came from abroad and asked for Mar'ia's hand.

Vereshchagin, Mikhail Nikolaevich (1790-1812). *War and Peace* (3, 3, 25). The son of a Moscow merchant who translated a speech by Napoleon from a Hamburg newspaper and was accused of treason by Rastopchin. When the French were approaching Moscow, Rastopchin allowed a mob to hang Vereshchagin.

Vereshchagin, Nikolai Gavrilovich. *War and Peace*. A Moscow merchant, who was the father of Mikhail Vereshchagin.

Verzhembitskaia. "Lebedian'," in *A Hunter's Sketches*. An actress who was performing in the town.

Veselovskii, Grisha. *Anna Karenina*. A soldier who was going to the Turkish front.

Veslovskii, Vasenka. *Anna Karenina*. A second cousin of the Shcherbatskii family. He was a flashy man-about-town and a keen sportsman.

Vesenii. *War and Peace*. The name some cossacks called Vincent Bosse.

Veuillot, Louis François (1813-1883). *Smoke* (5). The French publicist whose pamphlet Prince Koko was reading at Mark's bookstore.

Viazemskii, Count Andrei Ivanovich (1750-1807). *War and Peace* (2, 1, 2). A Russian statesman who was a habitué of the English Club in Moscow.

Viazemskii, Prince Petr Andreevich (1792-1878). *Evgenii Onegin*. The epigraph to Chapter One is from his poem "The First Snow" (1822). The well-known poet was a friend of Pushkin. He was supposed to have met Tat'iana Larina in Moscow. *On the Eve* (34). The Russian poet Lupoiarov quoted Insarov while visiting in Venice.

Viazmitinov, Count Sergei Kuzmich (1749-1819). *War and Peace* (1, 3, 2). The administrative official who was left in command of St. Petersburg in 1805, 1812, and 1815 when Aleksandr I was involved in military affairs outside the capital.

Viceroy. See Beaugarné, Eugène.

Vikhorev. *Virgin Soil* (3). A character with Slavophile tendencies in *Stick to Your Station*, an 1853 play by A. N. Ostrovskii (1823-1886).

Viktor Aleksandrovich. "The Meeting," in *A Hunter's Sketches*. The boy who was the spoiled valet of a rich master and who treated his girl roughly when saying goodbye to her.

Victorinka. See Osinina, Princess Victorinka.

Vikulov, Mikhailo. "The Office," in *A Hunter's Sketches*. The peasant who was the overseer of the countinghouse.

Villeneuve, Pierre de (1763-1806). *War and Peace* (1, 1, 13). The commander of the French navy who committed suicide after losing to the English under Admiral Nelson.

Vinesses. *War and Peace* (1, 3, 1). A celebrated miniaturist who lived in St. Petersburg in 1812 and made many portraits of Russian aristocrats on snuff boxes.

Vinet, Alexandre Rodolphe (1797-1847). *Resurrection* (2, 23). The critic and theologian whom Nekhliudov read to try to understand questions on religion and humanity.

Vinnikov. "The Death of Ivan Il'ich." The candidate for Alekseev's post.

Vinovskii, Petr. *Anna Karenina*. The man who sent Levin and Oblonskii champagne while they were lunching.

Violetta. *On the Eve* (33). The heroine of the opera *La Traviata*, by Verdi, which Elena and Insarov saw in Venice.

Viotti, Giovanni (1753-1824). "Tat'iana Borisovna and Her Nephew," in *A Hunter's Sketches*. The violinist and composer who was worshiped by Polikarp.

Virchow, Rudolph (1821-1902). *Smoke* (4). The German physiologist and founder of cellular pathology who was mentioned by Voroshilov when he finally interrupted Madame Sukhanchikova.

Virgil (Publius Virgilius Maro) (70-19 B.C.). *Evgenii Onegin* (5, 22), The Roman poet whom Tat'iana was not reading in bed. *Virgin Soil* (14). Sipiagin prided himself in knowing some quotations from the Latin poet's works.

Virginia. *Rudin* (7). *Paul and Virginia* was the book by Benardin de Saint-Pierre (1737-1814) which Lezhnev mentioned.

Virsavia. "The Kreutzer Sonata." Uriah's wife.

Vladimir. "L'gov," in *A Hunter's Sketches*. The huntsman who was a liberated house serf and fairly well educated.

Vladimir, Saint. *Fathers and Sons* (21). The Russian saint whose name was used for a medal of honor in the Russian civil service.

Vladimir Petrovich. "First Love" (4). A chief of police known by Princess Zasekina.

Vladimir Sergeich. "First Love." The host in whose house the gentlemen relate the history of their first loves.

Vlas. "Raspberry Spring," in *A Hunter's Sketches*. Fog's brother, who came to the spring. *War and Peace*. One of the peasants who were plundering Moscow during the fire.

Vlaseva. *Anna Karenina*. A girl mentioned at Princess Tverskoi's who was supposed to be in love with Sir John.

Vogel'. *War and Peace*. The dancing master in Moscow who gave parties for his students.

Vogelmayer, Karolina. *On the Eve*. A name Insarov thought up as a typically anonymous one when he was having trouble obtaining a passport. Later he saw a woman of that name in a dream.

Voinitsin. "A Hamlet of the Shchigrovskii District," in *A Hunter's Sketches*. The young man who lived in Aleksandr Mikhailovich's house in a capacity which one would find difficult to describe, according to the narrator.

Voitov. *Anna Karenina*. An acquaintance of Iashvin's who came to buy a horse from Vronskii.

Voldemar. *Virgin Soil*. The governor to whom Sipiagin went in regard to the arrest of Markelov.

Volgin. *On the Eve*. One of Anna Vasil'evna's rich relatives.

Volkonskii, Prince Petr Mikhailovich (1776-1852). *War and Peace* (3, 1, 9). The field-marshal general who was a minister of the court in St. Petersburg. In 1805, he was deputy commander under Kutuzov. In 1812, he was in Aleksandr I's personal suite and, in 1813, served as chief of the Emperor's staff.

Volodia. A diminutive of Vladimir. "The Death of Ivan Il'ich." Ivan's brother. Also Ivan's thirteen-year-old son.

Voltaire (1694-1778) (pseudonym of François Marie Arouet). "Chertopkhanov and Nedopiuskin," in *A Hunter's Sketches*. Pantelei knew that he was a great writer but never read him. *A Gentry Nest* (8). Fedor Lavretskii's father studied Voltaire's works in his youth. "A Hamlet of the Shchigrov District," in *A Hunter's Sketches*. The Russian Hamlet talked about a tragedy by Voltaire. "My Neighbor Radilov," in *A Hunter's Sketches*. Radilov thought that Voltaire said "All that happens, happens for the best." *Resurrection* (2, 23). Nekhliudov did not believe that Voltaire could help him in his philosophical quest. *Virgin Soil* (19). Fomushka Subochev defended Voltaire's philosophy.

Volynskii, Artemii. *The Captain's Daughter* (14). A minister of the Empress Anna Ivanovna (1730-1740). He was at the head of a plot against the Empress's favorite, Biron. Volynskii was executed. See Khrushchev.

Volyntsev, Sergei Pavlich. *Rudin*. The quiet and plain nobleman who opposed Rudin for Natal'ia Lasunskaia's affections. He accused all intellectuals of being despots.

Vonifatii. "First Love." A servant of the Princess Zasekina.

Vorkuev. *Anna Karenina*. An acquaintance of Anna's in Moscow.

Vorobev, Baron. *Resurrection*. The influential official on the Petition Committee who was a kindly man and who had received his title in an amusing way. See Pavel I.

Voronskaia, Nina. *Evgenii Onegin*. A friend of Tat'iana Larina. She was described as being as beautiful as Cleopatra.

Voronzova. *Resurrection*. The countess who was discussed at Maslinnikov's party.

Voroshilov, Semen Iakovlevich. *Smoke*. An intellectual who was mentioned by Bambaev as the first on the honor roll of the Corps des Pages of the tsar.

Vorotinskaia, Countess. *Smoke* (1). The woman who was the talk of the town before Irina Osinina appeared in court circles. Turgenev had in mind the fictional society lioness by that name created by Count V. A. Sollogub (1813-1882) in his tale "High Society" ("Bol'shoi svet") (1840).

Vrbna, Count Rudolph (1761-1823). *War and Peace* (1, 2, 10). The Austrian diplomat who was the imtermediary between the French and Austrians after the former occupied Vienna in 1805.

Vronskaia, Countess. *Anna Karenina*. Once a famous beauty in higher aristocratic circles, she was delighted that her son was having an affair with Anna Karenina. Later she tried to break up the destructive romance.

Vronskii, Count Aleksandr Kirillovich. *Anna Karenina*. Aleksei's brother who tried to stop the affair between Aleksei and Anna Karenina.

Vronskii, Count Aleksei Kirillovich. *Anna Karenina*. The wealthy, handsome aide-de-camp to the Emperor who became Anna Karenina's lover and lived openly with her in society until her suicide. Tolstoi's dislike of young men of Vronskii's type is seen in the depiction of the hero: he is prematurely balding; he falls from his horse in a prestigious horse race; he tries to commit suicide and fails; and after Anna's suicide,

he has a toothache, a problem considered distasteful in
the nineteenth century.

Vronskii, Count Kiril Ivanovich. *Anna Karenina*. Aleksei's father.

Vulich. "The Fatalist," in *A Hero of Our Time*. The Serbian whose
passion was gambling with money and his life.

Wagner, Richard (1813-1883). *Anna Karenina* (7, 5). The great German
composer, whom Levin criticized for wrongly "trying to
make music pass into the province of another art form." Tolstoi's dislike of Wagner is evident in Levin's remarks.

Wandering Jew. *Evgenii Onegin* (3, 12). The literary figure of a
widespread medieval legend which told of a Jew who refused
to allow Christ to rest at his door while carrying the cross to
Calvary. The Jew was condemned to wander over the face of
the earth till the end of the world. The Jew was usually
named Ahasuerus, a cobbler, in the legend.

Washington, George (1732-1799). *On the Eve* (10). The first American president, who was the subject of the harangue which
Bersenev's father gave him and his schoolmates.

Weber, Karl Maria von (1786-1826). *On the Eve* (4). The German composer of "La dèrniere pensée," which Zoia played for Anna
Stakhov. *Spring Freshets* (11). Gemma hummed a beautiful melody by Weber.

Weirother, General Franz von (1754-1807). *War and Peace* (1, 2, 13).
The Austrian general who was headquarters director of the
Austrian army.

Wellington, Arthur Welsley (1769-1852). *Fathers and Sons* (7). The
famous English statesman with whom Pavel Kirsanov had
once dined at the court of Louis Philippe.

Werner. "Princess Mary," in *A Hero of Our Time*. The Russian doctor of German ancestry who befriended Pechorin but did not
approve of his carrying out the duel with Grushnitskii. The
doctor was a skeptic and a materialist, and had a caustic
tongue.

Werther. *Anna Karenina* (2, 18). The hero of Goethe's *The Sorrows
of Werther* (1774), who was mentioned by Tolstoi in regard
to Vronskii. Werther committed suicide over unrequited
love. Vronskii did try suicide but was unsuccessful. *Evgenii
Onegin* (3, 9). Tat'iana read *Werther* after Onegin visited the

first time. *On the Eve* (26). Zoia read Goethe's novel when Anna Stakhova was ill.

Willarski, Count. *War and Peace.* The person to whom Pierre Bezukhov was sent by I. A. Bazdeev when he wanted to learn more about Masonic teachings.

Wilson, Mrs. *Anna Karenina.* An acquaintance of Anna's in Moscow society after Anna left Karenin. She accepted Anna in society when others were ignoring her.

Wilson, General P. *War and Peace* (4, 4, 4). The English representative on the Russian general staff who was one of the men who complained against Kutuzov for inaction, waste and weakness.

Wintzengerode, Ferdinand Fedorovich (1770-1818). *War and Peace* (1, 1, 1). The Russian general sent on a mission to the King of Prussia. In October, 1812, he was captured by the French but was rescued by Chernyshev's battalion.

Wittgenstein, Petr Khristianovich (1768-1842). *Fathers and Sons* (20). The Russian field-marshal general in the War of 1812 whose pulse Vasilii Bazarov once took. *War and Peace* (4, 1, 1). In the beginning of the War of 1812, General Wittgenstein commanded the First Corps, which defended the roads to St. Petersburg. After the death of Kutuzov, He was Commander-in-Chief of the Russian Army.

Wlocki. *War and Peace* (3, 2, 1). An adjutant general who demanded that Barclay de Tolly fight the French as they advanced on Moscow. Barclay dispatched him to St. Petersburg.

Woldemar. *A Gentry Nest.* The name which Maria Kalitina called Panchin.

Wolf, Vladimir Vasilich. *Resurrection.* The senator to whom Nekhliudiv went for help with Maslov's case. He was known as a dandy and liked the reputation. He voted to accept Maslova's appeal.

Wolmar, Julie. *Evgenii Onegin* (3, 9). Julie is the heroine of J. J. Rousseau's novel *Julie, ou La Nouvelle Héloïse.* However, Pushkin made a mistake. Julie had the last name of d'Étrange, not Wolmar, when she was the mistress of Saint-Preux.

Wolzogen, Baron Ludwig Ustus von (1774-1845). *War and Peace* (3, 1, 9). A Prussian general in the headquarters with General Pfühl. Together, they composed a war plan which brought on much criticism in military circles.

Wrede. *Anna Karenina*. The old acquaintance whom Anna said she was going to see when she left Princess Tverskoi's gathering, but she was actually going to see Vronskii.

Wurst. *Anna Karenina*. A name thought up by Tolstoi to designate an author who wrote on the subject of perception. Koznyshev discussed the subject with Levin (1, 7).

Württemberg. *War and Peace* (3, 1, 7). A German family name mentioned by Napoleon at dinner with Balashev. The Württembergs ruled the duchy by that name from the eleventh century.

Württemberg, Count Alexander Friedrich (1771-1833). *War and Peace* (3, 2, 35). The brother of the Empress Maria Fedorovna, the wife of Pavel I of Russia. He was also the brother of the King of Württemberg. The Count participated in the War of 1812.

X____, *Smoke*. A Madame X____ was at Irina's party. Also a Count X____ was an amateur musician who could not tell one note from another.

Y____. *Smoke*. Prince Y____ was a friend of some people who had amassed a huge fortune by selling inferior liquor.

Yorick. *Evgenii Onegin* (2, 37). "Poor Yorick" is an exclamation Hamlet made over the skull of a jester. Lenskii used the phrase by Larin's tomb.

Z____, Baron. *Smoke*. An orator and administrator who was an example of the "fine fleur" of society in Baden when Litvinov went there.

Zadeck, Martin. *Evgenii Onegin* (5, 22). The author Tat'iana was supposedly reading in bed. Nabokov regards this personage as the anonymous German-Swiss ephemerist whose name appeared in 1814 in Moscow on the title page of a 454-page "Oraculum." (See *Evgenii Onegin*, Comentary One to Five. V. 2. Trans. by Vladimir Nabokov. Princeton University Press, 1975.)

Zakhar. *War and Peace*. A coachman at the Rostov country estate.

Zakhar Ivanovich. "The Death of Ivan Il'ich." The friend who found Ivan Il'ich a very prestigious position.

Zakharchinko. *War and Peace*. Tushin's sergeant major during the fighting in the War of 1805.

Zakharich, Prince Mikhail. *War and Peace*. An acquaintance of Pierre Bezukhov in a Moscow club.

Zakharov. *Resurrection*. Shustova's cousin.

Zakurdalo-Skubyrnikov. *A Gentry Nest*. A retired guardsman who was an admirer of Varvara Lavretskaia in Paris.

Zalataev. *War and Peace*. A soldier in the Fifth Company bivouac during the French retreat from Moscow.

Zaretskii. *Evgenii Onegin*. The friend of Lenskii who served as his second in the fatal duel with Onegin.

Zasekin, Prince. "First Love." A well-educated aristocrat who went broke. When he died, he left his wife in financial trouble.

Zasekin, Vladimir (Volodia). "First Love." The twelve-year-old son of the Princess Zasekina.

Zasekina, Princess. "First Love." The decadent old mother of Zinaida Zasekina.

Zasekina, Princess Zinaida Aleksandrovna (Zina, Zinochka). "First Love." The beautiful and clever daughter of the old Princess Zasekina. She enticed men by her voluptuousness. Enslaved by their emotions, her suitors became adversaries toward one another. She died in childbirth.

Zdrzhinskii. *War and Peace*. The officer who related a tale about General Raevskii at the Battle of Saltonov.

Zeus. *Evgenii Onegin* (1, 2). The Greek king of the gods and men who was the ultimate source of justice. Evgenii Onegin thought it was the will of Zeus that he was the heir to his relative's estate.

Zhilinski, Count. *War and Peace*. The wealthy Polish adjutant with whom Nikolai Rostov lodged when he went to Tilsit for the meeting of the two emperors, Aleksandr I and Napoleon I in 1805.

Zhivakhov. *Anna Karenina*. An aristocrat who lived well even though he was 300,000 roubles in debt.

Zhukovskii, Vasilii Andreevich (1783-1852). *Fathers and Sons* (20). The noted Russian poet whose pulse was once taken by Vasilii Bazarov. "Rattling Wheels," in *A Hunter's Sketches*. The narrator remembered a line from the poem "Maid of Orleans" (1821) by Zhukhovskii when the brigands would not allow his coach to pass their vehicle. *Rudin* (1). According to Pandalevskii, the Russian poet considered Lasunskaia an expert on the Russian language and even consulted with her on the subject.

Zikin. *War and Peace.* A soldier who was weighed down by his knapsack during the Russian rout through Austria in the War of 1805.

Zinaida. "First Love" (14). A character in A. S. Khomiakov's tragedy *Ermak* whom Valdimir B____ recalled in a conversation with Zinaida Zasekina.

Zinaida Dmitrievna. *War and Peace.* A name mentioned as a face in a crowd in the Sloboda Palace in Moscow when the gentry and nobles gathered to hear news about the French advance into Russia.

Zipporah. *Anna Karenina* (5, 6). The Biblical wife of Moses. She was mentioned in the ceremony at Kitty Shcherbatskaia's wedding to Konstantin Levin.

Zizi. *Evgenii Onegin* (5, 32). Pushkin referred to Evproks'ia Vul'f (née Osipova) of the Osipov family that lived near his estate, Mikhailovskoe. *Smoke.* A Mlle. Zizi was mentioned in conversation.

Zluitenkhov. *Smoke.* When Litvinov's servant asked the lady who brought flowers what her name was, she answered Zluitenkhov.

Zoia. *On the Eve.* See Müller, Zoia.

Zola, Émile (1840-1902). *Anna Karenina* (7, 10). The French writer whom Anna mentioned in a conversation with Vorkuev and Levin. The latter was pleased that she had liked his remarks on art. "The Death of Ivan Il'ich" (5). Ivan picked up a novel by Zola but could not read for thinking of his illness.

Zosima. *Virgin Soil.* The priest who married Solomin and Mariana after Nezhdanov's suicide.

Zozo. *Smoke.* A young Mlle. Zozo was mentioned in conversation.

Zubov, Platon Aleksandrovich (1767-1822). *War and Peace* (3, 2, 4). A favorite of Ekaterina II who was remembered by Count Nikolai Bolkonskii.

Zubova, Countess. *War and Peace.* An old aristocrat who was recalled by Princess Liza Bolkonskaia because she wore false curls and false teeth.

Zurin, Ivan Ivanovich. *The Captain's Daughter.* The captain of the hussars who taught Grinev how to play billiards and won one hundred roubles from him.

Zverkov, Aleksandr Silych (Koko). "Ermolai and the Miller's Wife,"
in *A Hunter's Sketches*. Arina's former master who refused to
allow her marriage to the man she loved.